†

E. R. CHAMBERLIN

Marguerite
of
Navarre

The Dial Press   New York   1974

Design by Lynn Braswell

Library of Congress Cataloging in Publication Data

Chamberlin, Eric Russell.
    Marguerite of Navarre.

    Bibliography: p.
    1.   Marguerite de Valois, consort of Henry IV, King of France, 1553–1615.   I.   Title.
DC122.9.M2C45   944'.031'0924 [B]   74–6095
ISBN 0–8037–5207–5

Contents

v

†

Marguerite
of
Navarre

†

I

The Italian
Woman

After ten days of great agony, the king died. Almost his last act was to pardon his involuntary slayer, for his death, after all, lay on his own head. It had been he who had insisted that they should run another course, deeming it unfitting that a king of France should be bested by his own captain of guard. Reluctantly, the Scotsman had obeyed. There had been no shrilling of trumpets and thundering of drums to mark this second tourney. It was as though the watchers had been touched with prescience, and men remembered afterward the sudden silence that enveloped the tourney ground as the metal-clad horsemen lumbered toward each other. The lances were shivered in the correct manner, but in the last millisecond of contact, Montgomery's shattered weapon had glanced up from the king's shield toward his head, and the slender, jagged edges easily entered the visor.

During the ten days that the surgeons probed for the sliver of metal that was approaching the brain, France held its breath. Henri II had not been a great or good or particularly popular king. His subjects judged him, accurately enough, to be cold, bigoted, indifferent alike to their well-being and the larger affairs of state, content to leave matters in the hands of that grim old man, Anne de Montmorency, while he indulged himself in the Valois passion for chasing wild animals. But he had been the king, the sole catalyst who could make one of this vast and variegated land, the sole governor who could prevent the hurtling off of the components by the centrifugal force of their own power and independence and pride. Even those who stood to gain most from confusion, who could best defend themselves during the chaos that must fall upon the land, feared what such an untimely death might bring. There was wild talk of impeaching the constable, old Anne de Montmorency himself, because he had let the king wear an unsuitable visor. The talk passed over the old man's head. Mumbling, wild-eyed, he haunted the door to the sick chamber like some brooding ghost. Somewhere, he found a corpse and dragged the king's surgeons to it one by one, insisting that each should demonstrate upon the inert thing the exact position of the wound and afterward sat staring at it by the hour as though his brain, bred and shaped in countless battles, might yet make some dizzying leap and seize upon a surgeon's miraculous cure.

The king's heir, his eldest son François, was sick with weeping. "What shall I do if he dies? What shall I do if he dies?" he cried again and again, and no one could find any answer that comforted him. He was sixteen, but with his gentle, pouting mouth and soft, rounded cheeks he seemed a child, an overtrustful child. His wife, Mary, though the same age, seemed startlingly adult by contrast. She was a beauty—fair-haired, lively, intelligent, and perhaps owed her greater maturity to her consciousness of the fact that she was already a queen in her own right. Soon she would be Queen of France, but history would ever remember her as Mary, Queen of Scots. Now she comforted her trembling husband with genuine pity, for she was fond of him, but there was excitement behind the pity. She was made of tougher stuff than the gentle François and, to do her justice, was only remotely connected to the dying king and so could indulge in the soaring dreams of ambition not too much hampered by filial sorrow. Behind her stood her uncles, brothers of the great House of Lorraine—François, Duke of Guise, and Charles, Cardinal of Lorraine —who a few months earlier had placed her feet on the path that would end at the block at Fotheringhay, for they had persuaded her to adopt the arms of England as well as of Scotland. They were as perturbed as the rest of France at the approaching death of the king: he had come to rely more and more upon them, and they, and their house, had grown great in his shadow and no man could guess where the dice would fall on the death of a king. But their dutiful niece was the wife of the heir, and their ground was as secure as intelligence and a total lack of scruples could make it.

"I pray God that he make you a happier man than I have been" was the king's parting benediction to his son. He died in the early afternoon of July 10, 1559, and the cumbrous ceremonial machinery ground into action. The surgeons who could not save his life were at least capable of beautifying him after death, hiding the ravages of their scalpels with wax and cosmetics so that, in the open lead coffin, he looked much as he had in life—handsome, disillusioned, weary. The coffin was moved to Notre Dame, the forest of candles lit, the guard detailed. In the palace where he had died, a garishly painted effigy of him presided over the mourning feast where, for forty days, the poor of Paris would find sustenance in their bereavement. And while they ate and drank hastily, not really believing their luck or the power of custom, by that same custom the king's widow remained, almost literally immured, in a black-draped bedroom in the Palace of the Louvre.

Henri was not quite forty-one when he died: his widow, Catherine de Médicis, was just thirty-nine. But where contemporaries looked upon him as a young man untimely snatched from the world, if they thought of Catherine at all, it was as an aging woman. Grief now placed decades upon her. Other, more fortunate women might be touched by sorrow with a transient pathos and charm: it merely made the dumpy little Italian somewhat repellent, bagging the limp and sallow skin, making bloodshot the protuberant eyes. For hours she would sit staring blankly in front of her, deaf to all remarks or answering them in a dead, mechanical voice; every so often her body would be wracked by painful, dry sobs, for she had long gone beyond tears. So profound, so shattering was that grief that even those who disliked her—and they were probably in the majority—could yet find time for pity and alarm among their own preoccupations. Even the sprightly Mary Stuart, who habitually referred to her mother-in-law as "that Florentine shopkeeper," wrote to her own mother saying, "She is still so troubled and has suffered so much during the sickness of the late king that, with all the worry it has caused her, I fear a grave illness." It was not pity alone which moved Mary to urge the grieving woman to rest and eat. The new king was, technically, of legal age but so young and pliable was he that, in practice, he would be the tool of whoever could claim governance over him. Mary's uncles had thrust themselves forward quite illegally; but if the boy-king's mother could be persuaded to sanction their usurpation at least with her presence. . . . Indifferently, Catherine assented, although well aware that she and her son were being used as puppets. It did not matter. Nothing mattered. The most extraordinary demonstration of the depths of her sorrow, of the extent of her desolation, was the way she treated her husband's mistress. The court had waited agog to watch the humiliation of Diane de Poitiers, the woman who had exercised a fascination over the king even though she would never see fifty again, and had done so almost throughout the marriage. Catherine had restrained herself for a decade and more. "He was the king, yet even so I always let him know that it was to my great regret," she remembered afterwards. "Never has a woman who loved her husband liked his whore—for even though this is an ugly word one cannot call her anything else."[1] But now that she had the opportunity of total and justified revenge, she contented herself merely with forcing the ex-mistress to return the crown jewels which the besotted Henri had given her. And even this she did for the sake of her son, passing the jewels immediately over to Mary. She obliged Diane to give up the château of Chenonceaux, that delicate miracle astride the waters of the Cher, but gave her in exchange the château of Chaumont. Incredibly, Catherine's love for her husband, it seemed, could extend even to tolerance for his mistress.

She was married at the age of fourteen.

Her uncle, the melancholy Pope Clement, arranged the marriage and gave her away and stood in the bedchamber while the union was consummated, for all her other closer relatives were dead. Dead was her mother, the pretty little French girl with the beautiful name—Madeleine de La Tour d'Auvergne—who had scarcely survived childbirth to succumb to puerperal fever. Dead was her father, the dashing Lorenzo, with his mobile, handsome, deceitful face, his ambition, his incompetence, who survived his wife for only five days before succumbing to a complication of pleurisy and syphilis. Death, indeed, beat its wings near her throughout her babyhood and childhood. The tough old grandmother who had whisked her away after her mother's death died when she was scarcely six months old. The great Pope Leo, brilliant pinnacle of the Medici fortunes, who had planned such great things for the Medici family, died while still a young man. Death came close to her personally, first through the ubiquitous "fever" and then through the sword, for the raging Florentines, finding themselves betrayed by the family which had also brought them glory, came close to revenging their lost freedom on the shrinking body of the last of the Medici of the elder line, the great-great-granddaughter of Lorenzo the Magnificent. But the mob, as fickle in wrath as it was in loyalty, was deflected from its purpose, and the sickly child survived to grow into an unattractive girl. But though Catherine lacked almost every physical grace, she excelled in the flashier Medici talents. She read voraciously and, with a remarkably retentive memory, could quote appositely, giving an appearance of learning. She picked up French and Latin, could talk glibly enough about the new arts and artists, though never in her life did she display any real insight. A succession of foster parents had made her anxious to please and skilled in the little arts of ingratiation; a succession of homes had made her pliable, capable of settling down rapidly in the most unlikely places.

In October 1533, she sailed, with her uncle the pope, to Marseilles and there became the bride of Henri, Duke of Orléans, second son of the King of France. She was, perhaps, too young to appreciate fully the diplomatic niceties that had brought this marriage into existence. It was the crown of her uncle's career, the consolatory domestic prize after a series of disasters of State. In rebellious England the arrogant King Henry might defy him and marry the witch Anne Boleyn in the teeth of the Church's anathema. In Italy, Italians might curse the name of Medici, which had brought upon them the most disastrous of all wars of modern times, a war which had ended with the sack of Rome and Clement's own flight from the Vatican. He had brought his disasters upon himself, and his dark, handsome face was set now in a permanent expression of melancholy and disillusion. But though he might have failed as priest and as monarch alike, he had triumphed brilliantly as a loyal son of the House of Medici by placing this dumpy niece of his into the foremost royal house of Europe.

Exactly how clever he had been became apparent after his death a year later. The king's ministers had had some sharp things to say regarding the size of the girl's dowry and the fact that she was to waive all rights to the Medici inheritance. But it was understood that her uncle would make it easier for her father-in-law to claim certain possessions in Italy. He may perhaps have intended to do that, although one could never be certain about any contract drawn up by a Medici. There were rumors that, safely back in Rome, Clement had repudiated any such suggestion. But his own early death finally eliminated the secret clauses, for his successor was hardly likely to surrender Italian cities for the sake of a Medici marriage. Pope Clement's foxiness saved the Medici coffers at the cost of his niece's good name even though the financial juggling was demonstrably none of her doing. There was talk of repudiating the marriage, but her unpredictable father-in-law came to her aid, even though King Francois took her part probably as much because it would irritate his son as because he thought it just.

And that was the first of the clouds that lay over the marriage of Catherine de Médicis.

The second was Diane de Poitiers.

"I have read the histories of this kingdom, Madam," the bristling little Italian queen once informed the calm, unmoved beauty, "and I have found in them from time to time at all periods whores have managed the business of kings." It was an accurate enough summary of one aspect of French history, but Diane merely laughed and went about her affairs. There was something inhuman about Diane de Poitiers's self-control, even as there was something magical —eerie—about her beauty. She was thirty-eight when she first came into Henri's life—more than twice his age and entering that period which, for most women of her day, was the beginning of old age. Twenty years later, however, the influence she exercised over the king was as great as ever, and it seemed even to those closest to her that time had not made a mark upon that peerless skin, upon that full but graceful form. Her relationship with Henri was, at first, platonic. The uncouth youth, searching for he knew not what, responded with pathetic eagerness to the culture and sophistication of the beautiful, mature woman. On her side, Diana knew well enough what she was about: that fabled, tender beauty of hers was an instrument, the means whereby she could gain those tangible, measurable values for which her cold heart hungered. The dauphin died; Henri became the heir to the throne; Diana passed from mentor to mistress.

Catherine endured the situation. She was genuinely in love with her husband: he was courteous and kind and that, perhaps, was all that could be expected in a purely dynastic marriage. She even endured being nursed by Diane when she contracted scarlet fever. Henri congratulated himself on establishing such a civilized relationship between wife and mistress; Catherine learned just a little more about the art of dissimulation.

The third cloud that lay over her marriage virtually obscured the other two, rendering them of passing interest, no more. She was barren—sterile—and remained so for ten years.

The discovery did not so much terrify her as stun her. It was, literally, unbelievable. Her uncle had been so naively certain of her ability to conceive that he had postponed his departure from France day by day for nearly three weeks, expecting each morning to be told the news. His knowledge of gynecology was doubtless even less than his skill in statesmanship, but even so Catherine was not unduly worried during that first year. But at about the time that Clement died, and it became obvious that the marriage contract was a swindle on the French, so did the girl's sole remaining justification for marriage disappear. Diane de Poitiers appeared on the scene and all that Catherine had to combat that dazzle of beauty was her transient youth; her husband had a child by a peasant woman, underlining the fact that the fault lay with his wife. Her enemies—and already they were many—went to the king urging him to put an end to this unfertile marriage, a marriage born in fraud and now incapable of producing the vital heir to the Valois throne. Characteristically, the girl tackled the threat head on. She threw herself literally at the king's feet, offering to free his son, begging only that she not be sent back to Italy but remain as servitor to her successor, if necessary. Francois, touched by some whimsy, perhaps, or stirred to admiration by the sight of a lone fighter, lifted her up and assured her that it was all the will of God and she must be of good cheer.

The danger had receded but was not eliminated. The king might yet repent of his chivalry, or be pressured into placing the interest of France before the interest of Catherine de Médicis. So she tried prayer, prayer and endless pilgrimages to the shrines of Our Lady of Conception. Faith remained unanswered and imperceptibly, at first, but inevitably, she turned to darker sources of comfort and aid.

It was probably at about this period that her vague, uninformed interest in the occult became crystallized into practice. The line between legitimate and forbidden medicine was, in any case, hazily drawn: any worthwhile doctor would naturally base his diagnosis and prognosis on an astrological interpretation of his patient's condition and would choose his medicines as much for their spiritual as their physical qualities. It was easy to step a little beyond that hazy line as the more conventional medicines proved useless, to turn to astrologers and magicians and frowsy old women in back street hovels instead of the physicians who took their fees and shook their heads. It speaks much for her constitution that it survived under the continual assault of nauseating compounds. It speaks perhaps even more for her husband's tolerance and sympathy that he took part in the rituals—the midnight sacrifice of a black cock, the concoctions of hen's blood and bull's sperm, the raw fish, the intercourse at forbidden times—in a desperate attempt to justify his wife's existence.

And they were successful at last. In June 1543, Catherine was overjoyed to notice the first signs of pregnancy; on January 19, 1544, she was brought to bed of her firstborn, the boy François, who would in time become François II. Then, incredibly, after having waited more than nine years for her first child, she bore a child almost every year for the next decade. The bells of Notre Dame joyfully proclaimed each occasion. Te Deum was sung, incense arose in clouds of thanksgiving as was right and proper—but there were mutterings that the Italian woman owed her late and abundant fertility not to the Christian God but to some other, less wholesome cause. Sensibly, she dismissed the mutterings as the product of rage and envy, but as the years slid into decades and time itself provided a perspective and comment upon the tragedy that gripped this hard-won family, so even she must have wondered whether she had not transgressed the law in bringing this family into existence out of nothingness.

Death or insanity would touch almost every member of the brood. François, the longed-for firstborn—dead before his seventeenth year. Elizabeth, gentle, loving, lustrous—dead in her early twenties. Claude—crippled from birth and welcoming death, in her twenty-seventh year, as release from an intolerable burden. Louis, Jean, Victoire—all dead within months of their baptism. Charles—balanced on a knife edge of sanity and at last pushed over it by his mother's action; his death at the age of twenty-four was perhaps the most fortunate event in his life. The stunted little gnome miscalled Hercule, who was to earn the mockery of Europe as he wooed England's virgin queen—dead at thirty. Henri, potentially the most intelligent of the lot, but touched eventually by the Valois madness, descending into grotesque perversion and dying, with an assassin's dagger in his bowel, at the age of thirty-eight. Of all the ten children of Catherine de Médicis, Marguerite alone appeared balanced and healthy. Yet time would show that she, too, paid the price of her heritage both physically and mentally, both in her lifelong barren-

ness and in the desperate hunger with which she moved from lover
to lover.

The families began to gather for the rites of funeral and coronation.

First, as ever, were the Guises. "They will strip my children
to their waistcoats and my poor people to their shirts," François I had
complained a generation earlier, but there was little that he, or his
son, or now his grandson, could do about that, for the abilities of the
Guises were as great as their ambitions. Yet, securely placed though
they were in the uppermost level of the French aristocracy, confidently jostling around the throne itself, there was still something
indefinably alien, indefinably parvenue about them. They came from
Lorraine, that borderland that was not quite France, not quite Germany; with courage and skill and a complete lack of scruple, they had
clambered to the top. Or almost to the top, for above them loomed
the unsurmountable peak of royalty, the throne itself, which could
be occupied only by a Valois of the Blood Royal. Outwardly, they
seemed content with their undefined role of shield to the monarchy,
but ambition, far from being quenched by this proximity to the
source of all honors, became ever more enflamed. They let it be
known, lightly but with a steely undertone, that they were, in fact,
descended from Charlemagne himself and so were at least as good as
the Valois.

There were six Guises now, all brothers—big, fair-skinned
men who tended to marry small, fierce wives. Dominating the family
as he dominated everyone was François, the second duke—not yet
forty but so scarred, seamed, and craggy that he seemed a patriarch.
They called him Le Balafré—Scarface—because of the livid weal that
ran from eye to chin, whose gaining must have taken him to the very
edge of death. Head thrust downward and forward, eyes glaring
blue-gray beneath beetling eyebrows, he was a figure from a cruder
heroic past, and the jostling crowds tended to melt away before him
as he shouldered his way about Paris, grimly intent upon family
business. But sometimes, too, people would stop on recognizing him

and raise a spontaneous cheer for the hero of France, the man who had kicked the English out of Calais at last and defended Metz against the Spaniards and plundered Italy like a Frenchman should. And he would acknowledge the cheers, doffing the shabby bonnet that he affected, bending the knee to the stinking mob who were the natural ally of his family against the purse-proud merchants and the pretensions of his fellow aristocrats.

A pace or two behind the duke walked the cardinal—Charles, Archbishop of Rheims, Cardinal of Lorraine, at thirty-five the most important figure of the Church in France, for Rheims was the premier see and he was therefore Primate of France. The office was now virtually hereditary in the family, having passed from uncle to nephew throughout this century, but though Charles might have gained it through the accident of birth, he held it by the merit of intelligence. The contrast between the two brothers exactly illustrated the reason why the Guises had soared to the top in so short a time: in François the family energy was expressed in force, in Charles it was expressed in intelligence, the strength of each neatly supplementing the weakness of the other. Charles's intelligence had nothing to do with morality; as a social animal, he was a disastrous failure—greedy, cowardly, snobbish, tyrannical toward subordinates, groveling towards those who could hurt or help him. But as a political tactician he was supreme, faithfully working out his brother's bold plans in meticulous detail, choosing the allies, marking down the more dangerous enemies for assassination.

Charles and François were the architects and planners of the family fortunes and their four brothers obediently lined up where they were instructed. One of them, Louis, was a high ecclesiastic in his own right, for he was Cardinal of Guise and was outranked only by his brother Charles. Efficiently, they protected each other's backs in that most lethal of political arenas, the Sacred College in Rome. The other brothers were rough and tumble soldiers, intelligent enough and with the fashionable tincture of culture but lacking their elder brother's ferocious dedication to Guise interests. Neither was it expected of them, for the Guises worked on the principle of the wedge, and Duke François was more than adequate in the forward position. And when time and death should remove him, his son Henri would take his place.

The Guises were firmly in possession of the game within hours of the king's death—for was not the new king, François, the loving husband of their niece Mary? Even so, they awaited the coming of the Bourbons with a certain unease, for the Bourbons, too, were of the Blood Royal, being cousin to the Valois and destined to succeed them on the throne in the unlikely event that the House of Valois ever failed. Long-standing tradition had decreed that the Bourbons should act as adviser to their cousin the king, should he be a minor or youthful, and the Guises had delivered a direct challenge by their usurpation of that role.

The head of the house now was Antoine, King of Navarre. The title was splendid even though the reality meant, simply, the tiny mountainous state between France and Spain whose heiress he had been fortunate enough to marry. He was an extraordinary character, steering a dizzy course between buffoonery and nobility, quick to anger, quick to laughter, his head stuffed full of ideas to make his own and other people's fortune, a generous friend on whom it was quite impossible to depend, so wayward and rapid were his changes of mood and motive. Anger now dominated all other emotions on his mobile face; no preparation had been made for his suite. He alone could be lodged in the Louvre, and lodgings had to be sought for his followers even in the outlying villages. Shortage of accommodation was nothing new in Paris; stewards of the great townhouses made a comfortable income by letting them out—quite unofficially—during the absence of their masters. But it was unthinkable that a Bourbon should have to scurry around and look for a bed for the night.

Accompanying Antoine were his brothers—Louis, Prince of Condé, dark, wiry energetic, and Charles, Cardinal of Bourbon, a slow-moving, slow-thinking man who was universally known as the Red Ass. Like chess sets, each of the great families had equivalent pieces to set upon the political board. Thus François, Duke of Guise, was exactly matched by Antoine, King of Navarre; Charles, Cardinal of Lorraine, was matched by Charles, Cardinal of Bourbon; Louis, Prince of Condé, was matched by Louis, Cardinal of Guise, while the lesser brothers or cousins of each helped to make up weight. Each family was, in turn, linked by blood or marriage to other clans who played a greater or lesser part in the game according to the needs of the moment. Behind the Guises stood the Lorraines—the elder branch of the family and therefore tending to hold themselves somewhat aloof from the hurly-burly into which the cadet branch threw itself so wholeheartedly. The Bourbons, apart from their connection with the throne, looked upon the Châtillons as their natural allies. The head of this clan was the constable himself, Anne, Duke of Montmorency, but old age was relaxing even his enormous sinews and it was his nephew, Gaspard de Coligny, to whom the clan now looked for leadership.

Guise, Bourbon, Châtillon, Montmorency—and, at the middle, like a dusty, plump, black duck, Catherine de Médicis and her brood of orphans. When at length her grief receded somewhat and she was able to take stock of her surroundings, it was to find herself in a position of no little peril. The Guises, outwardly all sympathy and condolences, were firmly in the center of the stage and as firmly, if discreetly, were edging all other rivals off in the name of the king. Anne de Montmorency, utterly loyal to the memory of the late king and therefore the natural protector of the king's widow, was dismissed like a stableboy. He withdrew, muttering, to his estates at Chantilly, a formidable unexploded mine. His nephew, Coligny, gravely watched the turn of events with his habitual serene expression and his hand not far from the hilt of his sword. Antoine of Navarre blasphemed and threatened and had a tremendous quarrel with one of the younger Guises and altogether behaved like a match on a powder keg. The young king himself unhappily looked on. His wife's uncles had persuaded him that the Bourbons would not hesitate to spill his sacred blood if that would bring them to the throne. It had proved more difficult to get him to believe that even the old constable was a rival and a danger, but they had succeeded. They had even neatly detached him from his mother while yet outwardly according her additional honor: proudly, François announced that all laws were to be enacted in her name, believing that she was thereby made the chief power in the land. He was, after all, only sixteen, and a young sixteen at that.

Catherine drew her remaining brood closer around her. Already they were leaving the nest, journeying far beyond her influence. Elizabeth, the loving, lovely Elizabeth, left for Spain as bride to its gloomy monarch Philip. In a way, she had been responsible for her father's death, for the fatal tournament had taken place to honor her proxy marriage. She seemed an incongruous successor to Mary Tudor in the bed of Philip of Spain, but dynastic marriages made such incongruities a commonplace. Her sister, the crippled Claude, went northward not long after as bride to the Duke of Lorraine. The Guises could bask in at least a reflected glory and congratulate themselves on making another link with the royal family of France. Catherine could only contemplate her encirclement and make what provision she could for the future. She kept the ten-year-old Charles— next in line for the throne—and his nine-year-old brother Henri with her, but sent Marguerite and the six-year-old Hercule to the comparative safety of Amboise.

Marguerite was eight years old at the time—old enough to be aware of the tensions around her and the fact that her mother was afraid, not old enough to know the causes. Years later, when she came to write her sprightly *Memoirs,* she drew freely upon hindsight to fill the gaps—in a curiously roundabout manner. She opened her *Memoirs* a few days before the accidental killing of her father, but though she made an editorial nod in the direction of "the ill-fated blow which deprived France of peace and our house of happiness," she went to great trouble to record what seems to be a totally trivial incident. During the tournament which ended with the king's death, he took her on his knee: "I was then only four or five years of age, and to try and make me talk, he asked me to choose which I should like best for a sweetheart—Monsieur le Prince de Jounville, who afterward became the great and unfortunate Duke of Guise, or the Marquis of Beauprés. Both were at play close to my father the king, and I was watching them. I told him that I liked the Marquis best. 'Why?' said he. 'He is not so handsome.' I replied that it was because he was a better boy whereas the other was never satisfied unless he was doing harm to somebody every day, and that he always wanted to be master—a true prophecy of what we have since seen fulfilled."[2]

It is a pretty scene: the bright-eyed, dark-haired little girl upon her handsome father's lap; the two sturdy little boys so engrossed in their game that they are unaware of being under observation; the cheerful bustle and clatter of the court *en fête*—small wonder that the disappointed, disillusioned woman in her late forties should nostalgically conjure it up in memory and conversation. What was, however, surprising is that she should have given such pride of place in her memoirs to the commonplace little story. Marguerite de Valois ran her life largely on impulse, but like most impulsive, disorganized people, she had a rather wistful vision of herself as a cool, practical person, and her memoirs were the outward expression of this vision —the place where her messy, unsatisfactory life was transformed into a balanced whole. Every sentence, every paragraph, every anecdote was supposed to contribute to this ideal picture of a woman who was the victim of fate and not of her own actions. And she included this story of the little girl's good taste and prescience in order to dissociate herself, in retrospect, from perhaps the only man she ever really loved and who, incidentally, brought France to the very edge of destruction.

But in 1560 Henri de Guise was simply a cruel little boy whom she, though well able to give a good account of herself on the children's battlefield, was glad enough to escape. And Amboise, too, was a welcome change from the stinking streets of Paris and the cramped quarters of the Louvre. The great château stood high above the smooth, full-bodied Loire, one of the royal residences that studded Touraine like jewels. It was here that her grandfather, François I, had brought his most famous possession, the great Italian Leonardo da Vinci, and given him a mansion in the grounds of the château and a princely pension, and courteously waited for him to make a return by painting a picture or devising an entertainment or perfecting a machine. As a child, Marguerite's eyes passed uncomprehendingly over those strange and glowing paintings—passed over the Gioconda and the Pomona and the Holy Family; in her maturity her lively intellect would respond to the mysticism that clothed itself in conventional outward forms but there was no one at court to direct the childish, questing mind, and the paintings of Leonardo da Vinci were simply slabs of color to decorate a gray stone wall. Far greater pleasure she received from the comparative freedom possible in Amboise —scrambling up the steep bluffs above the river, wandering among the water meadows or—and this was a great treat—crossing the river in a clumsy tub to land, like some explorer, on the Isle d'Or that was visible from the château. And always tagging after her, desperately trying to keep up with the goddess-like big sister, the pale, stunted little Hercule. His presence would sometimes irritate and, cruelly, she would abandon him and leave him sobbing and then, as precipitately, her heart would melt and she would swoop upon him and kiss and comfort him and lead him away—the protector's role she would play all his life.

But while their characters unfolded in their little green and gold universe of water and grass and flowers, in the stony urban world beyond, the pressures increased, the tensions heightened, and suddenly the empty château was filled—crowded—with the fearful court from Paris. Her mother was here together with the other children and maids of honor and ambassadors and the king and queen and the Guises. But not the Bourbons; not the Châtillons, not the Montmorencies or their allies. Marguerite added another word to her rapidly growing vocabulary, a word usually uttered in contempt or hatred, the French equivalent of the German *Eidgenossen* or "companion"—Huguenot.

Martin Luther had been fourteen years in his grave: in four years' time Calvin would follow him, but was now Lord of Geneva. In the Netherlands the new faith was a banner and a trumpet to a despairing people in the iron grasp of Spain. Across the Channel, the Reformed Church, having gone underground during the reign of the queen who would go down for all time as Bloody Mary, emerged into triumphant daylight when her half-sister ascended the throne. In Germany, religion was polarizing: across the Alps, in the provincial town of Trent, ecclesiastics and theologians had been meeting for fifteen years, and would go on meeting for another three, in an attempt to paper over the widening crack in Christendom.

In France, the new religion had at first been greeted, at the highest possible level, as an intellectual novelty. A generation earlier, Marguerite's great-aunt and namesake, Marguerite, had wholeheartedly adopted the Religion, as it became to be called—and she was not only the sister of the brilliant François I but also a formidable bluestocking in her own right. With that aristocratic backing, Calvinism spread rapidly. Its appeal was strongest among the newly emergent middle classes and the more intelligent of the nobility, weakest among the peasantry and the urban proletariat—Paris remained fanatically Catholic from start to finish of the bloody Wars of Religion.

The court itself was split, affecting even the children. Marguerite remembered how her brother Anjou tried to force her to become a Huguenot, even throwing her cherished book of hours into the fire. It is likely that Henri of Anjou tormented his little sister as much out of sheer love of deviltry as from any innate religious belief. But the anecdote demonstrated, better than any thesis, how controversy had once again entered religion. As with Christianity itself during its emergent decades, violent and bloody argument again garnished theological debate. It seemed that the most illiterate of men could once again chop logic, could once again advance hairbreadth arguments in defending or attacking Transubstantiation, or Justification by Faith, or Predestination, or this or that esoteric aspect of religion which hitherto had been the province of technicians. Government grew alarmed. The tolerance of François I was followed by the fear and hatred of his son, Henri II, reacting in a manner identical to that of his sister-sovereign Mary Tudor across the Channel. The stench of burning flesh ascended to God in France as it did in England.

Persecution had its traditional and predictable result: the unorthodox grew ever more fervent in their unorthodoxy and religion became inextricably entangled with politics. After Henri II had been carried off the tourney ground, there had been a brief breathing space. But rapidly the hatreds polarized and intensified. The Guises were Catholics of the fanatical, instinctive variety. Doubtless they were sincere enough, convinced that earthly happiness and future salvation did indeed lie exclusively in the hands of the pope. But equally doubtless they were confirmed in their beliefs by the fact that their great rivals, the Bourbons, were Huguenots. And Antoine, King of Navarre, though sincere in his effervescent, dashing way, probably remained faithful to Huguenotery because his small, bustling, tight-lipped wife was, incidentally, a fanatical Protestant as well as Queen of Navarre in her own right. From these two centers, Guise and Navarre, the twisted lines of family alliances snaked out to entangle the religious and irreligious, the committed and the uncommitted alike. One of Navarre's brothers was a cardinal: that was essential to maintain the ordinary pattern of politics, but the other, the Prince of Condé, was a Huguenot. So too were their natural allies the Châtillons and the Montmorencies and—very importantly—Gaspard de Coligny. But the Guises could count on even more august support— the royal family itself. Young King François was a good Catholic and so was his little sister Marguerite and his brothers and his mother.

It is highly doubtful whether a purely altruistic thought ever passed through the mind of Catherine de Médicis. She was a Catholic, certainly; at a deep, purely instinctual level, it was unlikely that she, the niece of two popes and the daughter of a great Italian house, could be anything else. At the more conscious level, she chose Catholicism, quite coldly, as a political tool: it was, and always would be, the party of the majority, the rich ground in which the monarchy was eternally rooted. Eventually, she would be forced to declare outright for it, and, in so doing, commit a bizarre and enormous crime. But she would have preferred to have it neatly balanced in the State by its opponent, with herself controlling the fulcrum at her good-will. Religion, in any emotional sense—in the sense in which it could stir even her ten-year-old daughter—was probably meaningless to her, and when, in the autumn of 1559, the Guises claimed to have discovered a Huguenot plot, she was left floundering. There was the ever latent fear of the Bourbons, those heretics with their irritatingly legal claim to the throne; but there was the fear, too, of the Guises' very obvious lust for power, mixed with relief that they formed a shield against the world outside. She fled to Amboise with them, clutching her children to her, peering myopically and fearfully at every bush which might hide a ravening Huguenot.

It was, after all, a most curious kind of plot—at once international and parochial, somehow amorphous and yet directed toward a single, malicious goal. A sceptical mind might, perhaps, have suspected that it was directed not against the king's royal person but against his in-laws, the Guises. The Guises would have countered such an unworthy thought with the retort that they had only the good of the crown at heart and what was good for the Guises was hence unquestionably good for France. And from the safety of Amboise, search began for the silent leader—the shadowy figure who menaced the Catholic faith and the crown alike. Troops in their tens of thousands were supposed to be gathering on the frontiers of the State, supplied by those hostile Protestant princes who ringed France. The craggy Duke of Guise took over the defense of Amboise, the crown, and the State with only a perfunctory nod of recognition toward the Most Christian King, his sixteen-year-old nephew, cowering wide-eyed while he listened to the hair-raising tales of Huguenot ferocity.

And on a morning in March 1560, suspicions appeared to be substantiated. A patrol returning to the château—marching behind the royal standard but recruited entirely from the ranks of Guise—encountered a body of men descending the hill toward the château. They were armed—but only as all men were armed these days. They replied freely to the questions. They were discharged soldiers, unemployed artisans—hungry men who had accepted a little money to make a demonstration. Yes, they would gladly accompany the patrol back to the castle. That was what they were hired to do—protest about Guise arrogance before His Majesty.

In the château they were questioned again and then executed.

Duke François thought it prudent that the royal family should be closely involved with his loyal defense of their interests and invitations just this side of commands were issued for the family to attend the execution. So it was that, at the age of ten, Marguerite had her first experience of violent death, looking down with her brothers from a window into the courtyard, watching the grotesque dance of suffocating men on the end of a rope, listening to their strangled grunts and squeals. It was the first of many such lessons over the next few weeks. Daily, hourly, the Guise patrols found victims—nobles as well as peasants, urban as well as rural, their only common denominator being that they were Huguenots. Daily, hourly, blood spurted from the severed necks of the quality, breath rasped in the throats of the common. It proved difficult to kill quickly enough to keep pace, for it was no easy task to dispose of the bodies until an ingenious executioner introduced the system of roping the victims together and tipping them into the Loire. Those downstream later complained because of the stench of stranded, decaying bodies, but the technique cleared the area around Amboise efficiently enough.

Extreme action eventually bred reaction. Even the friends and allies of the Guises were beginning to look thoughtful, for apparently it was Duke François and the family council who now decided when a heretic became a traitor. And Catherine de Médicis was stirring from her lethargy. For nearly two years she had wept; for nearly two years she had recited the virtues of her dead husband to her restless children, to courtiers, to whoever had no alternative but to listen; for nearly two years she had dressed in black. There was politics as well as emotion in her behavior, for in the present uncertainty the prudent person remained in the background. But the scales were beginning to tilt, if only temporarily, against the Guises, who had her son in their pockets. Simultanously, too, the burden of grief began to lift from her. The court marked one particular day when the female dwarf of the Dowager Duchess of Guise—a hideous little creature barely three feet high—came chuckling into Catherine's presence, clapping her minute, pudgy hands with simulated glee. "Madam, Madam. What luck, what luck. I've just been served twenty-four times by the biggest lackeys in the court." Catherine's indignant ladies hushed the dwarf, apprehensively glancing toward their mistress. But to their astonishment she was smiling broadly. It was not the world's most exquisite joke—but Catherine de Médicis was not the world's most sensitive person, and the dwarf's flow of bawdy, unsubtle conversation so exactly suited her that she bought the creature from the duchess.

Moving cautiously into the field of action, Catherine found allies. She was, after all, the mother of the king, and even he was beginning to question, if timidly, the Guise assumption that their well-being and that of France were coterminous. And Duke François, courageous though he was, in private had confessed himself suprised —appalled—by the force of hatred directed against the family. He welcomed it, interpreting it as tribute to the Guise loyalty—but perhaps it was as well for him to move into the protective background for a while and transfer the burden of controlling this volatile country to the plump black shoulders of the Queen Mother—as, more and more, she was being called. And Catherine accepted the burden and with a group of the more temperate evolved an edict of conciliation between Catholic and Huguenot. The States General—the nation met in Parlement—were summoned by her "to find the remedy for the present evils and appease the troubles which we see in the realm" and peace seemed about to return. And the king died—of a mastoid— aged seventeen.

†

II

The Grand
Tour

Monday, March 13, 1564, was a still, mild day with a pearly mist that cleared by midmorning. At Fontainebleau, the casual knots of idlers had coalesced into a sizable crowd by the time the sun broke through. Most people present had been involved, in some capacity or another, with the forthcoming spectacle, for life in the little town was utterly dependent upon the castle. Familiarity might perhaps have dulled the edge of wonder but, even so, it was not every day that the entire royal court took to the road in all its gaudy splendor, and the townsfolk intended to make the most of the occasion.

They were not disappointed. Shortly after 2 P.M., the great gate of the castle that looked toward the town creaked wide open and the first colored wave of the flood frothed out—one hundred Gentlemen of the Household, dressed for peace despite the long, elegant sword each carried, richly embroidered coats swirling, plumes nodding. Behind them came their apprentices, the pages and grooms attached to the royal household to gain a wider view of life and learn their place in the hierarchy. Following these gaudy male butterflies, the mercenaries struck a somber note of realism: they were foreigners—Swiss and Scotsmen gleaming in polished steel and backed up with mounted archers dressed simply in plain leather helmets and jerkins.

The Grand Tour
†

They rode by looking straight ahead, indifferent to yet another crowd, and some of the crowd muttered, audibly indignant that a king of France should be hedged in by foreign steel. But most had become accustomed to such a spectacle, and the bodyguard passed on to be succeeded by the technicians of the household—the stewards and butlers and cooks and carvers and physicians, sufficient men to have efficiently administered an entire city.

After them there was a gap, for it was not fitting that the next group should mingle with domestic servants. Richly dressed, heavily scented, magnificently equipped, they were the nucleus of the court, its reason for existing—the princes of the blood, marshals, ambassadors, secretaries, councillors. And at the center of this gaudy group, like some improbable diamond in a too ornate setting, came the person who had triggered off this vast pilgrimage, whose will alone had uprooted eight hundred people from their comfortably familiar surroundings and would keep them unrestfully moving for more than two years, Catherine, the Queen Mother and Queen Regent. She rode in a giant coach, one of the first the country had seen—an impressive crimson vehicle which nevertheless swung sickeningly on its thick leather straps so that, long before each day's journey was over, she would be glad to hoist her massive body onto horseback. But there was no doubt that it conferred prestige, and Catherine de Médicis hungered after prestige and would endure any discomfort for its sake.

Apart from that incredible moment when she had found herself pregnant for the first time, perhaps the most fortunate moment in Catherine's life to date was when the breath finally rasped out of the body of her seventeen-year-old son, François II. In that moment an equivocal situation came to an end, for in that moment the Guise claim to control of the throne through their nephew-in-law also came to an end. The new king, Charles IX, was indisputably a minor, for he was only ten years old and the law unequivocally recognized his mother as Regent. She picked up the scepter that she would wield, through three reigns, over the next thirty years. At the age of forty-two, after a lifetime spent in the background, she stepped into politics as though she had been preparing for it all her life. She summoned the leading Catholic and Protestant theologians to a great council—the national equivalent of the Council of Trent, which was still laboring to bring forth its mouse. Her own council broke up in rancor and disorder, but still she held to the path of mediation, privately contemptuous of those for whom religion meant anything more than a set of ceremonies. Skillfully, she set about neutralizing the center of opposition—the consecrate and natural leader of the Huguenots, Antoine de Bourbon, King of Navarre. She brought his small son Henri to her court. She tempted Antoine from his virtuous, vinegary wife with the plump, rosy Mademoiselle de Rouet, one of her very special attendants. Antoine suffered a crisis of conscience, speculated on the nature of his claim to Navarre, contrasted the delicious little commoner with his undoubtedly angular wife, and fell exactly as Catherine had hoped and expected. She sent messages and compliments to that other queen across the Channel, the twenty-nine-year-old virgin who had few more physical charms than the Queen of Navarre but who was ruler of a great country and therefore was assumed to be possessed of devastating sensual attraction. And Elizabeth of England returned the compliments and the messages and perhaps pondered on the personal advantages of a social position that obliged her to consider a ten-year-old French boy as bedmate. In Spain, Philip seethed and muttered to his beautiful and anxious young wife: her mother should be burning heretics, not debating and negotiating with them. And Elizabeth of Spain, who was not only a dutiful wife but also a good Catholic, humbly agreed with him and wondered how to bring up the business of her sister Marguerite, whom her mother was most anxious to marry off to Philip's nephew, the heir to Portugal, in order to stop his marrying the widowed Mary Stuart. Catherine was in her stride, already using that technique which she would polish over the next three decades, employing her children as extensions of herself, regardless of their desires.

And for nearly two years she patiently made her careful and complex moves. Later, her thronging enemies would claim that not only had she brought a gluttony for ice cream and cock's livers from Florence but also the parochial habit of mind which tried to run a nation of thirteen million people in the same way that her forebears had governed a city of eighty thousand. And the charge was true in essence—but the system worked. Until a Sunday morning in March 1562 when a band of Guise men-at-arms fell upon a group of Huguenots at prayer and slaughtered them. And in that hour, peace departed from France and would not return, except for brief, uneasy intervals, for the rest of that century.

The massacre of Vassy might have been planned by Duke François; it might have been the product of spontaneous hatred. Whatever the cause, it was the pebble which started the avalanche. By the time that Catholics and Huguenots gathered for their services on the following Sunday, France was plunged into civil war, the first of the so-called Wars of Religion, in reality the curtain-raiser for a continuous and bloody struggle. Catherine watched, impotent, while her carefully erected structure was dashed to the ground by the fury of fanaticism. Antoine of Navarre awoke from his dream of scented dalliance, remembered that he was the leader of the Huguenots, and took himself off to his death with his undoubted courage and equally undoubted lack of common sense. He died not so much in the cause of freedom of religious worship as, typically, in pursuit of a joke. He was urinating derisively against the wall of an enemy town when an indignant citizen got him with a lucky shot. Not long after, his great rival in life, the Duke of Guise, joined him in death, shot down by a Huguenot assassin. The first generation was departing from the stage, but others took their place, leaving no break in the feud. Young Henri of Navarre replaced Antoine, and Henri de Guise, now an eleven-year-old stripling, golden-haired and as handsome as his father had been ugly, became duke.

But that had been a year ago. Peace, of a sort, had been patched up at Amboise, and though realists were fully aware that it was only the breathing space between rounds, the ebullient Catherine decided to treat it as the dawn of a splendid new age. And what

better way to celebrate such a dawn, to celebrate the passing of a
night of civil discord and terror, than to make a grand tour of the
wounded kingdom so that Catholics and Huguenots alike could pay
homage to their king, their divinely appointed protector.

That divinely appointed protector, her fourteen-year-old son
Charles IX, now sat immediately opposite her balancing himself un-
comfortably on the hard, crimson velvet seat of the coach. Strictly
speaking, he should have had his own coach—this very coach, in fact,
sprinkled so liberally as it was with the royal fleur-de-lys. But it
would have required an unusually bold youth to draw attention to
such a point of etiquette. And King Charles was not bold. There
were, indeed, times when he could fly into such a shrieking, trembling, white-faced rage that those around him feared equally for their
lives and his sanity. But after such a storm he would relapse into his
sullen, lethargic state in which he would obediently perform the
treadmill tasks of royal office. Looking at him now, Catherine's maternal heart might well have warmed toward him—for when there
were no other pressing considerations, she could be a loving and
solicitous mother. The boy looked so pale, so ill at ease. Even now,
she could blush at the contretemps during his coronation four years
before. The great crown of state had borne heavily on his childish
head and he had cried out and tried to remove it. They had stopped
him, but throughout the gorgeous, lengthy ceremony he had sni-
velled at its weight, and at the weight and stuffiness of the coronation
robes that seemed to press him to the ground. She had taught him
to keep a stiff upper lip in public, at least, but there was nothing she
could do about his woebegone expression. He looked beyond her
with his beautiful, golden, unhappy eyes, past her to the coach that
followed them, making no secret of the fact that he would willingly
have changed the honor of being with his mother for the pleasure of
being with the children in the following coach. Charles IX had forgotten how to be a child, but had not yet learned to be a king.

There were four children in the coach behind. Henri, Duke of
Anjou, was a year younger than his brother the king but seemed, in
fact, considerably older. Maturity sat easily, naturally upon him al-

ready: the brown face with the dark sparkling eyes could assume an expression of arrogant superiority, and the childishly shrill voice could lacerate in contemptuous anger. But the same voice could enchant with a cascade of wit and fantasy, the same face could be warmed and rendered curiously touching by a heart-moving smile. Charm, and the desire to be loved, were first to serve Henri of Anjou as very useful tools and then, like some lethal drug, destroy him. Beside him, his small brother Alençon sat in his shadow as he always had and always would. He was now ten years old and as ugly, as unprepossessing, as his brother was attractive. He had been pleasant enough as a very young child, but a bout of smallpox had left its ineradical mark upon him—exactly the sort of thing that would happen to François, duke of Alençon. Even his name was not his own. He had been christened Hercule, and when his brother, François the king, had died, his mother had changed his name through some obscure belief in avoiding the evil eye.

The third boy, also called Henri, was just eleven years old. There was the faintest, the most fleeting of resemblances between him and the other boys. He, too, was a prince of the blood, for he was a Bourbon, cousin to the Valois. He was also a monarch in his own right now that his father Antoine, King of Navarre, was dead. His splendid title sat lightly upon him, however, partly because he realized that his presence here, at the heart of the royal court and at the very peak of social excellence, was only on sufferance. But partly, too, because he was lighthearted by nature, with the mouth of a poet but the eyes of a clown. He laughed easily, regarding the world from beneath a wheat-sheaf shock of hair as a place where, if one looked hard enough, entertainment could be found somehow. Certainly he had found variety enough in his short life. When he was born his grandfather had roared with delight, snatched him up, and moistened his lips with garlic and wine "to make a man of him." As a young child he had run wild with the goats and mountaineers' children, barefoot as they—tough, cheerful, and undeniably odorous. Then he had been swept up, only half comprehending, and deposited in the heart of the most prodigal, most sophisticated court in Europe; but whether as guest, as cousin, or as hostage, nobody quite knew. When his father had dallied with Catholicism and Mademoiselle de Rouet, young Henri found himself summoned to mass; afterward, he reverted to Protestantism without anyone in the court being particularly disturbed. He learned a lot in his eleven years—above all, how to be externally pliable in order to maintain an inner core of steel.

The fourth person in the coach was Marguerite, four months younger than her cousin and future husband, a gay, witty child much liked by those who had to deal with her. Throughout the previous, vital, years when imperceptibly she changed from baby into girl, her mother had been something too preoccupied with state affairs to trouble much about the upbringing of her youngest daughter. It was, perhaps, fortunate for Marguerite in the long run for as governess she had Charlotte de Vienne, Baronne de Curton, a lady who, in her time, had been *gouvernante* to seven queens and princesses and had a lively knowledge of the strengths and weaknesses of the breed. "A wise and virtuous lady, greatly attached to the Catholic religion," Marguerite remembered her affectionately long afterward. The streak of earnestness and genuine piety in the little girl's nature responded eagerly, warmly to the elderly woman's own piety and gentleness. It would have been expecting too much of any mentor to turn a daughter of the Médicis and Valois into a well-behaved young lady. But Baronne de Curton did manage to instill certain old-fashioned virtues into her—in particular the virtue of being self-sufficient: of keeping her own counsel and making her own judgment. Perhaps, if the baroness had only had her charge longer, she might have been able to eradicate the fatal weakness in the girl's character, the hedonism which was to destroy her. But now that she was emerging from her puppy fat into the first glow of that astonishing beauty of hers, her mother decided upon her new role. At the age of eleven she was taken out of the baronne's loving care and suddenly thrust into the heart of perhaps the most corrupt court in Europe.

But on this mild spring afternoon, she was still essentially a child embarking on a prolonged treat, gazing with wondering eyes on a suddenly widened and colored world. Precocious, her attention inevitably would be attracted to the scented, giggling, beribboned occupants of the carriages which followed her own. To the casual eye they seemed to be the usual empty-headed young girls who fluttered prettily and uselessly round any court. The knowing already had a name for them, the queen mother's "Flying Squadron"—the shock troops of her highly specialized form of warfare. They entered legend, but it is highly unlikely that Catherine ever sat down and created her *escadron volante* in cold blood. She was a naturally gregarious woman, delighting particularly in the company of the young and the beautiful, and ambitious girls whose beauty was not equaled by their dowries naturally gravitated toward such an open-handed court. Most continued as simple maids of honor but, in each batch of newcomers, one or two would find themselves singled out for the queen mother's confidence—girls, for example, like the Mademoiselle de Rouet, who had so prettily charmed Antoine of Navarre. Gradually, unobtrusively, such girls would find themselves as part of an inner circle that was marked by no especial titles or costume, but whose members could be counted on to take part in any necessary cutting-out operation, ultimately receiving rich husbands as rewards.

The head of the cavalcade was entering the billets for the night not long after the last stragglers had left Fontainebleau. And so it was to continue for nearly two years, a great sluggish snake stolidly wriggling its way across France. Eight hundred members of the court required a corresponding number of baggage animals and wagons to transport their clothes, their entertainment, even their food. Only the favored members of the royal family could hope to "live off the country," a euphemism for being entertained at the expense of some unfortunate landowner. The rest had no choice but to pay the suddenly high prices in the marketplace, or laboriously cart their supplies with them. Matters were made no easier by the havoc caused by the late civil war. Again and again the enormous cortege would find itself lumbering through an apocalyptic landscape, an area where every crop had been delivered to the flames, where vines were slashed, rivers choked and only ashes marked the site of farmsteads. The young king looked upon his country with wide and horrified eyes, stammering his determination to bring the perpetrators to brook, to usher in eternal peace. His mother nodded and planned and ordered her Master of Horse to find another route. But still the court could not escape the stories. They differed in but one aspect from region to region: here the villains were Catholics and the innocent victims Huguenots; elsewhere, the roles are reversed. But the obscene details remain otherwise unchanged—eviscerated babies, men, women, children buried alive, burnt alive, hanged, strangled, bludgeoned.

The route of the procession was planned in a vast, shallow curve running first eastward to Lyons and then southwest to the Spanish border where the queen mother had some very pressing business to transact. But she was in no hurry to get there. France had to be shown to her son, and her son to France, she herself the plump tutelary deity of both. At Troyes there was an immense ball to celebrate the peace with the English: one of the Flying Squadron, Mademoiselle de Limeuil, distinguished the occasion by giving birth to a "fine splendid boy" at the height of the festivities and was promptly packed off to a nunnery for her trouble. The queen mother set great store by decorum. At Bar-le-Duc she had the delight of dandling her first grandchild—the future Duke of Lorraine, son of the poor, crippled Claude. She and the silent king and her other children were entertained there right royally, Claude briefly enjoying her role of chatelaine instead of humble daughter. But after the procession had moved on out of that rich, equivocal land of Lorraine, the billet master was hard put to find lodgings even for those of the Blood Royal. On more than one occasion Catherine found herself bedding down for the night in some stark, ruined house; she was not a nervous or even an imaginative woman, but on these nights her children slept near her despite protocol. Marguerite, as her brothers, had her own household, but the regent's mandate calmly swept aside such distinctions, and the princes and princess slept, as they had when babies, in a single room. Marguerite took it lightly; so did the young King of Navarre, while her small brother Alençon showed his delight. But Anjou hated it, hated the enforced intimacy and the loss of privacy.

The Grand Tour

†

The plague was raging in Lyons and so the party was forced to skirt the most comfortable town outside Paris. It crossed the Rhone a few miles downstream and met disaster, for a sudden storm sprang up, overwhelming one of the barges. There was no hope for any who fell into that roaring yellow-green current—particularly if they were young girls wrapped in voluminous cloaks and shawls and scarves. The barge which sank had been carrying members of the Flying Squadron, and for a little time the giggling was stilled as the survivors looked wild-eyed at each other. But the memory of death vanished with the scudding storm clouds and others took the place of the dead.

Outside Salon, the royal family parted company with the rest of the court and rode into the little town. The city fathers, astonished and delighted at such unexpected honor, welcomed their monarch and his mother and brothers and sister on a platform of white and crimson velvet. Charles, gauche and embarassed, cut short their fulsome speech of welcome. "We've really come to see Nostradamus," he blurted out.

The detour had been made at Catherine's express desire, and it was in this manner that Nostradamus saw, for the last time, the extraordinary family whose fate he had hinted at in his enigmatic prophecies. He had first met them eight years earlier when Catherine's husband was still alive. It was, indeed, to explain a curious prophecy which seemed to refer to the king that he had been summoned to Blois. It was one of the quatrains in his recently published *Centuries* which had attracted Catherine's attention for, it seemed to echo a warning that her own astrologer, Luc Gauric, had made about a duel. The quatrain ran

> *The young lion shall overcome the old*
> *In warlike field in single fight.*
> *In a cage of gold his eye will be pierced—*
> *Two wounds one, then die a cruel death.*

What did it mean? The seer could only shrug: his verses were probably as impenetrable to him as they were to the reader, products of some unknown and unknowable faculty of his mind. But Catherine, with her passion for the occult, had welcomed him; he must at once erect horoscopes for all her children. He did as instructed and she was pleased, if puzzled, by the result: three of her four sons would be kings and two of her daughters would be queens. It was not only possible but likely that Marguerite and Elizabeth would be queens precisely as he prophesied, for they would be much sought after by European monarchs. But how could François and Henri and Charles *all* be kings? Nostradamus, if he knew the answer, prudently kept silent.

Three years afterward, the king received his fatal wound on the tournament field—and suddenly all France was talking about that quatrain, enigmatic no longer, for was not the "cage of gold" the gilded tournament helmet? And "two wounds one" could only mean the wound in the throat and the wound in eye caused by one thrust of the lance. The students of Paris burned Nostradamus in effigy and there was talk of bringing him to trial, but it came to nothing. And now Catherine was hungry for more wonders. The horoscopes for some of her children were already working out, for two of the three sons had been kings, precisely as he had promised, and Elizabeth was a queen now in distant Spain. Could he show her more? And that night, it was said, the queen regent humbly waited upon the Christianized Jew in his shadow-filled library-cum-laboratory, and there he showed her a mirror and in it three of her sons circled round, each circuit equaling one year of his reign. There was the dead François, making his solitary circuit; there was the still living Charles, making fourteen circuits, followed by Henri of Anjou, making twenty-four circuits. But that was not all, for when the shade of Henri of Anjou dissolved into deeper darkness, its place was taken by a curiously familiar face with the mouth of a poet and the eyes of a buffoon— Henri of Navarre. She did not have the heart to ask for more—to ask, among other matters, how *la p'tite Margot* was to become a queen and when.

The immense cortege rumbled on from Salon, running due west now. Tempers were short, for they had been fifteen months away from base, fifteen months of dubious meals and endless traveling on rutted roads, and now the baking heat of summer was again arising round them. Catherine placated those whom she could placate, and dismissed those who remained intractable and somehow kept the whole circus on the move. For it was now approaching the climacteric, the true goal of its wanderings. She was going to meet her daughter Elizabeth and the King of Spain himself at Bayonne, near the frontier with Spain, and to bring that meeting about she would have prodded and cajoled and threatened the cortege into hell itself, if necessary.

But long before they arrived, there came disturbing news of Philip's frame of mind. It was made known to Catherine, Queen Regent of France, that Philip, King of Spain, could not breathe the same air as heretics. Reluctantly but firmly Catherine dismissed all Huguenots from her train, save only for the little King of Navarre. Philip was still not satisfied. He had no real desire for this meeting, he told Fourquevaux, Catherine's ambassador in Spain. They had nothing to discuss until the regent began to take a firmer line with the Protestants who were undermining the stability of kings. As the cortege moved slowly westward, slowly but steadily closing the gap to Bayonne, couriers hastened through the heat between Madrid and the peripatetic court of France. Philip sent word that he would not come in person—and neither would his dutiful wife. Catherine wept few tears on news that she would not, after all, be meeting her son-in-law for the first time, but that she should be denied her only chance of again holding her daughter in her arms. . . . Passionately she protested in one of her racy, vehement letters and coldly Philip agreed that Elizabeth should go by herself, though he declined to pay out any money to dress her and her ladies in a fitting manner for such an occasion. The Duke of Alva would come in his stead, and with Alva Catherine would have to be content.

It was on a day of terrible heat that France and Spain met at last. It was on the banks of the Bidassoa, which marked the boundaries of the two states, but the presence of water had no effect on the temperature. By midday that awful hammer heat had killed six men of the bodyguard, and though their deaths were obviously caused by the fact that they were in full armor, inside which they had literally broiled, the quality were little better off, dressed as they were in costumes of rich and heavy stuffs. Despite the heat, Catherine ushered her brood down to the water's edge and then, unable to contain her impatience, put out in an open boat to meet Elizabeth coming from Spain. And so it was at last that Marguerite saw, coming out of the heat haze like some legendary figure, the elder sister who had so long been held up to her as a species of goddess.

Elizabeth had left home when she was fourteen—only a year or so older than Marguerite was now. Over these past five years she had rounded and blossomed from an attractive child into a truly beautiful woman. In Madrid, common citizens would go home in a glow of achievement and pleasure if they had caught sight of her; they had grieved tempestuously when, a year before, she had given birth to a stillborn child and then, a few months afterward, had contracted smallpox—that terrible disease which usually disfigured permanently those whom it did not kill. That was the first thing Catherine had looked for, but the only scars on her daughter's delicate skin were a couple of faint marks on her nose. The Franco-Spanish alliance, founded on Elizabeth's beautiful body, was unimpaired. It was unlikely that such a self-consciously virtuous man as Philip would have put his wife from him because of smallpox scars, but it was also good to know that the political alliance was buttressed by sexual pleasure.

The fact that Philip loved his wife was unsurprising: it would have taken a far more dedicated misanthrope even than he to remain unaffected by that warm and gentle charm. But, curiously, Elizabeth returned that love. It did not mar the delight of the family reunion: after sunset, when the earth began again to breathe in a velvet darkness, there was an intimate dinner party with an abundance of wine and flowers and laughter, when the Valois wit flashed and even Charles laughed like the child he was, and Marguerite and her small brother Alençon were permitted to remain until far into the night. Elizabeth was, for the moment, a part of the family again. But occasionally behind the banter and good-will and private jokes there would sound a steely undertone, particularly when they touched on religion. "What cause have you to think, Madam, that the king my husband mistrusts your Majesty?" Elizabeth said on one such occasion. "Only evil-minded people could give you such ideas." "My dear daughter, you have become very Spanish," Catherine retorted. "I am Spanish, I own it," was the reply, "and in truth it is my business to be. But I am always your daughter, the same that you sent into Spain." Except on any matter concerned with religion, Catherine noted, and thereafter avoided the topic with her daughter.

They moved on to Bayonne the following day and the observers noted how shabbily the Spanish escort was dressed—a deliberate insult to Catherine. She affected to be unaware of it, and, on her side, poured out money for the most elaborate entertainments. One of these occasions so impressed her younger daughter that she must have jotted down an account of it within a few hours, for thirty years later she was able to give a lively and detailed account. The entertainment took place on an island in the middle of the Adour. "The shape of a room was designed in the middle of the island as though by nature, in a large oval meadow enclosed by stately trees, around which the queen my mother had arranged niches in each of which was placed a circular table for twelve persons whilst that of their majesties was raised at the end of the enclosure, upon a dais approached by four grass steps. All these tables were served by different sets of shepherds, dressed in cloth of gold and satin, according to the various costumes of all the provinces of France. Upon alighting from the magnificent boats—in which, all the way from Bayonne, we were accompanied by several seagods who sang and recited verses to their majesties—these shepherds were discovered, each group apart, in meadows upon either side of a grass alley leading to the aforesaid enclosure. They were dancing each after the manner of his province —the Provençals with shawms and cymbals, the Poitevines with the bagpipes, the Bourguignones and Champenoises with small hautboys, round fiddles and rustic tambourines, the Bretonnes dancing the passepieds and branlesgais and so on with respect to all the other provinces." In the evening, after the banquet, there was a torch dance

by heavily jeweled girls, a brilliant barbaric spectacle that was suddenly cut short by an extraordinary storm of wind and rain. The
revellers dashed unceremoniously for the boats "and the confusion
of the retreat, by boat, in the darkness gave occasions for more
diverting stories than even the splendours of the festivity afforded."
Marguerite's debut as a reporter is an impressive one. Sparsely, and
with a refreshing touch of feminine malice, she builds up her picture
—the chattering, laughing boatloads on their way to the picnic; the
raucous, plaintive peasant music that greeted them, the richness of
costumes, the glint and glow of precious stones seen by torchlight,
the rush and spatter of wind and rain.

But after the entertainments and compliments, the bargaining,
the horsetrading between Alva and Catherine. The position of each
was quite clear-cut, quite simple. Catherine, like a good bourgeois
mother, wanted to marry off her children to their best possible advantage—and the best possible advantage was a husband or wife
with Hapsburg blood. She wanted to marry Marguerite to Don Car-
los, Philip's son by his first wife, and she wanted to marry Henri of
Anjou to Philip's elderly sister, Juana. Alva listened coldly and made
evasive remarks and presented his own simple, clear-cut case: he
wanted Catherine to kill, convert or exile all Protestants in her own
lands and help him to do the same in the Netherlands. Catherine was
voluble and evasive and day after day in the crushing heat of
Bayonne their followers watched discreetly from a distance as they
walked up and down, up and down the cool, shaded gallery of Catherine's palace—the one immensely tall, bony, angular, the other,
short and dumpy, yet alike in their intransigence to each other's
demands. The conference came to an end with nothing resolved,
foundering on interests that were too diametrically opposed. Philip
of Spain had no particular desire to tie himself even closer to this
dubious family; Catherine had no intention of pulling his religious
chestnuts out of the fire. She kissed her eldest daughter and Elizabeth
returned to the south to the golden heat and dust of Spain and to the
death that awaited her two years later. Catherine's cortege, shrunken
now, gathered itself together and began the painful journey north-

ward. There was an embarrassing episode when they passed through the tiny kingdom of Navarre and the court was besieged by Catholics, bitterly protesting against the treatment they had received from Henri's mother Jeanne. She had clamped down a regime that, for its bigotry and severity, surpassed anything they had yet seen, and on their arrival at the capital, Catherine reprimanded the tight-lipped Jeanne and uncompromisingly demanded that she restore freedom of worship in her lands precisely as existed in the rest of France. She did so. She had no choice, but her expression gave warning enough of what would happen to Catholics in Navarre when war again loosened the control of the crown.

The bitter little exchange was the last affair of state that the peripatetic court discharged. On May 1, 1566, the court of France entered Paris, nearly two years and three months since it had left Fontainebleau.

†

III

Daughter of France

At nineteen, Henri, Duke of Anjou, was wholly adult, the last uncertainties of childhood and adolescence thrust firmly behind him. He retained, as he always would, a certain gay inconsequentiality which sat gracefully enough upon him but which only lightly concealed a steely core. His was a fantastical nature, delighting in the bizarre, moving effortlessly from affection to cruelty and back again, avid for novelty. But all these characteristics were courtiers—outriders—to a ravening central ego. Gaily, but quite mercilessly, he exploited his mother's love for him. Catherine de Médicis loved all her children, but she held a particular affection for this, her third son, the most Italian of them all. Mother and son communicated at a level that seemed almost telepathic, so sensitive and instantaneous was the response of one to the other, creating a rapport so close that enemies hinted at an even more intimate, forbidden relationship.

These two formed a kind of double star around which the rest of the family—Alençon, Marguerite and even the king himself—revolved. Charles smouldered: he accepted, perforce, his mother's tutelage, for it would have taken a far stronger character than his to break that velvet chain. But bitterly he resented the effortless social dominance of his brother, and no great skill was needed to predict that such virulent personal jealousy must, eventually, have political repercussions. Alençon shared the Valois blood and therefore shared the jealousy, even though he was scarcely fourteen. But Marguerite, who had actually been injured by this brilliant and dashing brother, idolized him—for a few years. The childish bigotry which had led him to persecute her was long since forgotten: he was now more Catholic than the pope, with an exaggerated, swashbuckling piety. Her religion meant much to Marguerite, and therefore, with this barrier between them removed, she could become his warmest and most uncritical partisan. Even after their brief-lived love was succeeded by an enduring mutual hatred, she could yet look back upon it with nostalgia. She held a curious and genuine respect for the unfortunate Charles, "my brother the king"; for Alençon she varied between exasperation and a kind of motherly solicitude; but Anjou was, in a very real sense, her alter ego, the kind of person she might have been had she had the freedom of a man. When the mood took them, they could fascinate the court with a cascade of wit, each striking sparks from the other, building higher and ever more elaborate structures of fantasy while Charles looked on glumly and their mother smiled benignly and pondered yet again on whom to chose for their marriage partners. To watch them dancing together was an aesthetic delight of a high order, for whether they were moving in the stately pavane or the uproarious branle, they were ideally matched, their movements as fluid as one.

Marguerite, approaching seventeen, was at the dawn of a beauty that was to become legendary. It was a beauty that, apart from what it owed to her personality, must have been founded upon bone structure, for it defied not only the ravages of time but the crude cosmetics with which she punished her skin, eventually leaving it coarse and pitted. Yet, curiously, it was a beauty which somehow escaped the foremost artists of her day. Catherine de Médicis, like the good bourgeois mother she resembled at so many points, delighted in having the portraits of her children around her, and dozens must have been sketched or painted in her lifetime. Marguerite, in her maturity, was indifferent to portraiture and bothered to have only two or three commissioned on her own account. But these, together with those executed for her mother, provide a more or less continuous picture of her from childhood to near old age. The little girl who looks out of the earlier portraits has a poignant sweetness with her huge eyes and gentle, rather shy expression; the woman in late middle age has a certain massive and amiable dignity. But the young lady in her twenties—in the full bloom of that legendary beauty—appears to be possessed of simply a commonplace prettiness, marred, moreover, by a very definitely sly expression. On the evidence of her portraits alone, Marguerite de Valois, Daughter of France, appears to owe her beauty to the sycophantic praise of courtiers, by no means an uncommon phenomenon.

But the evidence of other contemporaries tells an entirely different story, and the most dramatic is that provided by the dashing Don John of Austria. He was crossing France clandestinely to take up a dangerous appointment in the Netherlands, but nevertheless broke his journey to attend a ball at the Louvre simply in order to see this fabled princess with his own eyes. She was then in her early twenties and, after watching her dancing for some time, Don John nodded a somber agreement to his escort's eager question. "The beauty of that princess is more divine than human, but she is made to damn and ruin men rather than to save them"—an oddly prophetic remark. Rather similar was the reaction of the Polish nobleman who arrived in Paris as part of an embassy. He, too, gazed his fill upon her, then swung upon his heel and marched away: "Never do I wish to see such beauty again." A Neapolitan hung about Paris for more than two months solely on the chance of seeing her, and as soon as he had done so, left for his long journey home. "If I had returned without seeing this princess I could hardly have claimed to have seen France."[3] The elaborate conceits that Pierre de Ronsard, the court poet, wove around her seem intolerably arch and sugary to a later generation— her mouth "filled with a thousand roses, where gleam twin rows of pearls," the "shell-like ear," eyebrows like "ebony bows," the comparisons with Venus, who flushes red with jealousy and chagrin, are perhaps the small change of court poetry. But they seem almost sober by contrast with the extraordinary adulation of that gallant warrior-priest, the Seigneur de Brantôme. Nowhere in his gallery of illustrious contemporary women, *The Book of the Ladies,* is Brantôme exactly sparing with adjectives and superlatives, so that when he comes to his brief biography of Marguerite he is forced to pile hyperbole upon hyperbole and extravagance upon extravagance to obtain his effect. Even Marguerite was slightly taken aback when she read the book, and smilingly reproved him for his flattery. Brantôme's eulogies of Catherine de Médicis, Mary Stuart, Elizabeth of Spain and the rest were more or less standard exercises in court flattery. But behind the fulsome flood of words describing the appearance and career of Marguerite de Valois, the reader can detect a very personal, very sincere admiration. It rather looks as though the Seigneur de Brantôme was more than a little in love with the subject of his biography, and the Seigneur de Brantôme was no mean judge of feminine charm and beauty.

She dressed with flair and dash. In this, at least, she owed her initial confidence to her mother, who had neither time, inclination nor ability to trouble much about fashion and was, if anything, rather proud of her daughter's talent. Upon one occasion, when they were absent from Paris, Catherine remarked upon the frequency of her daughter's change of dress. "I'm wearing out those I brought from the Court so that, when I return, I can dress according to the fashion," Marguerite replied. "Nonsense," was Catherine's answer. "It is you who invent fashion. Wherever you go the Court will copy you." She may have meant nothing more than that the ladies of the court would prudently copy the daughter of the queen regent, but Marguerite took the words at their face value and thereafter dressed as she pleased. Now she was demurely clad, from tip to toe, in shimmering white satin; now in a bold confection of swirling orange and black with a great gem-sewn veil; now in encrusted brocades with waist drawn in to vanishing point, bared breasts and towering hairstyle. Perversely, she favored blond wigs, though she had most luxuriant black hair of her own; in later years, when she became undeniably freakish, she actually kept blond footmen who were periodically shorn to provide her headpieces. Brantôme worshipped, recording each minute change for his own delight and the education of posterity, even though posterity might have concluded ungratefully that the fashions as set by the daughter of France were undeniably garish. "I have often heard our courtiers dispute as to which attire became and embellished her the most, about which each had his own opinion. For my part, the most becoming array I ever saw her in was, as I think, and so did others, on the day when the Queen Mother made a fete at the Tuileries for the Poles. She was robed in a velvet gown of Spanish rose, covered with spangles, with a cap of the same velvet, adorned with plumes and jewels of such splendour as never was. She looked so beautiful in this attire, as many told her, that she wore it often and was painted in it."[4]

A superb figure, a beautiful face, a generous nature and a flair for fashion: it was perhaps Marguerite's misfortune that she should have added to these social advantages a restless, wide-ranging and somewhat mocking intelligence. She was, after all, granddaughter to the splendid François I and a descendant of the superb Medici. The family intellectualism had by no means passed her mother by: Catherine de Médicis's capacity for concentration was phenomenal— awed courtiers reported how she could absorb complex state dispatches at first reading, frequently while being jolted and swayed in a clumsy coach. But the pure love of learning for its own sake did, undoubtedly, skip over her, while it appeared and flourished in her daughter. Marguerite's formal education was decidedly sketchy, broken again and again as it was by civil turmoil which enforced flight. But it was this very lack of formality that eventually made her literary style so vivacious and dashing, expressed though it was in the weirdest of spelling and the clumsiest of calligraphy. Brantôme grotesquely exaggerated her very real talent for writing: "Her beautiful letters are the finest, the best couched, whether they be serious or familiar and such that the greatest writers of the past and present may hide their heads and not produce their own when hers appear —for theirs are trifles beside hers. No one, having read them, would fail to laugh at Cicero with his familiar letters."[5] But he was on solid ground when he went on to claim that "whoever would collect her letters and discourses would make a school and training for the world," if not quite in the manner that he fondly imagined. Marguerite's letters certainly make delightful reading; they are also masterpieces of deviousness.

She was a linguist of a high order. She never seems to have learned Greek—still a fairly rare accomplishment—but Latin was virtually a second, and certainly a living, tongue to her: on one occasion she astonished the court by spontaneously replying to an ambassador's Latin oration in the same language. Italian and Spanish came to her "as if she had been born and brought up in those lands"; her mother still spoke a thick, heavily accented French and tended to lapse into her native tongue, so Marguerite's command of Italian was unsurprising. Presumably, she was taught Spanish against the very high likelihood of making a Spanish marriage as her sister Elizabeth had done.

Dancing came to her as naturally as breathing, and her mother personally taught her to embroider and insisted that she learn both to sing and to play the lute. In this matter, at least, the queen mother was very much a Florentine.

It was her mother who supervised what there was of the girl's education, but it was through her brother, Henri, that she stepped into the lethal political arena.

In September 1567, the delicate balance which Catherine had established between the conflicting religious parties collapsed in bloody ruin. It was by no means the regent's fault: she had not only resisted the coldly arrogant demands of Alva but she had even raised a force of Swiss mercenaries to protect France's eastern frontier against a Spanish invasion. Ironically, it was the very movement of these troops marching to the Netherlands which aroused the alarm of the Huguenots. The hotheads among them decided on the desperate plan of kidnapping the king and holding him as a kind of hostage. It was a mad scheme whose success would have been even more damaging than its failure, for it would have totally alienated even those favorably disposed to them. And it very nearly succeeded. The

court was at the undefended château of Monceau at the time that
news came of the plot. Charles was at first totally unbelieving and
then, when his advisers managed to persuade him that his subjects
were actually planning to lay hands on his sacrosanct body, he lapsed
into one of his rages. But this was no sudden, flaring rage that died
down as rapidly as it rose: rather, it was a cold, sullen, diffused hatred
that remained with him long after the ostensible cause was ended.
With his mother and sister, he hastily retired to the defended city of
Meaux, awaiting the Swiss, and then, hedged around by foreign
pikes, the King of France and his family advanced on to the capital.
There was an indecisive engagement just outside Paris: the Prince of
Condé, reluctantly backed up by Gaspard de Coligny, who regretted
the whole tragic situation, seemed disposed to prevent their entry.
But the Swiss, "lowering their pikes, ran at them like mad dogs, at
full speed," and brought them home at last.

So began the second round of the Wars of Religion. The old
constable, Anne de Montmorency, was killed early in the new war,
going down like a great oak, taking with him half a dozen men more
than thirty years his junior. And with him ended something from a
larger, more spacious past. Catherine debated as to whom to put in
his place. The office was perhaps just a little too powerful to re-create
in these uncertain times; in addition, her second son, Henri of Anjou,
was clamouring for better outlets for his energies. She made him
lieutenant-general of the kingdom, effectively filling the constable's
role, for Anjou was now in command of all the royal forces. Despite
his whimsicality, his silks and his perfumes, the young man had a
distinct military flair. It was dashing, based on intuition rather than
logic, and, without the sober guidance of the grizzled old Marshal
Tavannes, Anjou would undoubtedly have been brought to grief. But
for some weeks the Catholic armies under their handsome young
leader happily cavorted across the battlefields of France, routing the
sour-faced heretics, bringing chivalry and romance back again into
the butcher's business. The king heard the news with ever increasing
bitterness, his normal dislike of his brother now fed to bursting point
with jealousy. He had pleaded with his mother to be allowed to take

the field at the head of his own armies: he had never wanted to be a king, but he had always wanted to be a soldier—and he would have been a good one, less brilliant but more reliable than the vaunted Anjou. Catherine refused to listen to him; war was simply an instrument of policy, and a bad one at that as far as she, the Florentine shopkeeper, was concerned. So Charles had to fight in his imagination. He showed the gentlemen of his bedchamber the curious birthmark on his shoulder: they should note it because it would identify his dead body on the battlefield. But he was aware of reality. When a courtier poet praised him, the king, for the armies' victories, he turned fiercely upon the man. "Stop writing your stupid lies and flatteries about me. Save them for my brother—he'll cut you a better pattern." And when ever more splendid news of victories came in, he threw himself upon horseback and hunted like a madman until consciousness left him and oblivion gave him a kind of peace.

In March 1569, with the Huguenots massing for a last, desperate stand, Henri sent a flowery, swaggering message to the court. The coming battle might be his last, "but he would quit the world with less regret" if he could but have a last audience of the king his brother, the queen his mother, and the princess his sister. "I leave you to guess how these words touched the heart of so excellent a mother," Marguerite recorded tongue in cheek. She decided to set off immediately, taking the king with her and the small party of ladies she was accustomed to travel with—Madame de Rais, Madame de Sauves and myself. Borne upon the wings of impatience and maternal affection, she accomplished the journey from Paris to Tours in three days and a half." Swiftly though the queen mother moved, the battle of Jarnac took place before they arrived. The royal forces were totally triumphant and the Prince of Condé, the peppery, old-fashioned and honorable leader of the Huguenot faction, was taken prisoner. He was slaughtered almost immediately afterward with a bullet in the back of the head. Henri, Duke of Anjou, was rapidly learning the correct way to wage a civil war.

It was during a lull in the festivities that followed that Anjou took his sister aside for a quiet and confidential chat. They happened to be strolling in the beautiful garden of the château at Plessis-lez-Tour, as were many others of the court on that mild spring day, and Anjou unobtrusively directed their steps to a kind of ornamental alley of shrubs. Satisfied that they were unobserved, he began to talk seriously. Over the following years Marguerite returned again and again to that conversation, dissecting it for hidden meanings, brooding over its outcome, polishing and repolishing it for eventual publication. In her final version, the opening of it sounds like the opening of a conversation in one of the convoluted novels then becoming popular, and certainly the words she put into her brother's mouth could never have been uttered by him. "Sister," she made him say, "early associations no less than close kinship constrains us to love one another and you must have been well aware that I, of all your brothers, have been the most solicitous for your welfare while I have remarked that you, too, were disposed to return me a like affection."[6] But while it is highly unlikely that the lively Anjou would ever condescend to speak like some peculiarly sanctimonius preacher, he undoubtedly did begin with the heaviest of flattery, for he wanted her to do him a favor. And as Marguerite's report approaches the central point of the conversation so the stiltedness drops away, something of the urgency of Anjou's own tone and words comes through and a brief and vivid tableau is created—two young people, gorgeously dressed as they stroll through a springtime garden, heirs to the greatest luxury and pleasures the world could afford, engrossed in their first maneuverings in the murky world of politics which would eventually kill the one and exile the other.

Anjou wanted his sister to be, quite literally, a friend at court by "influencing the Queen our Mother to retain me in my present good fortune." He pointed out, with justified pride, that the new war had burdened him with sudden and heavy responsibilities whose discharge would keep him more and more away from court. In his absence, enemies would plot against him—above all, his brother the king. And in a vivid simile that was all his own, he spelled out his fear: "The king my brother, growing up and becoming brave, may not always continue to amuse himself with hunting but may become ambitious and hunt men instead of beasts and deprive me of the post of king's lieutenant which he bestowed upon me." How could Marguerite help? By attending constantly upon their mother, the true source of all power, in order to defend his interests. "Be always present in her cabinet, at her *lever* and *coucher*. I shall tell her that you speak for me and she will confide in you. Rid yourself of your timidity. Talk to her freely as you do to me and, believe me, she will listen graciously. You will greatly advantage both yourself and me, and I shall be beholden to you, after God, for the maintenance of my good fortune."

The proposal completely astonished Marguerite. "I had existed, until then, without any purpose in life thinking only of dancing or hunting and having been brought up with so much constraint with regard to my mother that not only did I dare not speak to her, but I trembled when she even looked at me for fear that I might have done something to offend her." The awe with which Catherine de Médicis was held by intimates and courtiers alike was well expressed by her young daughter, who could find only a biblical parellel to it. "I was very nearly answering him as Moses replied to God upon beholding the vision of the burning bush 'Who am I to go unto Pharaoh?' " But Marguerite was not quite so frivolous and thoughtless as she would have her readers believe. She was perfectly well aware that Anjou was their mother's favorite child—it might, perhaps, have crossed her mind that it was odd that he should need anybody to sing his praises to his mother, for Catherine was already doing that to whomever would listen. But whatever his reasons, this was an unrivaled opportunity to penetrate into the inner court where, armed with her brother's credentials, there would be nothing to prevent her looking out for her interests as well as his own. The Valois learned the art of survival at a very early age. Prettily, she accepted the commission, they exchanged some more ornate compliments and shortly afterward they parted, Anjou to return to the wars and Marguerite to plan her political career.

A few days later she was summoned to her mother's closet. They were at Blois at the time, Catherine de Médicis's favorite château, and this elegantly paneled room was, in a very real sense, the seat and heart of government. Marguerite had visited before but rarely, and then usually to receive a reprimand for some misdemeanor. She, like the rest of the court, must have heard of the legend of those secret panels in the gilded wainscotting which would open on the touch of a hidden switch—panels which contained the queen mother's stock of rare and terrible poisons for the swifter dispatch of her enemies. The cupboards, in fact, contained nothing more lethal than certain documents which Catherine had particular reason to keep private, but the legend added to the mystique of government which the queen mother cultivated so assiduously.

Catherine graciously welcomed her daughter. Anjou had told her of the conversation he had had with his sister. "He no longer regards you as a child. I likewise will do so no longer. It will give me great pleasure to converse with you. Be obedient to me and do not fear to talk to me openly, for I wish it to be so." Marguerite took her place near the great black table which served as her mother's desk and sat there, outwardly demure, inwardly bubbling with excitement, hugging herself with delight, as the business of state went forward. She was now at the very heart of things, "and looking back to the past with a contemptuous eye, to the amusements of my childhood—the dancing and hunting and the associates of my own age—I despised them all as things utterly vain and unprofitable."

And so, for some months, she continued in that agreeable state of being privy to secrets of which the common herd knew nothing. Conscientiously, she had herself awakened before daybreak so that, her own toilet completed, she could attend her mother's ceremonial *lever*. And the last thing at night, although her own eyes were heavy with the fatigue of youth, she accompanied the queen mother to her bedchamber and, struggling to keep awake, conversed brightly and intelligently with her while the ladies of the bedchamber disrobed her and prepared her for the night. "She did me the honour, sometimes, to talk to me for two or three hours. I spoke to her continually of my brother and he was faithfully informed by me of everything that took place." There was one jarring note in the otherwise delightful symphony of mutual admiration: the reaction of her other brother, Charles IX. His impotent hatred and jealousy of his brother was transferred to his sister, Anjou's spy. His gloomy, suspicious gaze followed her about the court, and he responded to her respectful greetings either curtly or by swinging on his heels in tight-lipped silence. Marguerite's political career was hampered—as it would always be—by a warm and loving heart. She was torn now between respect and pity for her tormented brother the king, and admiration and gratitude for her brilliant brother the duke, who had gained their mother's confidence for her and so placed her feet on the path to a brilliant future.

And then, overnight, her little amateur structure collapsed. Anjou had again, with the utmost respect and loyal courtesy, commanded the presence of his monarch to witness another of his triumphs. He was laying siege to the town of Saint-Jean-d'Angely and claimed that the presence of the royal family was indispensable to success. Away went Catherine de Médicis on one of her breathless careers across the country, dragging with her the reluctant Charles, the delighted Marguerite and a handful of intimates who had long since become resigned to setting out on long journeys on short notice. Marguerite's disillusionment came on the very first night of the family's reunion. Anjou and her mother had been closeted together in earnest consultation before she joined them and she was aware at once of a strained atmosphere. Reasonably, she had expected that her brother would display a becoming gratitude at the very least, for she had faithfully kept her part of the bargain. To her astonishment and humiliation, he greeted her with the utmost coldness and thereafter studiously avoided talking to her. Her mother seemed embarrassed and uneasy: three or four times she ordered Marguerite to go to bed, but indignation and bewilderment gave the girl courage to disobey. At last Anjou withdrew from the room and Marguerite threw herself before her mother, imploring her to explain the cause of the obvious breach between them. Catherine for once seemed to be at a loss for words, but when Marguerite continued to insist, she said at last, "My daughter, your brother is wise: you must not bear him any ill-will.

What I am about to tell you can only lead to good." Then she told Marguerite that she had indeed warmly praised her daughter to her son during their private consultation. Anjou, however, had been almost hostile and commented that what was prudent at one time was dangerous at another. When Catherine demanded a reason for his change of front, he blurted out that Marguerite and the Duke of Guise were probably lovers, and because of the arrogance and overweening ambition of the Guises, it was now highly unsafe to entrust any confidences to Marguerite.

Marguerite exploded. Passionately she protested her innocence, and when her mother remained unmoved, adopted the same tone of cold contempt. "I begged her to believe that I should always remember my brother's behaviour to me. She grew angry at this and ordered me to show him no sign of what had passed. From that day forth she greatly diminished her favours to me, making an idol of her son."

Such was Marguerite's own account of the crucial quarrel with her brother which shattered their adolescent alliance and was to have profound repercussions throughout their lives. She laid the blame squarely upon one of her brother's friends, the red-headed, supercilious Louis du Guast, "a bad man, born to do mischief, who had at once fascinated my brother's mind and filled it with a thousand tyrannical maxims—that one ought to love and trust oneself: that one should not involve even a brother or sister in one's destiny, and other fine Machiavellian precepts." It was du Guast, she claimed, who had made up the story out of sheer devilment and jealousy of the bond which existed between Anjou and herself, and Anjou had swallowed that story uncritically. Marguerite probably knew at the time, as she hinted, that her brother was a homosexual and that du Guast was the first to make capital out of it. But although du Guast's talebearing might have been founded in malice and ambition, that did not prevent its being founded also in truth. The story as Marguerite tells it is pure melodrama, with the innocent young girl, caught up in the murky world of politics, traduced and betrayed by those of her very blood. The reality was considerably different: not for the first time did the novelist overcome the chronicler in those famous memoirs of hers. The impression she desired to convey was that she had barely set eyes on the Duke of Guise since the time they had been children together at her father's court; in fact, their love affair was the gossip of half the courts of Europe.

Henri, Duke of Guise, was reputedly the handsomest man in France. Like Marguerite herself, he was half Italian by blood, tracing his ancestry back to that Duchess of Ferrara better known to history as Lucrezia Borgia. He was huge—over six foot six in height, blond and blue-eyed in the traditional Guise manner, a devastating combination with the grace and subtlety of movement of his southern ancestry. But great physical strength and beauty were only part of the advantages heaped upon him. He excelled in every activity he undertook—fencing, swimming, horsemanship, tennis. He was as genuinely at ease among peasants as among princes, addressing all in the same courteous, smiling manner. It was said that he was the greatest usurer in France, for there were few who were not in his debt, either for some loan given or for some favor requested and promptly granted.

And to all this, he added not only personal courage of a high order but also the role of Catholic champion of France inherited from his father. He had succeeded his father when only thirteen, but after the briefest period of tutelage emerged to lead his own forces against the heretics. His military exploits were characterized more by courage and dash than by skill, and no Guise ever learned to take orders: twice his disobedience of old Tavannes's orders nearly led to disaster in the field. But his defence of Poitiers had something of the epic about it, and at the age of nineteen Henri, Duke of Guise, was the idol and hero of France. It seemed as though the passionate royalism of the French, cheated by the lacklustre qualities of the recent occupants of the throne, was seeking a new outlet through this handsome and undeniably noble youth. The crowds ran after him in the streets to touch his cloak as though he were some living saint; old women were known to invoke him in their prayers, kneeling before his portrait as before an icon—portrait artists did a thriving trade in crude representations of him. On one occasion the cry of *"Hosanna filio David"* actually mingled with the more conventional *"Vive Guise"* when he entered Paris in state.

It would have taken a very strong and somewhat cynical mind to remain unaffected by this adulation. Henri, Duke of Guise, did not possess such a mind. Indeed, apart from a certain lack of imagination, the one great flaw in this young demigod's personality was a ravening egoism, a wholly boundless ambition. His father, who had not been among the world's most modest men, had confidently predicted that his son would destroy himself in attempting to reach the ultimate heights. And in France in these closing decades of the sixteenth century, the ultimate heights were represented by the somewhat theatrical splendor of the throne of the Valois.

When, therefore, the handsome, popular, ambitious nineteen-year-old Duke of Guise became aware that the beautiful, popular, generous, seventeen-year-old Marguerite, Princess of France, was regarding him with an increasingly speculative gaze, a match was lit above a powder keg. Guise's initial reaction was by no means a cold-blooded calculation of the political value to be gained from sharing the bed of a Daughter of France. He was as generous, in his way, as Marguerite, easily fired by beauty, responding spontaneously to the still innocent attractions of a singularly attractive girl. But even if he had been blind to the political advantages, his uncle would have opened his eyes. The Cardinal of Lorraine had dropped somewhat into the background since his brother's murder and, like a good politician, had long since washed his hands of his niece, for Mary Stuart was now obviously sliding down to her grave. But his nephew, the handsome lad who could make any girl's pulse beat faster, who was not troubled with too many brains or too subtle an imagination —here was an instrument well worthy of attention. Marguerite's older sister Claude was already married to the head of the House of Lorraine: there was no reason why Marguerite should not marry the head of the junior branch. Juggling the destinies of his relatives, the cardinal came to a momentary pause. There was in fact an excellent reason why Marguerite should not marry the Duke of Guise—two

excellent reasons. The first was the long-standing marriage negotiations which the Portuguese were conducting for the hand of Marguerite; the second was the fact that the queen mother would react
like a tigress at the slightest possibility of the Guises' increasing their
influence and disturbing the hard-won equilibrium. A tricky business, the cardinal decided, but on balance it was just worthwhile
taking the chance. He moved his nephew onto the game board, but
warned him to pursue his lovemaking with all possible prudence.

On her side, Marguerite undoubtedly welcomed the atten-
tions of Guise. She would scarcely have been human to have done
otherwise, for the little that she had heard about Dom Sebastian, her
royal suitor in Portugal, would have done nothing to inflame her
desires to become Queen of Portugal. "Dom Sebastian is sixteen or
seventeen years of age," the French ambassador wrote to Catherine
de Médicis. "He is fair and stout. He is thought to be untrustworthy,
bizarre, obstinate and of the humour of the late Don Carlo [a euphemism for half-mad]. He has been brought up in the Portugues
manner—that is to say, nourished on superstitions and vanities.
Some say that he can have children: others judge him useless for this
purpose and dissuade him from marriage for to marry would be to
shorten his life. All are in accord in believing that he has not long to
live."[7] There was no comparison between this fat, impotent, priest-
ridden boy, whose main attraction was that he would leave his bride
a widow, and the blond giant who had all France at his feet. Marguerite, who never put politics above personalities even when it was to
her personal advantage to do so, was unlikely willingly to sacrifice
herself on the altar of such a dynastic marriage. But she also knew
enough of court politics to realize that the Duke of Guise was about
the last suitor to be welcomed by her family. She, too, was very
happy to conduct her love affair in secret.

The shock of the discovery that it was, after all, no secret
threw her into a "severe and continuous purple fever, a distemper
which was then raging and which had already carried off the king and
queen's two first physicians—as though seeking to do away with the
shepherds in order to make shorter work of the sheep." The death

roll soared, but Catherine, terrified though she was of disease, sub-
dued her fears and doggedly sat with her daughter as though atoning
for what had happened. It was an uncharacteristic action for Catherine de Médicis, who never apologized, but it was all of a piece with
the tangled, obscure business. She was not the only frequent visitor
to her daughter's sickbed: Anjou, too, stayed by the hour, attending
to Marguerite's every want as though, she said, "we had been at the
period of our warmest affection" instead of at the beginning of a
deadly hatred. She put it down to hypocrisy, using one of her ornate
classical allusions: "I could only reply to this hypocrisy by sighs—as
Burrhus did to Nero, whilst dying by the poison that tyrant had
administered—showing him plainly enough that my illness had been
brought about by the contagion of slander, and not by that of in-
fected air." She may have been right: Anjou might, indeed, have
attended her bedside simply to gloat over her—almost any motive
could be ascribed to the members of that strange, unhappy family.
But Anjou might just as well have been moved to contrition. His
maneuver had been designed to cut out the Duke of Guise: the fact
that it hurt Marguerite was an unfortunate by-product, and he might
now have been making a last, deeply sincere attempt to restore the
old love and trust between himself and the sister with whom he had
so much in common. But if such was his hope, he was disappointed.
Marguerite rarely bothered to hate anyone, but when she did her
hatred was as wholehearted as her love, and considerably more permanent.

After a fortnight, the physicians agreed that their patient
could be moved, and the slow journey back to the Loire began. She
was carried in a litter and, every night, her brother the melancholy
king personally helped to bear it to her bedside. Charles said little.
No one had yet told him about Marguerite's indiscretion—the courtiers because they did not dare to do so, Anjou because the time was
not yet ripe. But Charles was no fool, and he was perfectly well aware
that the conspiratorial intimacy between the sister he liked and the
brother he hated was at an end. The signal honor he paid her—an
anointed King of France descending to menial labor—was his own,

inarticulate attempt to acknowledge the fact and establish some sort of communication. Marguerite was touched; but this brother of hers, who wielded almost absolute authority over her, was as unpredictable as a child, and her compassion for him did not lessen her fear of his reaction should he ever learn of her affair. That fear suddenly became very real when the party rode into Angers and encountered the Duke of Guise with his uncles. The meeting was completely accidental but Anjou, urged by some devil of malice or thwarted affection, went out of his way to plague his sister with hints and double meanings. He greeted the young duke effusively, slapped him on the back, insisted that together they should go to the bed of his sick sister and, before her frightened gaze, threw his arms around the man he hated more than any other, declaring, "Would to God that you were my brother." Guise was as frightened as Marguerite and could do nothing but smile in a somewhat sick fashion, avoid the king's puzzled gaze and leave as quickly as he could.

And so back to Paris, back to the cramped, odorous streets and the cold confines of the Louvre, claustrophobic under a lowering winter sky. The palace was huge, but so were the demands upon its resources. The French nobility had not yet descended to that extraordinary parasitic existence which spelled social death for the nobleman who absented himself from court, but, more and more, the heads of families were leaving their estates to be run by servants of greater or lesser ability and taking up residence within the magical ambit of the crown. Privacy was nonexistent. When custom decreed that courtiers should attend the monarch when he arose and when he went to bed, when he ate and when he bathed—even when he sat upon the close-stool—there was small opportunity for lesser people to perform any function in private. Such a desire, indeed, would have appeared either eccentric or treasonable. The Louvre was a hive of people, a murmurous complex of opinion and gossip where, during long hours of tedium, the smallest actions were dissected and magnified and eventually transmitted, if of scandalous interest, to every part of Europe. The royal court gave rich employment to actors and singers and dancers, but the best drama of all was that provided continuously by the court itself. Under these circumstances it seems unbelievable that Marguerite and Guise should have continued their affair. In a sense, they had little choice, for Guise's official office of Master of the Household forced him to reside in the bosom of the family, throwing him in frequent and close contact with Marguerite; they were genuinely attracted to each other and it would have required superhuman willpower to conceal the fact. Early in the spring of 1570 the Spanish ambassador wrote to his master that "there was nothing talked of publicly in France but the marriage of Madame Marguerite and the Duke of Guise." He exaggerated, for while there was much speculation and whispering in corners, there was certainly no public discussion. In Rome, the news sped round that the Cardinal of Lorraine had taken the papal legate to one side and with many a nod and wink given him to understand that soon the Guises would be linked even closer to the throne. The news trickled back to France and was picked up by a furious queen mother, who burst in on the cardinal, despite the fact that he was on his sickbed, and demanded an explanation. Pale with fright, the cardinal denied everything: he had been misrepresented; Her Majesty must know that Romans loved gossip above everything; his nephew would not dream of holding anything but the most respectful and loyal sentiments for a Daughter of France. Unconvinced, but lacking proof, Catherine swept out again, brooding over the troubles that this daughter was already causing—and she not yet eighteen.

The queen mother was beset with family griefs and troubles. Sharpest, most unbearable of all was the death of Elizabeth. The news had arrived when Catherine was presiding over her cabinet: wordlessly, she rose and left the room. Her councillors milled uneasily about for over two hours, unable to depart, for they had not been dismissed, unable to proceed without her. Then she returned with a face like stone, quite dry-eyed, and went on with the business in hand without reference to the cloud that would remain with her to the end of her days. She had loved Elizabeth above all her daughters: Claude was too timid; Marguerite, too bold, too much like her mother for there to be anything but friction between them. But Elizabeth, loving but firm, loyal at once to her husband and her mother—she was irreplaceable. And after the personal grief had moved into the background, there was the political problem. The king had raised his head out of his melancholy and, believing that Philip had poisoned his wife, swore to be revenged on him. It had taken Catherine hours of patient argument to put the mad idea out of his head and substitute another of her own: would it not be a splendid achievement if Marguerite could take her dead sister's place in the royal bed of Spain? Her son was indifferent and her late son-in-law, when the matter was put to him, was insultingly adamant that he wanted no other kin of Catherine de Médicis as his bride. Reluctantly, Catherine dropped the idea but clung still to the hope of making a marriage alliance with the all-powerful Philip, for Dom Sebastian of Portugal was his nephew, and the proposed marriage with Marguerite would take place—or not—according to his will. And now here was the headstrong girl busily compromising herself with the Guises. She summoned Marguerite to her closet.

The last time that Marguerite had been closeted with her mother was on that heady day when she had become Henri's confidante. Now, she was simply an erring girl again. Catherine looked at her with reluctant approval and admiration. The Portuguese ambassadors had arrived that day at court especially to look over the potential bride, and she had dressed herself in cloth of gold to receive them. The more impressionable ambassador had been overwhelmed by this radiant princess, golden as in some antique myth, her black hair for once falling simply to lie upon the golden shoulder and frame the startling, living pallor of her face with its warm, affectionate smile. The other man, less chivalrous or more experienced, had muttered darkly that beauty was not the first importance in a dynastic marriage and was even now writing a report which combined the skillfulness of a courtier and the penetration of a psychologist. Something of a similar nature probably passed through Catherine's mind. Marguerite might be—and probably was—the most beautiful girl in France, if not all Europe; nevertheless, she was not yet married, although approaching the age of eighteen. Elizabeth had been married at fourteen, Claude at fifteen.

The queen mother abruptly brought up the question of the

Portuguese marriage, "asking me what was my will, expecting to find therein an excuse for being angry with me. I assured her that my will was subservient to her own, and that whatever was agreeable to her would be agreeable to me."[8] Catherine refused to be placated, suspecting—with some justice—the sincerity of her wayward daughter's sudden obedience and accusing her outright of compromising herself with Guise.

The interview ended on that bitter note. Despite her lip service to the idea of the Portuguese marriage, Marguerite had not the slightest intention of abandoning her lover, and he was as eager as ever. Later slanders insisted that their intimacy proceeded to its logical conclusion and that she eventually had a child by it. But there were small opportunities for such dalliance, and indeed the pair, aware of the multiplicity of eyes upon them, the multiplicity of ears awaiting the lightest whisper, took to corresponding by letter.

It was a mistake that very nearly proved fatal to both for, until then, there had been no concrete proof of their relationship. Du Guast intercepted one of the letters and took it gleefully to his master: Anjou, in turn, took it triumphantly to his brother the king.

Charles's reaction was eccentric to the point of madness. He seems to have spent all that night brooding on the matter; about dawn, something snapped in his brain and, still dressed in his nightshirt, he stormed into his mother's bedroom. Catherine, struggling up out of sleep, was met with a torrent of enraged accusations: her daughter was a whore who was not only besmirching the family name but was endangering the crown, for all knew of the boundless ambition of the Duke of Guise. Marguerite must be sent for immediately. Catherine dispatched one of her Italian confidants, the Count of Retz, and he, sensing that danger was brewing for Marguerite, awakened his wife and made her accompany him back to Catherine's bedchamber. The Countess of Retz, however, was promptly ordered out, and the sleep-dazed Marguerite found herself in the presence of her mother and enraged brother without witnesses. What happened next was conveyed in a dispatch of Alava, the Spanish ambassador, to his master, confirming Philip's intention to have as little as possible to do with this lunatic family. Alava must have learned it from Retz, who had been ordered to stand guard outside the door but was able to hear almost everything that happened inside. Everyone else remained very tight-lipped about the affair—even Marguerite, thirty years afterward, shrank from its memory and did not record it in her memoirs.

As soon as she entered the room, Charles began again to shriek his accusations and reproaches and then, literally choking with rage so that further speech failed him, he threw himself upon the girl and began kicking and punching her, tearing her hair and rending her nightdress. According to Alava, after a moment's hesitation, Catherine took part in the physical assault upon her daughter. It seems unlikely, but it is possible that she judged it safer to do so—or pretend to do so—rather than incur Charles's rage by an implied criticism. It was only when the girl was beaten senseless that Charles desisted and, after one last volley of curses, left the room. Catherine revived her daughter and spent nearly an hour trying to repair or to disguise the effects of that terrible beating so that the outward proprieties, at least, should be observed: it would not do to have the world say that the future Queen of Portugal had been beaten up by her brother.

Charles had barely begun his revenge. He was in the manic stage of his malady, a stage in which it was not enough merely to chastise his erring sister. The cause of her deliquency would be removed. Early that same day he sent for his bastard half-brother, Henri d'Angoulême, and when the young man arrived he pointed dramatically to two swords which had been carefully placed upon a table. "Choose! One of those swords is to kill the Duke of Guise, the other to kill you if you fail." Reluctantly the young man picked up one of the swords: whatever happened, he seemed to be condemned to death. Even if he were to succeed in dispatching Guise, a formidable swordsman, the inevitable blood feud would spell his own end. Over the next few days he somewhat half-heartedly pursued his errand. Guise had wisely abandoned the palace for his own hotel, and the only real opportunity for assassination would arise if he went hunting, when he would probably be separated from his followers. But warned of the turn of events, he remained within his hotel. Charles stormed at the wretched Angoulême as day after day passed and no corpse of Guise was produced to assuage the affronted Valois honor; but gradually the first, fierce reaction was succeeded by the usual sullen, all-encompassing melancholy.

But Marguerite remained terrified: terrified for her life, terrified for the life of the man whom she seems genuinely to have loved. Throughout the affair she may have hoped that her family could, eventually, be brought round to her own way of thinking, but Charles's violently hostile reaction spelled out the danger in which both she and the duke stood. As far as she was concerned, the affair was at an end. But Guise lacked alike her imagination and her common sense; he was convinced that the whole thing would blow over and that there was yet an excellent chance to unite the Guises with the royal house of France. He continued to pay his court, if slightly more discreetly and, in desperation, Marguerite sought the most unlikely of allies—her timid, crippled sister Claude. But though Claude might be, personally, a nonentity, she was also the Duchess of Lorraine, wife to the head of the clan of which the Guises were only the cadet branch. Responding immediately to her sister's urgent plea, Claude contacted Guise's mother, begging her to urge her son to cease his hopeless and dangerous suit and to take, instead, a wife —the Princess of Porcien whom he had been courting, off and on, over the past two years.

But Guise was still reluctant to abandon the game he was playing for such high stakes; it was the king who made up his mind for him. The duke had not appeared in the Louvre since the abortive attempt to assassinate him; then a state ball was planned and, as Master of the Household, he had no choice but to attend. In an antechamber near the ballroom the two men met for the first time since the king had discovered the affair. Charles turned pale with rage and, putting his hand to his sword hilt, demanded to know why Guise dared to appear in the palace. Guise replied, conventionally, that he had come to serve His Majesty. "I have no need of your service," the king cried. "Get out!"

And Guise left, glad to save his neck and his estates, as convinced now as Marguerite had been that the king would prefer to see either of them in the tomb rather than allow the house of Guise to loom even closer over the Valois. Like Marguerite, the duke realized that the only way of ending the royal displeasure was to remove himself totally from the matrimonial field, and this he did by announcing, shortly afterward, the betrothal of himself and the Princess of Porcien. And at the wedding which followed in the autumn, the royal family was all smiles and generosity, with the king actually presenting a dowry of 100,000 livres from his own purse. But afterward Henri, Duke of Anjou, remarked to a friend, "If he should ever cast his eyes upon her again I will proclaim him renegade and miscreant and make him bite the ground with a dagger in his heart."

IV

Eve of Saint
Bartholomew

Marguerite had been a child—barely seven years old—when the first suggestions were made that she should marry the young King of Portugal. Portraits were exchanged as custom demanded, and the French ambassador in Lisbon was able to report that the little girl had made a conquest. "Madame's portrait has so pleased those of this court that nothing could possibly be better. I have been informed that as soon as the King saw it he kissed and hugged it and that since then he has declined to part with it." Over the next ten years, Dom Sebastian was apparently content to continue kissing and hugging the portrait instead of its original, despite the growing pointedness of French remarks and the fact that the pope himself wanted to bring this marriage about to create another barrier against the riding tide of heresy. It was puzzling: here was perhaps the most eligible princess in Europe—a girl who was not only possessed of wit, charm and great beauty but was also the loved and loving sister of the Continent's second most powerful monarch—here was a matrimonial prize of the first order being treated with a lethargy that amounted to insult.

It was no fault of Marguerite's; had she been Cleopatra herself, the negotiations would have come to exactly the same end, for the Continent's most powerful monarch and his nephew, the potential bridgegroom, were alike opposed to the marriage, although for very different reasons.

Dom Sebastian, King of Portugal, might have begun life with normal tendencies, but by the time he, too, reached seventeen and was technically ready for marriage, they had been fairly well leached out of him. The cause of the change was his tutors, two monks who foresaw accurately enough that their influence over him would dwindle and vanish on the arrival of a bride and studiously sought to prevent such a happening. "They have made the king conceive a perfect horror of women," a papal envoy told the French ambassador in Madrid. "While they are there he will never marry." But even if they had been removed, Marguerite's marriage would not have been brought any closer. Despite the exchange of fulsome compliments, despite the lip service which Philip of Spain paid to the idea of the marriage, in private he was working steadily to prevent it. His opposition did not arise so much out of dislike of his late wife's family as from the knowledge that Dom Sebastian was highly unlikely to leave an heir, and he had no intention of allowing Catherine de Médicis to place her hungry hands, by means of her obedient daughter, upon the crown of Portugal. That was plain good politics, but Philip of Spain was also preeminently a faithful son of Holy Church, and he did not like the way things were going in France. In August the Peace of Saint Germain had brought an end to the third civil war, and the Catholic world had confidently waited the legal crushing of the Huguenots. The war had been nothing but a series of disasters for them, and they would have had no choice but to accept a dictated peace. Instead, the queen mother was dispensing privileges and concessions as though it were she who was suing for peace—or was a Huguenot at heart. A general amnesty, the restoration of all confiscated estates, the free exercise of their detestable heresy everywhere except in Paris and the royal residences, equal rights in the courts and —as though all this were not enough, they were actually to be permitted to retain the four towns of La Rochelle, Cognac, La Charité, and Montauban which they had conquered and which would now indubitably serve as a rallying point for disaffection. It was bad enough for Catherine to countenance the heretical enclave of Navarre on the very border of Philip's own kingdom, but to create even more such enclaves. . . . So Philip brooded among his priests and his soft-footed councillors and at last made an almost imperceptible gesture which sped along the lines of communication to Lisbon. And in October 1570, a few days after the marriage of the Duke of Guise, the court of Lisbon announced that the marriage negotiations between Dom Sebastian and the Princess Marguerite were at an end because of the king's youth. The court regretted any inconvenience that this might cause but was convinced that so rare and admirable a lady as the Princess Marguerite would have no difficulty at all in finding a husband elsewhere.

The court at Blois had expected little else. Charles might have begun to cherish doubts regarding his sister's entire suitability for marriage, but they were private doubts, whereas Lisbon's long procrastination was an open and public insult. Just before the Portuguese had broken off the negotiations, he had announced regally that, if they did not immediately come to a decision, he intended to dispose of his sister's hand to a more appreciative recipient. It is highly unlikely that he meant anything particular by the threat, for he had no one special in mind. But the rumor that the king was seeking another bridegroom for his sister sped through the court and came to interested ears. And within a week of the abandonment of the Portuguese marriage, there arose the most remarkable rumor of all— that the court was considering marrying off Marguerite, sister of the anointed leader of all Catholics, to her shock-headed seventeen-year-old cousin Henri de Bourbon, King of Navarre and titular leader of all Huguenots. Rumor, for once, was accurate.

The kingdom of Navarre was an anomaly, a gallant archaism, a political fossil that should long since have been absorbed into the body of either France or Spain and yet, remarkably, continued to survive independently. It belonged to the heroic period of the Continent's history when men thought of their loyalty in regional or even tribal terms, indifferent to the large and cloudy claims of nationalism.

A century earlier it had been one of the Five Spains, equal in pride if not in wealth to Aragon and Castile and Catalonia and Andalucia, its tough Basque hillmen speaking a language that was neither French nor Spanish. Then came Ferdinand and Isabella, intent upon welding the Five Kingdoms into one, and all that part of Navarre which lay south of the Pyrenees became, finally, Spanish. But beyond the mountains, the truncated kingdom, consisting mostly of the province of Béarn, continued not merely to survive but to flourish beneath its ruling family, the Albrets. They were a swashbuckling race, prepared to undertake any activity that would involve swordplay and would yield a little income. Their victims called them bandit lords but the epithet was neither fair nor accurate, for they were, after all, recognized nobility, with their seat in the pleasant little town of Pau and an impressive ancestry. Navarre's enormous neighbor could have ended its existence with an absentminded gesture, but Basques were a notoriously stubborn people with a tenacious fondness for old customs, and the House of Valois had found it simpler to tie Navarre to the crown by matrimonial alliances rather than by anything so crude and unsatisfactory as physical force. Ironically, it was one of these clever matrimonial alliances that had created the present anomalous position.

A little over a generation earlier, the beautiful, bluestocking sister of François II, the Daughter of France whose name was also Marguerite, married Henri d'Albret, King of Navarre. Hers was a restless, brilliant, contradictory intellect: she gave the world the delicate bawdry of the *Heptameron* but she plunged, too, into the craggy theological arguments of Martin Luther and John Calvin and eventually declared herself to be not a Huguenot, certainly—it would be another thirty years before that term was coined—but a follower of Calvin, a member of the Religion. It was a slightly eccentric but wholly respectable action which, in most other parts of the country, would have had little effect on the people as a whole. But these mountaineers of the Pyrenees were as slow, as loath to give up an idea as they were slow to adopt it in the first place. The heiress of Marguerite and Henri, the pretty little girl who grew up to become

Jeanne d'Albret, Queen of Navarre, was born, lived and died a fanatical Huguenot.

Catholic execration and Protestant hagiography later combined to throw a veil over Jeanne's character. The Vatican longed to see her decently burnt and the aberration of Navarre cauterized from the body of Catholic Europe: pamphleteers did the next best thing and turned her into a female Antichrist. On their side, the Protestant apologists made of her the greatest martyr since the Maid of Orléans, investing her with all that was sweet, feminine, holy and courageous. As a young girl Jeanne undoubtedly had her share of magnetism: she had a capacity for poetry and sufficient physical attraction to charm even that gay libertine Antoine de Bourbon, who might have married her for her title but certainly loved her in his own peculiar fashion. But when the burden of the state fell upon her shoulders and she endured first the bitterness of Antoine's desertion and then the shock of his death, the steely element in her nature came to the fore. Not the least tragic aspect of the Wars of Religion was the way in which the brave generosity of thought which characterized the Religion in its formative years became soured and narrow under pressure. Freedom of conscience was about the last thing in which Jeanne, Queen of Navarre, was interested. She demanded it for herself: but she demanded, too, that all who were her subjects should share her religious beliefs down to the last comma or else—"It is putting a high value upon our opinions to be prepared to burn somebody for them," the Sieur de Montaigne murmured, but his soft and civilized voice was drowned in the impassioned yells of Catholic and Protestant bigotry. Navarre was vassal to the crown of France, and the crown of France was fiercely Catholic; Jeanne was therefore forced to tone down the more extreme of her measures. But Catherine de Médicis must have felt that she was chaining a she-wolf.

There were those who thought that the projected marriage, like the remarkably generous Peace of Saint Germain, was simply a device of Catherine's to lull the Huguenots before destroying them. But Marguerite, the highly reluctant bride, made it clear that the first suggestions for the marriage did not come from Catherine but from the Montmorencies, kinsmen of Jeanne. Charles de Montmorency, third son of the great constable, was dining with Catherine when, with studied casualness, he raised the idea. Montmorency belonged to that party which, in time, came to be known as the Politiques, the moderate, middle-of-the-road men who watched with increasing incredulity and horror as Catholic and Protestant extremists disemboweled France between them. And Catherine—even now, after the third civil war and after the undoubted insults and threats that the Huguenots had presented to the royal family—even now Catherine hoped to make a concord between Protestant and Catholic, unwilling or unable to believe that others could prefer the chimaera of religion in place of the reality of political stability. She listened eagerly to Montmorency's suggestion and then told him to speak to Marguerite about it. Marguerite affected a dutiful indifference. "I told him that I had no will but my mother's—but she should certainly take into account the fact that I was a good Catholic and would be exceedingly distressed to marry anyone who was not of my religion." Marguerite said the same thing again to her mother when Catherine summoned her to her closet later that evening. But Catherine remained dry-eyed at the prospect of her daughter's distress: she had ascertained that Marguerite would at least remain passive, and the negotiations were promptly put in hand.

The possibility of a marriage between Marguerite and her cousin had been in the air for more than a decade: such a marriage, like that of her great-aunt and namesake, was the obvious means of tying together the sundered branches of the family. Marguerite's father had first raised the idea, lightheartedly, when both she and Henri of Navarre were just five years old. The little boy was being formally presented to the king and he, engaged by the child's sturdy independence, leaned forward and asked smilingly, "Would you like to be my son?" "I have a father," the boy replied. "Well, then," said the king, "would you like to be my son-in-law?" The boy beamed at his five-year-old cousin. "O bé!" he answered in his dialect, "Yes, willingly."[10] It was a slight if charming incident, forgotten almost immediately by most who were present. But it was obviously at the back of the king's mind when he arranged that young Henri of Navarre should receive at least part of his tutelage at the court of the Valois.

The potential bride and groom therefore knew each other well, extremely well compared to others of their class, who could find themselves facing a total stranger on their wedding morning. They not only knew each other, but actually liked and admired each other: it was to be their personal tragedy, and a large part of their country's affliction, that their mutual liking was not infused and strengthed by the mysterious alchemy of sexual attraction. The situation had all the elements of high tragedy and the lowest of bawdy comedy: the two most celebrated lovers of their day—the one eventually collecting at least sixty known mistresses, the other influencing politics according to whose bed she graced—these two were incapable of striking a spark in each other.

The upright, ascetic Jeanne d'Albret was apalled when the idea was put to her. The Valois represented to her everything that was rotten and hateful—moral corruption, priest-ridden tyranny, foreign dominance—and what she had heard of the potential bride did not make her exactly anxious to entrust her beloved son to such a family. But the saner, more moderate Huguenots prevailed upon her to make the very real sacrifice, arguing that the marriage would buttress that astonishingly generous Peace of Saint Germain and give the Religion time to draw breath before proceeding to the inevitable triumph that awaited it. Jeanne was a fanatical little woman, but she was also highly intelligent, capable of taking good advice even when it clashed with her own desires. "Alas, I have few friends," she sighed and prepared to go to Blois to negotiate in person. She left Navarre in January 1572, taking with her her small daughter Catherine—but firmly refusing to allow her son to leave Navarre until the matter was settled one way or the other.

Halfway along the journey to Blois her party was overtaken by a cavalcade, coming up fast from the southwest. In the center of the group of horsemen was a portly, scarlet-clad figure, Cardinal Alessandrino, nephew to His Holiness himself, hastening to the court of France to stop this diabolical marriage. As he came abreast of Jeanne he looked stonily through and beyond her, deliberately omitting the salutation due to her as a woman and as a queen, "deeming it a crime and an impiety to offer any greeting to an excommunicated person." Jeanne's thin lips tightened: this was how she was going to be treated in a Catholic land. At Tours she was given even greater grounds for indignation: would Her Majesty, the Queen of Navarre, graciously consent to remain in Tours until Cardinal Alessandrino had finished his business in Blois? But she had no desire to meet the legate in the confines of Blois and so remained, fuming. She did not have long to wait. Alessandrino had been charged not only to protest against this monstrous and unnatural proposal to unite Catholic and Protestant in marriage but even bore a message from Dom Sebastian of Portugal. His Holiness had condescended to put direct pressure on the young man: the court of Lisbon, too, was alarmed at the prospect of the marriage and Dom Sebastian was now pleased to consider accepting the hand of the Princess Marguerite. Charles declined the honor, courteously and with due regard to diplomatic niceties but with a scarcely concealed relish. Two days later Catherine and her daughter met Jeanne and the bargaining started.

At first Jeanne was favorably impressed with her future daughter-in-law. "She is beautiful, discreet and graceful—but she has been reared in the midst of the most vicious and corrupt society that ever existed," she wrote to her son. "When you are married you and your wife must withdraw yourselves from this corruption it is worse than I even expected. Here it is not the men who solicit women, but the women the men. If you were here you would never escape." Henri might have wryly regretted escaping this particular fate, but his mother continued adamant that he was not to come to Blois. Catherine, for her part, exerted every persuasion and pressure possible to bring the boy to court, shrewdly certain that, exposed to its scented luxury, surrounded by the voluptuous members of her Flying Squadron, he would become as malleable as his father had been and make her task so much easier with his pigheaded mother. For after the first exchange of fulsome compliments, the two women barely troubled to conceal the contempt and hatred they had for each other. It could hardly be otherwise, for their age and sex was about the only thing they had in common. Catherine—plump, smiling, devious, born and brought up in the most sophisticated of societies, essentially indifferent to religion, fond enough of her daughter but not prepared to let emotion interfere with politics—might almost have belonged to another species compared with Jeanne—reed thin with permanently compressed lips, provincial in tastes and outlook, prepared to give her own life or that of anybody else for the Religion but so ambitious for her beloved son that she was prepared to make the greatest sacrifice of all. In Navarre they prayed for her, battling among the hosts of Midian, and hungrily awaited her letters. They were engaging letters, written with a caustic humor and irony, free of bombast or self-pity, giving a vivid picture of the courteous, deadly struggle in which she was engaged. "As for outward honours they show me quite enough of that sort. But if one wants any good thing here one must take it by ambush, before they think of it. As for me I fortify myself from hour to hour with the grace of God and show the most beautiful patience you ever heard of. I am amazed I can endure the vexations that I suffer for they scratch me and prick me and flatter me and brave me and try to draw me for all I'm worth without letting themselves go for a moment." And when the open struggle was over for the day, there were still other, insidious means to continue it. "They make holes in my room and in my dressing closet so that they can spy upon me."[11]

It was the clash of irreconcilables. Catherine personally cared nothing about the outward forms of religion but she had no intention of risking upsetting her Catholic subjects by making unnecessary concessions. And even those loyal, moderate Huguenots who had accompanied their queen into the lion's jaws occasionally had doubts about their purpose and confided them to Jeanne, adding to her burden. The Sieur de Rosny, whose son was to become her son's right arm, actually urged her to break off the negotiations. "Believe me, Madam, if these nuptials are ever celebrated in Paris the liveries worn will be blood coloured"[12]—which proved to be an unnervingly accurate prediction.

And through it all Marguerite stood to one side, pale, statuesque, unsmiling. She had indiscreetly confided to a friend that her heart was still in the keeping of the Duke of Guise and the friend had lost no time in passing the titbit on to the queen mother. But though Catherine's suspicion was aroused, her daughter gave her no grounds for complaint. Jeanne tried again and again to see the girl alone in order to find out what were her own, personal views on the all-important question of religion. But "I see her only in the Queen's apartments, from which she never stirs, and she never returns to her own chamber except during those hours when it is impossible for me to visit her. She is always attended by Madame de Curton, her *gouvernante,* so that it is impossible for me to utter a word which the latter does not hear."[13] The determined little woman did finally manage to have a few words with Marguerite, but it was of little value because "she speaks as she has been commanded to speak."

Winter slid into spring, into early summer. On Palm Sunday, 1572, Jeanne had to endure the chagrin of seeing her future daughter-in-law flaunting herself in a popish ceremony, the same ceremony which left Brantôme with mouth agape. His description has the freshness and vividness of a manuscript illumination. Marguerite was wearing a fantastic gown of crinkled cloth of gold, made of material which had been the gift of the sultan to the departing French ambassador. "He, not knowing how better to employ the gift of so rich a stuff, gave it to Madame, who had it made into a gown and wore it for the first time that day. She wore it all day long, although its weight was very great but her beautiful, full, strong figure supported it well." Gold sheathing her body, pearls and diamonds in her hair, she walked in procession "on that flowery Sunday with her face uncovered, bearing in her hand a palm branch as our queens of all times have been wont to do, with royal majesty, with a grace half-proud, half-sweet. . . ."[14]

So the ever impressionable Brantôme. But Jeanne was becoming disenchanted with this beautiful daughter of the Valois. "I own she has a very fine figure—but then she laces very tightly," she wrote grumpily to her son's tutor. "And when one comes to her face, the beauty is so much helped as quite to disgust me, for she will really spoil her skin. But paint is as common at this court as in Spain. You cannot think how pretty and unspoilt *my* little girl looks here." Her little girl, however, was as enthusiastic and as uncritical as Brantôme. Marguerite gave her a little dog, and she wrote to her brother, ecstatically describing the beautiful princess their mother was obtaining for him.

The deadlock continued and Jeanne turned to her co-religionists for help and advice. Sir Francis Walsingham and Sir Thomas Smith, the English ambassadors, were invited to dinner, and she poured out her worries to them. "She said to us that now she had the Woolf by the ears for that in concluding or not concluding the marriage she saw danger every way," Walsingham reported to Burleigh. Marguerite would not change her religion, but if she were allowed to have her popish masses in Navarre, then corruption would again be introduced into that godly kingdom. After dinner they joined a group of Huguenot ministers in an antechamber and the discussion turned to the wedding itself. Could they allow the priest to wear surplice and stole? Walsingham said shortly that it was an utterly trivial matter but it would "breed a general offence to the godly." In that case, Jeanne said almost hysterically, there would be no marriage. Nevertheless, Walsingham concluded, he was convinced that the marriage would take place because there was too much at stake for the negotiations to be allowed to fail.[15]

He was right, and the deadlock was broken by Charles himself, effectively exercising the royal power on his own account for the first time. He had watched in growing amazement and irritation as his mother and the Queen of Navarre became ever more entangled in theological niceties and personal dislikes. He took the matter out of their hands and passed it over to a commission, and when the commission, too, began to chop logic, he baldly stipulated the terms of Marguerite's marriage. They were favorable enough to the bridegroom, and Jeanne, after some quibbling, accepted them. The marriage was fixed for August 18.

On June 1, Jeanne arrived in Paris. She hated the city with a bitter and personal hatred, partly because she was essentially a countrywoman with a natural fear and dislike of the teeming crowds and the stinking air, but chiefly because she was a Protestant and Paris was the heartland of the enemy faith in France. She had tried to prevent the marriage from taking place in Paris, vividly aware of the danger to her son, but she had been overruled: the city, after all, was the metropolis of France, and it was unthinkable that a Daughter of France should be married anywhere save in Notre Dame.

Officially, Jeanne was in Paris on a shopping expedition: in fact, she was taking the temperature of the capital, trying to estimate the degree of danger to which her son would be exposed. On the afternoon of June 4, she called at the shop of a perfumer who had been warmly recommended to her by the queen mother; in the evening she fell sick, and five days later she was dead. She was just forty-four years old.

The sudden death of any eminent person tended to be put down to poison: when that person was a known opponent of the queen mother and, moreover, had been foolish enough to patronize the queen mother's apothecary, the assumption was inevitable. Richly imaginative stories circulated, describing exactly how the poison had been administered. In England, young Christopher Marlowe picked up one of these stories and worked it enthusiastically into his *Massacre at Paris:* the Old Queen of Navarre graciously accepts a gift of gloves from the wicked apothecary, draws them on and promptly dies in horrible torments, for the gloves were poisoned. It so happened, however, that Jeanne herself provided a defense for her enemy. She had long been tormented with what appears to have been a species of migraine and had left instructions that, after her death, her head was to be opened up and the cause of the malady discovered "so that if the prince her son or the princess her daughter were afflicted by the same, they might know what remedy to apply." It was typical of Jeanne's self-sacrificing approach to family life, and the doctors, in fact, found an abcess in the brain. Further examination, however, established that she had died neither from this abcess nor from poison but from the rupture of an abcess in the lung.

Catholic hatred encompassed her in death as it had in life. "There was nothing feminine about her save her sex," old Tavannes

snarled, and Marguerite, giggling and chuckling, tells her friend
Brantôme of "an amusing incident that is unworthy to be recorded
in history but may be privately mentioned between you and me."
She and other ladies of the court, including the Duchess of Nevers,
went to pay their formal respects to the body of the queen. "Madame
de Nevers whom the queen, in her lifetime had detested above every
other person in the world and who paid her back in the same coin,
stepped from among us and with sundry fine, humble and low curt-
seys approached the bed and taking the queen's hand, kissed it: then,
with another profound reverence, full of respect, returned to our side
—we, who knew of their hatred, appreciating all this."[16] The ritual
triumphing over a corpse at the court of the Most Catholic King was
just another commonplace demonstration of the coldly ferocious hatreds that moved behind the elegant façade.

Jeanne's son was on the way to Paris when he received the
news. Shocked, he paused to assess the situation. It was put about
that he was prostrate with shock and grief, but though he deeply
loved and admired his bantam of a mother, the illness was probably
diplomatic, lasting until it was established that Jeanne had died of
natural causes. There was talk of canceling the marriage, but again
the moderates were able to gain their point and Henri, too, was aware
of the high status of his bride. The wedding party continued northward—but with a difference: instead of the score or so members of
the family and kinsmen which originally formed it, the party now
consisted of more than eight hundred Huguenot knights, their horses
and themselves dressed in the deepest mourning. They entered Paris
like a great black cloud, riding through streets that were packed but
ominously silent. And throughout the next few weeks the tensions
between Parisians and visiting Huguenots increased. The citizens had
automatically resented the marriage, but the king was the king and
they had been prepared to accept the marriage that he wanted as long
as the bridegroom had conducted himself with a decent circumspec-
tion. But instead of the handful of family and retainers expected,
there had appeared this black-clad army of arrogant priest-slayers,
men they had been taught to hate and encouraged to fight, men with

the blood of the innocent upon their hands—baby killers, defilers of nuns. On their side, the Huguenots did nothing to make themselves popular. A year ago they had been the members of a defeated, demoralized party; then had come the miracle of the Peace of Saint Germain and, finally, this dazzling marriage of their young chief. It seemed as though the Catholics were suing them, and they reacted accordingly with arrogance and contempt while the churches resounded to thundering denunciations of this marriage and the crowds grew ever more threatening. People were pouring into the city for the marriage; the Duke of Guise was here again with his enormous following and his pale, plump wife; the Châtillons arrived with the Montmorencys; the Lorraines came, Claude submissively greeting her mother, then closeting herself with her sister to find out what had really happened last autumn. Marguerite kept her own counsel while the emotional and physical pressures in the city mounted higher and yet higher.

Preparations for the wedding went ahead despite the fact that a vital prerequisite—the papal dispensation—had not arrived. Marguerite and Henri were related within the forbidden degree and were, in fact, repeating history in a curious and, for posterity, confusing manner: Marguerite's grandfather, François I, had been brother to Henri's grandmother, Marguerite. Throughout, the Vatican had shown that it was singularly reluctant to countenance the marriage, eventually arousing Charles's rage. "I am not a Huguenot, but neither am I a fool. If Mr. Pope conducts himself too stupidly in this affair I will myself take Margot by the hand and have her married like a Huguenot." That was a threat not to be taken seriously, but Catherine swallowed her pride sufficiently to beg Guise's brother, the Cardinal of Lorraine, personally to intercede with the pope. "God alone can accomplish impossible things," came the cold reply. Catherine was to understand that the pope did not give two straws about the consanguinity, but the idea of a mixed marriage was utterly abhorrent to him, as it must be to any good Catholic.

The cardinal, France's major intermediary in Rome, was hardly the most disinterested. He was still licking his wounds over the disastrous attempt to marry the girl off to his nephew, Guise; now he was being asked to help to marry her to a hated Bourbon. Nevertheless, the Vatican's assent was at last grudgingly given and the wheels of bureaucracy began to turn to churn out the necessary documents. In France, the queen mother was beside herself with impatience. It became more and more obvious that the dispensation would not arrive in time for the ceremony, and it was equally certain that the Cardinal of Bourbon, who was to perform the marriage, would take no part in it without the necessary documents. Catherine decided upon a little discreet forgery and, to ensure that there was no embarassing consequences, ordered the Governor of Lyons to suspend all courier traffic to and from Italy until after the wedding. Marguerite's marriage was beginning with a technical, as well as an emotional, lie.

At three o'clock on the afternoon of Monday, August 18, the bridegroom's procession left the Louvre. The young King of Navarre had discarded his mourning for a somewhat garish suit of yellow satin smothered in pearls and diamonds, and he was accompanied not only by his own kin and followers but by the bride's brothers, the dukes of Anjou and Alençon. Anjou had treated the whole wedding in his usual half-mocking, wholly fantastical manner. Jeanne had found that "he attempts to domineer though in a very courteous manner, half in jest, half by deceit," and considered him the most likeable, if the most puzzling, of Marguerite's family. It was noted that the Huguenot nobles were dressed in the plainest, drabbest manner, contrasting painfully with the prodigal splendor of the Catholics—the pearls in Anjou's cap alone had cost him twenty-three thousand golden écus.

The procession moved to the archbishop's palace where, according to tradition, the bride had passed the night. Marguerite emerged now on the arm of her brother the king, followed by her mother and the ladies of the court; those close to her noticed that she was deadly pale and seemed recently to have been crying, but she walked regally, clothed in violet and gold. Looking back to that day, she remembered only—or chose only to record—the details of her dress, "all glittering with the crown jewels, and the large blue mantle with the train four ells long which was borne by three princesses."

The long months of negotiations had produced a compromise regarding the wedding: the actual ceremony was to take place outside the cathedral and afterward the Catholics alone would enter for the wedding mass. A kind of amphitheater, hung with cloth of gold, had been constructed along the west front, and it was there that the procession made its way while an enormous but eerily silent crowd looked on. The Parisians had come in their thousands, attracted by the gorgeous spectacle but hostile to it, so that the ceremony proceeded under a dead weight of disapproval. At the crucial moment, when Marguerite was asked if she accepted Navarre as husband, the Duke of Guise suddenly raised himself above his fellows and stared fixedly at her. The king intercepted the glance and rewarded Guise with a glare of such mad hatred "that he well-nigh lost consciousness." Charles then turned his attention to his sister; she was still standing as though frozen, the formal question left unanswered, and with a gesture he smartly rapped the back of her head so that, involuntarily, she nodded and so became Queen of Navarre.

That was on Monday. On Friday, at eleven o'clock on a morning of stifling heat, an assassin employed by the queen mother shot at, but only wounded, Gaspard de Coligny, the Huguenot leader.

†

V

Massacre

Coligny was the true architect of the marriage, the soldier-statesman who
had created the solid foundations upon which the lawyers and courtiers weaved their devious intrigues, the utterly devoted Protestant
who was yet the confidant and stay of the Catholic king. In that great
portrait gallery which François Clouet created—the gallery which
included most of the faces of those about the Valois court—the
portrait of Coligny is perhaps the most haunting because it is the least
equivocal. In all the other faces there is a play of duality, of uncertainty, as though the sitters, behind their mask of confidence and
aristocratic arrogance, looked out mistrustfully upon a chaotically
changing world. Coligny looks out calm, rock certain, the face untroubled by introspection but enriched by contemplation, for the
man himself was the product of more than a thousand years of
civilization, the Christian nobleman whose strength is controlled by
charity.

Controversy boiled around him both then and for centuries
afterward, at times obscuring his true character just as was the character of Jeanne d'Albret. Catholic propaganda inevitably cast him for
the role of archtraitor, the heretic who would put his heresy before
his country even if it meant selling out to the English; Protestants as

inevitably made of him a martyr, a sea-green incorruptible. Hagiography, for once, came nearer the truth than invective. His soldiers worshipped him, said Brantôme—a Catholic: "They owed him nothing but a salute, being neither his subjects, nor his vassals nor his mercenaries. And yet, when they were in his presence, one little word of anger confounded them and in his absence his signet alone made them do what he wished. And as long as he had to deal with people, he would never allow them any vice. Thus by all men, from highest to lowest, he was so loved an honoured that, when they had a single word from him in private, they were as pleased as if it had come from the king."[17] High praise, indeed, but substantiated from an unimpeachable source—the testimony of his enemies. During the negotiations which led to the Peace of Saint Germain, he fell ill and the Huguenots anxiously asked if his death would make any difference to the outcome of the conference. "You won't get so much as a cup of water from us if he dies," the royal commissioner replied cheerfully. "He is worth another army to you."

Coligny was a Protestant by conviction and not by birth; in this matter he was very much a man of the Renaissance. His mother had been a great friend of that enchanting bluestocking, Marguerite of Navarre, and much of Coligny's youth had been spent at the court of her brother François I. His tutor had been Nicholas Berauld, friend of Erasmus, and it was probably that gently sceptical influence which began to wean him away from traditional Catholic loyalties. There was then no political or social rift between the religions: one of Coligny's closest friends, indeed, was François, Duke of Guise, who later became his implacable enemy. "It is well known on what good terms we were at the beginning of the reign of Henri II," said Coligny himself, adding with a touch of sadness, "It would have been easy to continue so." And Brantôme gave an engaging picture of the two men at play. "Both were of a very jocund spirit, performing more extravagant follies than all the rest—and they did everything badly for they were clumsy players and unlucky at their sport." But as the religious differences in the land crystallized into factions and the factions hurled themselves into civil war, so Coligny and Guise passed from opponents to rivals to the bitterest of enemies. It was commonly assumed that Coligny was directly responsible for Guise's assassination, and though he denied it, the Guise faction swore revenge and young Duke Henri inherited a blood feud as well as the leadership of the extreme Catholic party.

Catherine's reaction to Coligny varied according to the ebb and flow of the wars, but under all circumstances it was quite passionless, devoid alike of hatred or admiration. She had as guide that excellent little treatise which Machiavelli had written for her father and faithfully followed its precepts in all matters that did not concern her immediate family, basing her actions on considerations of political efficiency, and not on irrelevant considerations of morality. When the Guises were in the ascendancy, then Coligny was wooed; when he became too successful, the Huguenots too powerful, then any form of attack upon him was permissible. At one stage he was formally and legally condemned as a traitor and his effigy was publicly executed—not beheaded as a nobleman, but hanged high as a felon. On another occasion she adopted an even more bizarre attack, as the Spanish ambassador reported to his master. A glib Italian persuaded her that he could destroy Coligny, his brother Andelot and his cousin Condé, by occult means. "Three bronze figures were made, of the shape of Condé, the Admiral and Ancelot, full of screws in the joints and the breast to open and shut them and to rivet the arms and the thighs, with the face upturned. Every day the Italian scanned the nativities of these three persons and consulted his astrolabe and screwed and unscrewed the joints," a complex, and highly expensive, version of sticking pins into a wax figure which amazed the Spaniard. "Even if we had no other evidence, by this we could judge what these people are worth."[18]

In 1571 Coligny was fifty-two—exactly the age of the queen mother. Together they had seen most of the first generation of the feud descend into the grave and watched while the heirs took up the quarrel. The Huguenot cause was almost wholly identified with Coligny, the senior survivor; Catherine, on her side, seemed to be wholly in control of the game, manipulating her children as it pleased her.

Until the autumn of 1571. In that year the twenty-two-year-old king moved hesitantly but quite definitely out of his mother's shadow, and his first act was to hold out his hand to Coligny and invite him to return to court after an absence of nearly seven years.

Charles was undoubtedly the most lovable, but also the most unhappy, of the sons of Catherine de Médicis. He was a young man of high and curiously varied gifts. His talent for music perhaps came from his Italian background: he chose his own choristers and sang with them; he divined the genius of the Amati brothers in Cremona and imported their superb instruments. His poetry he owed to his father, and the Pleiades who flourished at his court did not have to employ the usual courtier's tongue-in-cheek flattery to praise his verses. Physically, he was not very impressive, a lopsided young man with enormous shoulders and spindly legs who looked fixedly at his feet, or at the ceiling, when speaking to anyone. But his voice was beautiful and his very rare smile was a thing of sudden, warm charm. There was a hidden element of fantasy, a rather touching sense of fun combined with a hungry curiosity about the outside world. Once, he invited a gang of noted pickpockets to mingle with his guests at a great ball. Afterward they showed him their plunder—thousands of crowns' worth—and described their technique. He laughed, allowed them to keep their spoil and dismissed them—with the warning that he would hang them if they were ever caught at their trade. He liked working with his hands: in every one of his châteaux a room was fitted as a smithy where he would spend hours fashioning tools and equipment and ornaments in iron. His knowledge of natural history was immense: he hated buildings, "sepulchres of the living," he called them, and spent hours in the open air. His book on stag hunting would have been a small masterpiece if it had ever been finished, for he showed an instinctive, almost empathic knowledge of the habits of deer.

But his sanity was balanced on a knife edge: no one knew when, or for what cause, he would topple into raging madness. As a boy he nearly murdered the Duke of Guise; the young duke had been teasing him with a quarterstaff, ignoring his appeals to cease.

Suddenly, the fragile thread in Charles's mind snapped and he hurled himself upon the other boy, cutting and slashing with his sword in a wholly mindless frenzy. His language was habitually laced, and at times rendered almost incomprehensible, by the vilest, the most obscene of oaths. The violence with which he would throw himself into his ironwork, hammering hour after hour until he was bathed in sweat, was equaled by the immoderation of his hunting. At times he would spend twenty hours at a stretch in the saddle, his exhausted attendants following him in relays until the kill. And the kill itself —that purely technical end of the hunt—was conducted with a disgusting brutality that shocked even his unimpressionable huntsmen: as often as not he preferred to club the beast to death. Even domestic animals were not safe from him; his treasury again and again had to pay out for a pig or a dog or a horse which he had ripped up simply to watch the blood flow and the life ebb.

No one was more aware of his weakness than he himself, and after each such orgy of emotion he would be prostrated, writhing in fruitless remorse. And it was a curious but fortunate fact that this young man, whose berserk rage could keep the entire court in terror, loved and was loved by perhaps the two gentlest women in it. He was still a boy when he met Marie Touchet, the young daughter of an obscure provincial official. She was a Huguenot but he insisted on bringing her back to the court, treating that ribald company to the rare sight of a love affair so tender that Charles tried to avoid compromising his mistress, putting on an elaborate pretense of withdrawing to his private quarters when he was visiting her. Their love for each other survived his marriage to Elizabeth of Austria, even though his wife was as beautiful, as gentle and as loving as his mistress.

Catherine had gracefully given way regarding her son's little Huguenot mistress, even setting her up in a hunting lodge so that the young lovers could be undisturbed. How far she also acquiesced in calling Coligny to court she kept to her own inscrutable self. Certainly she supported it at the beginning, being well aware that his presence at Blois was a vital prerequisite in bringing about the marriage between Marguerite and Henri of Navarre, and after Jeanne's sudden death it was Coligny who urged the young man on to the altar. But what Catherine had not expected was the moral dominance which Coligny effortlessly assumed over Charles. It was as though the young king, after thrashing helplessly around in a morass, had suddenly found a solid rock and was clutching it desperately. Did Coligny make use of his position actively to warn the king against his mother and brother? Catherine believed so—or affected to believe so. And Anjou undoubtedly did at the time. Some years afterward, looking back on the events that led up to that nightmare August weekend, he spoke his thoughts aloud to his physician during a sleepless night. He described how he once entered his brother's chamber just as Coligny was leaving. "As soon as the king set eyes on me he began furiously pacing up and down, not saying a word but glaring at me, occasionally putting his hand on his dagger in such a threatening way that I expected him to rush upon me and stab me in the throat." Anjou became thoroughly frightened and, abandoning his errand, ran to his mother. "Thenceforward we were resolved to rid ourselves of the Admiral and to seek out in what manner we should do it." So the loquacious Anjou; but his mother kept her own counsel, leaving posterity to make what it could of her actions.

Friday, August 22, promised to be a busy day.

The wedding festivities were over, having ended the previous night with a brilliant ball. The festivities had been conventionally brilliant throughout: brilliant in the prodigal splendor and display of jewels, brilliant in costume, brilliant in the complexity and beauty of the ballets. The most exquisite food and wines in the world passed endlessly through the palace while the most exquisite music floated out into the sultry summer nights and the blaze of countless candles dispelled night for yards around. But to the more perceptive there had been a frenetic note to the gaiety. And sudden eruptions of violence, little vicious squabbles between Huguenot and Catholic, though swiftly suppressed by the king's officers, gave hint to the most sanguine of the currents which ran beneath. It had begun at the very hour of the wedding. Significantly, Marguerite's very talkative memoirs broke off in midsentence at this point, as though even the passage of years had not dulled the poignancy of that morning. She stood, alone, at the altar, receiving the solemn blessings of her Church while outside the bridegroom and his attendants strolled up and down, casually talking and laughing, ignoring the scowls and mutterings of the crowd watching these heretics desecrating the Holy Mass. The tables were turned that night by a beautiful ballet designed by Anjou in which the royal brothers defended Paradise from the bridegroom and his Huguenots—disguised as devils who were eventually beaten back into hell. A few nights afterward another ballet, designed this time by Guise, cast them as loathed and hated Turks. The insults apparently passed unnoticed over the head of young Navarre, who seemed oblivious to everything but the plenitude of drink and food and the opportunity for endless flirtation. Marguerite sullenly went through the motions of being a bride: later she claimed that the marriage had never been consummated, and though this was highly unlikely, her new husband certainly did his duty in only a perfunctory and absentminded fashion.

The more prudent Huguenots began to take their leave. The Lord of Montferrand, supposedly rather weak in the head, marched up to Coligny and said bluntly that he was leaving "because I prefer to be classed with madmen rather than fools. You can cure the one and not the other." Coligny merely smiled and gave him leave to go.[19] He dearly wanted to leave himself: he wanted to return to the cool shades of his beloved garden at Chantilly; he was anxious about his young wife, then far gone in pregnancy. But there was still much to be done in Paris as soon as these fatiguing and hollow festivities were ended. He had almost brought the king round to the belief that the best way to ease internal dissension was to launch a foreign war and wrest the godly Protestants of the Netherlands from the fierce clutches of Spain. He had been defeated on that issue, and had had a blazing quarrel with the queen Mother—"I pray God, Madame, that the King does not find himself embroiled now in a far worse war," heated words which Catherine was skillfully to use in her own defense a few days later—but he had every hope of being able to pin the king down on the matter of certain abuses of the peace treaty between Catholics and Huguenots. Charles, too, wanted to get out of Paris, his normal dislike of city living exacerbated by the stifling heat: his wife, like Coligny's, was coming near her time, and he wanted to move her to the relative coolness of Fontainebleau.

On that Friday morning, Coligny attended a meeting of the Council shortly after 9 A.M. Afterward he walked through to the tennis courts where the king was playing one of his violently energetic games and, after a few casual words with him, Coligny left the palace and began the short walk to his lodgings in the rue de Béthisy. He was surrounded by his usual entourage of friends and relatives —about ten or twelve people altogether—but only part of his attention was on their conversation, for he was reading a petition as he walked along. Suddenly, he made a wholly unexpected movement, bending and half turning to tie a shoelace. At that exact moment there was the roar of an arquebus and two bullets struck him in the arm. The marksman was obviously aiming at Coligny's chest, and had he not bent at that moment he would almost certainly have been killed outright. Two of his companions supported him while the rest rushed toward a house from whose upper window smoke was still curling upward in the windless air. They found an arquebus, still hot from the discharge, thrown down upon the bed and a coin-filled purse on the floor, which had presumably been dropped in a panic-stricken exit. There was no sign of the assassin, but there could be little difficulty in establishing his identity: the house belonged to the Duke of Guise.

Coligny was carried to his lodging and a messenger sent hurrying to the king. He was still playing tennis and his reaction was of childish petulance rather than royal anger. "God's death," he cried throwing his racket violently down. "Shall I never have peace?" He stormed off the court and into his private chamber. But a few moments later one of his gentlemen sought out Ambrose Pare, the royal physician, and instructed him in the king's name to go at once to the rue de Béthisy and do all that he could for Coligny.

Such were the bare bones of the story which had sped round

Paris by midday: the Huguenot leader had been wounded on the orders of the Catholic leader, Guise. It was long before the queen mother's name was even mentioned; Marguerite, certainly, had not the slightest idea that her mother was involved in any way. And during the following perilous hours, her mother made it very clear that she was prepared to sacrifice her daughter for the sake of a major political advantage.

The first that Marguerite knew of the affair was when her husband and Condé went off to the king, demanding justice on the assassin. At that stage, Charles was still convinced that it was entirely the work of the Guises, and he gave Navarre and Condé ample satisfaction, capping their oaths with his, swearing to wreak the most terrible vengeance on the person responsible. At about 2 P.M. he set off to visit Coligny; Catherine insisted on accompanying him and brought Anjou along with the firm intention of monitoring everything that Coligny told the king. She was frustrated. They found the house in the rue de Béthisy crowded with armed and truculent Huguenots, and as Charles approached the admiral's bed, he actually ordered his mother and brother to draw to one side. They endured the humiliation while a low-voiced colloquy took place between Charles and the man he called *mon père.* Anjou was frightened, as he frankly admitted afterward. "We were surrounded by more than 200 captains and gentlemen of the Admiral's party, who whispered among themselves passing and repassing before and behind us, and not with so much respect as they should have. We were startled and alarmed to be enclosed there, as more than once my mother has since admitted to me, saying that she has never been in a place where she had more reason to fear and from which she came out with more relief."[20] Fear and anger at last led her to break in on the conversation, remarking that the admiral's strength was being taxed. Shortly afterward they left and, as soon as they were outside the house, she began nagging her son, demanding to know what Coligny had told him. He kept sullen silence for a long time and then burst out with one of his explosive expletives. "God's death! He warned me against you and my brother. He told me that all power was going into your hands and I should suffer for it. By God, since you wanted to know it, that is what the Admiral told me!"

Arriving at the Louvre, Charles withdrew to his own apartment while Anjou and his mother went to hers to discuss this new and dangerous state of affairs, "stung and outraged by the language of the Admiral and by the faith which the king seemed to put in it, and fearing lest this lead to some change in the management of the state," as Anjou said frankly. "We were so bewildered that we could find no solution for the moment and parted, deferring the matter till the next day."

Early on the following morning Charles called a Royal Council and announced that he was immediately setting up a commission of inquiry into the attempted assassination. And with that announcement, his mother was forced into the open.

As far as the first attempt upon Coligny was concerned, Catherine had covered her tracks well—too well, perhaps, for it left her enemies free to ascribe to her the most varied and diabolical of motives. Some declared that she simply resented Coligny's influence over her son and coldly decided to remove him; others credited her with a more statesmanlike motive, arguing that by eliminating Coligny she would prevent her son's entering into a disastrous war with Spain. Others again saw her as the most finished product of Machiavellianism: in this view, she had deliberately incited Guise to arrange the assassination in revenge for the murder of his own father, knowing that the Huguenots would inevitably retaliate and the two factions would so weaken each other that they would never again constitute a threat to her position. This was the opinion which Marguerite held, if with some qualifications.

The queen mother's original motives were now merely academic. The violence of the king's reaction, and the fact that Coligny still lived, spelled immediate and terrible danger for both her and her son. Charles still believed that the attempted assassination was a crime committed by Guise alone; after the Council, the duke had asked permission to withdraw from Paris, and the king had replied savagely, "You can go to hell, for all I care. I shall know where to find you." But when the commission's inquiry showed—as it must show —that both Anjou and the queen mother were as deeply implicated, then his rage could be the end of them. It was unlikely that even Charles's madness would lead him to matricide—but there would be nothing to prevent him from banishing her and, for Catherine, banishment would be a kind of death. And as for his brother—the brother whom he hated, who had robbed him of military glory, who was the favorite of his mother, who moved effortlessly and gaily through life while he, the king, stumbled and was silent—he could not fail to take the opportunity of ridding himself of such an incubus, either directly with a dagger or through the machinery of law. Catherine and her son would have to go over to the attack.

Shortly after midday, a little group of people gathered in the newly planted gardens of the queen mother's Palace of the Tuileries, the only place safe from an eavesdropper. Apart from Catherine, there was only one other woman—the Duchess of Nemours, widow of the late Duke of Guise and the bitter enemy of the man whom she believed had assassinated him. Anjou was there, with his mentor the Marshal Tavannes. All the other men were Italians—two Florentines, Petrucci and Caviana, and three who bore French titles, Nevers, Retz and Birague. These three men formed Catherine's inner court, her only true confidants—men who had grown wealthy and powerful under her protection and repaid her by placing their subtle, wholly amoral minds at her disposal. The problem before them could be simply stated: how to finish what was begun the day before and avert the danger looming over Anjou, Guise and Catherine. For more than an hour, in the cool green shade in the sweltering heart of the city, they debated the problem in the Italian manner, balancing advantage with disadvantage, pressure with counterpressure, tracking the results of each move down dizzying potential vistas. "We could no longer use stratagems," Anjou remembered. "It had to be done openly but for this purpose it was necessary to bring the king around to our resolution."[21]

It was decided that Retz should open the attack and, accordingly, later that afternoon he waited upon the king. He came at once to the point: the king was mistaken in believing that only the Guises were involved. His mother and brother were also implicated and, as a result, the Huguenots were even now plotting a rising against the entire royal family. It was a risk: Charles might have rushed out screaming for the guard, ordering Anjou's immediate execution. But it was a calculated risk: ever since he had been a little boy, Charles had watched as the Count of Retz efficiently manipulated state affairs, and even though he was on the edge of frenzy, the ingrained respect for the man kept him under control. Retz withdrew and Catherine and Anjou entered. It was a tense moment as Charles eyed them sullenly, waiting for them to speak. Anjou wisely kept silent and his mother began. Ever articulate, she spoke now marvelously well, switching to Italian at highly emotional points, pleading, probing, frightening, encouraging. She spoke of the Wars of Religion, of the unquenchable antipathy between Catholic and Huguenot, of Coligny's boundless ambition. Yes—Coligny. Had he not displayed his true colors at that Council meeting when he had threatened them with civil war because they would not follow his lethal desire to make war on the terrible power of Spain? It was to save France—to save the king—that she had acted. As she spoke, the other members of her council of war entered the room, but they were scarcely needed. She returned again and again to the theme of death, of the ultimate threat that the Huguenots posed to herself and Anjou and the king, probing for that exposed nerve of his. At last she hit it. "The king flew into a rage and, as it were, a paroxysm of fury. At first he would not consent that the Admiral should be touched but finally, shaken by the danger that we had shaped, he wished to know whether there were no other remedy, and to have our counsel and advice."[22] And the advice he received was that only the admiral's death could save them—could save him—now.

Charles had been under great and growing strain over the past thirty-six hours. The nervous tension of the wedding and the hollow festivities that followed, the stifling heat, the clashes between Huguenots and Catholics, all had contributed to his unease, unsettling his precariously balanced mind. That balance had received a definite nudge the day before when he had visited the wounded man: he could not take his eyes from Coligny's bloodstained jacket, muttering to himself over and over again, "So that is the blood of the famous Admiral," his latent hemophilia revived on this occasion by human instead of animal blood. And now his mother was probing him skillfully, mercilessly playing on his fear of death, of desecration at the hands of his subjects. And, as she expected, the thin thread of sanity snapped. "God's death, kill him, kill him," he screamed. "But kill also every Huguenot in France so that none may remain to reproach me."

Phase II of the massacre began immediately.

Catherine ran her life on the sound engineering principle of applying no more pressure than was required to move a particular obstacle. There was no need to take the king's outburst at its face value and kill every Huguenot in France; all that was necessary was to remove a comparatively small handful of leaders and the great, headless mass would eventually become reabsorbed into the community. Coligny, of course, would be the first to go. The king's agonized cry had turned murder into execution, in effect activating the long dormant death sentence upon the admiral. Guise demanded, and received, the privilege of personally attending to the details of that execution. Then Catherine turned to the task of drawing up a list of those who would accompany Coligny out of the world. There were some automatic exemptions: little Marie Touchet, Ambrose Pare, Charles's old nurse—all these were dyed-in-the-wool Huguenots, but their executions would undoubtedly precipitate an explosion from the king and she passed them by. Her pen hovered thoughtfully over the name of Marguerite's new husband and his cousin Condé. The leadership of the Huguenots would automatically fall to Henri of Navarre when Coligny was killed: would it perhaps be best to eliminate young Henri now? But to do so would be to give an open field to the Duke of Guise, and she was already worried about that arrogant and confident young man. Henri of Navarre was a useful counterweight—and a safe one—a graceless, pliable youth whose only interests lay in chasing women and getting drunk. The pen passed on and it was as though the angel of death had paused momentarily over the first of the Bourbon kings, the king who would succeed the Valois and at last bring peace and unity to the tortured country.

And while, totally dispassionately, the queen mother went about her surgical work in her stuffy, shuttered room, Paris began to come to the boil under the sweltering August sun. The Huguenots, still convinced that the king was on their side, grew ever louder, ever more arrogant in their demands for instant justice; here and there the dormant hatreds began to come to the surface in sudden outbreaks of violence. Troop movements began to be evident: twelve hundred royal arquebusiers were brought in and stationed around the Louvre and near the rue de Béthisy. Anjou, as lieutenant-general, coordinated an action which was beginning to assume major military proportions: it was assumed that the king, nursing his despair in his own quarters, would approve all measures, and long before sunset the main outlines of the night's action were established.

"As for me, nobody told me anything of what was happening," Marguerite recorded ruefully. "I saw that everyone was in a state of excitement, the Huguenots desperate on account of the Admiral's wound, and Messieurs de Guise, fearing that justice might be done for it, whispering together in one another's ears." Despite the fact that she was at the very center of affairs, closely related to all the parties, she probably knew less about what was happening than an ordinary citizen. "The Huguenots regarded me with suspicion because I was Catholic and the Catholics because I had married the King of Navarre, who was a Huguenot."[23] She visited Coligny, but though the wounded man received her with his invariable grave courtesy, his attendants made it so clear that any member of the royal family was unwelcome that she was glad to leave, trailing back drearily to the Louvre where she spent the rest of that miserable day. Shortly after seven o'clock in the evening, Coligny's son-in-law Téligny went to the king and asked that a bodyguard should be set outside the house on the rue de Béthisy. Unfortunately, at that moment Anjou entered the room and heard the request. "I'll send Cosseins and fifty arquebusiers," he said with deceptive heartiness. Téligny was apalled: such an offer was tantamount to a death sentence for the admiral if trouble broke out, for Cosseins was a fanatical Catholic, hating Coligny with a religious fervor. He tried to persuade Charles to send half a dozen archers from the Royal Guard, but the king refused and Téligny returned to the rue de Béthisy profoundly disturbed. There was yet another conference among the Huguenot chiefs, a growing feeling that they ought to cut their losses and get out of Paris while they still had freedom of movement. Téligny, despite the shock he had received, was opposed to it: such a flight, he argued, would be an insult to the king, who had given his word that the murderous attempt would be avenged. Coligny also rejected the idea and it was decided to postpone any decision until the following day.

Later that evening Marguerite entered her mother's dressing room to take part in her *coucher* and bid her good night, as was customary. Her sister Claude was already there, "looking very sad" as she talked to her mother. As soon as Catherine caught sight of her daughter, she brusquely ordered her off to bed. Marguerite curtseyed and turned to withdraw, and at that moment Claude leaped to her feet, clutched her arm and, bursting into tears, said, "For God's sake, sister, do not go away." Claude had excellent reason to fear for her sister's safety, for, unlike Marguerite, she knew every detail of the plot that had been concocted, as her husband was a close kinsman of the Duke of Guise. Catherine swung viciously upon Claude, ordering her to be silent, but fear and sisterly love had given the poor crippled Claude a brief and unusual courage. "She replied that it was unseemly to send me forth to be sacrificed like that for there was no doubt if anything were discovered they would revenge themselves upon me. My mother replied that God would protect me from harm if it so pleased him—but that it was necessary that I should go for fear, if I stayed, that they should suspect something."[24]

Marguerite was now almost beside herself with fear. What plot were they talking about? Who would suspect? Who would take revenge upon her? And why? She stood, frozen, while her mother and sister continued the bitter argument. But such an unequal contest could have only one end. Claude's brief-lived courage evaporated and she fell silent. Catherine "again commanded me angrily to go off to bed. My sister, melting to tears, bade me good night without daring to say anything more and I departed, all scared and bewildered, without being able to imagine what I had to fear." She went to her own dressing room to pray, but even here she found no relief, for a messenger arrived from her husband, peremptorily summoning her to bed.

The reason for the summons was not that which a beautiful girl might have expected on the sixth night of her marriage. The marital bedchamber was full—crowded with men, thirty or forty Huguenot lords "who were unknown to me as yet for I had been married only a very little while." They ignored her as she crept into the great four-poster beside her husband. He did not explain why he had summoned her to bed and indeed, barely acknowledged her presence before turning again to the endless, fruitless discussion with his co-religionists. Shortly before midnight, Nançay, the captain of the palace guard, poked his head into the room and expressed surprise at the number of people there. "Gentlemen, if any of you want to leave, I warn you that the gates are about to close." No one left, and for the rest of the night the voices droned on and on, recounting the attack on Coligny, trying to guess the outcome, to plot future strategy. Marguerite lay awake through it all, uncomprehending, aware only of a terrible fear, certain only that whatever was impending must indeed be appalling if it had nerved poor Claude to oppose their mother.

At about the same time that Marguerite was bidding her mother good night, the king's own *coucher* was in progress. The last to leave was the Count of La Rochefoucauld, the plump, cheerful La Rochefoucauld whom everybody liked and who was the king's especial friend. Charles desperately tried to detain him. "Don't go, 'Foucauld. Let's talk the night through." The Huguenot laughed. "I need my sleep." "You can always sleep with my valets," the king replied. "No thanks, their feet stink," the other said lightly. "Good night, little master."[25]

Jean de Mergey, one of La Rochefoucauld's gentlemen, was

waiting for his master outside the king's bedchamber and so heard the exchange. Mergey then accompanied La Rochefoucauld first to the bedroom of the Dowager Princess of Condé "to whom he made love for an hour," and afterward they began the walk back to their own quarters. They were descending a staircase when the count was stopped by a man with whom he held an earnest whispered consultation. La Rochefoucauld then turned to Mergey and ordered him to go to the Navarre bedchamber with the news that the Guises were back in Paris and that their departure had obviously been a ruse. Mergey did so, but his master put so much importance upon the information that, shortly afterward, he personally went to Navarre's bedroom. No one seemed particularly worried, although Navarre said that, as soon as it was light, he would go and complain about the Guises in the strongest possible terms to the king. Mergey and La Rochefoucauld then left for their own lodgings in the town. Passing through the main courtyard of the palace they saw Swiss and Scottish mercenaries being assembled: surprisingly, neither man saw anything sinister about the midnight gathering of professional killers.

Charles had done his best for his old friend—far more than his mother had done for her daughter. That best had not proved enough, and he retired into himself, leaving the prosecution of the affair to others. His whereabouts were not again recorded until about 2 A.M.

His mother and brother ran matters quite efficiently on their own. Earlier in the evening, Anjou had satisfied himself that he could count on at least twenty thousand loyal Parisians to act as a kind of militia. At about 11:30 P.M. he summoned the Provost of the Merchants for a last-minute conference. All Huguenot doors were to be marked with a white cross and the execution squads should wear white armbands and white crosses on their hats, to distinguish them from Huguenots. The city gates were to be kept locked, instead of being opened at dawn. All boats on the river were to be chained up and a guard set over them. The provost hastened off to carry out his instructions, believing that they were designed to prevent a threatened Huguenot rising.

Midnight. In the rue de Béthisy, Coligny was still awake,

talking to his daughter and son-in-law. The date was now Sunday, August 24, the Feast of Saint Bartholomew, Apostle and Martyr.

In the queen mother's bedroom, Catherine, Anjou, Retz, Tavannes, and Guise agreed on a sudden change of plan. Catherine feared that the king might have a change of heart and cancel the arrangements. It was therefore decided that the signal for starting was to be advanced by an hour and a half and was to be sounded not by the palace tocsin, as had been arranged, but by the nearby church of Saint Germain-l'Auxerrois. The meeting then dispersed, Guise to see to the assassination of Coligny at the appointed hour, Catherine and Anjou to join the king in his room. They found him at the window overlooking the courtyard, lost in thought, and there the three of them looked out on the dark and silent bulk of the palace, "meditating the consequences of so great an undertaking which, to tell the truth, we had not considered clearly before," Anjou later recorded. At about 3 A.M., there was a single pistol shot, a sudden explosion of violence in the quiet summer night which, again according to Anjou, triggered off a remarkable reaction both in him and in his mother. "The sound struck us all, stunning us with fear of the great disorders which were to follow. We sent a gentleman in great haste to Monsieur de Guise, commanding him expressly to return to his lodgings and on no account to undertake anything against the Admiral. This one order alone would be enough to stop everything for nothing was to begin in the city until the Admiral had been killed."[26]

Anjou had no need to lie, and the statement that Catherine, at the very last moment, tried to stop the enormity of the massacre was not only true but inherently likely. There was no remorse in it, simply the fear that matters would get out of hand. Since the attempted assassination of Coligny, she had been forced to run ever faster to stay in the same position, and this was a desperate final attempt to maintain control. But it was too late. At about the time that the clumsy arquebusier had inadvertently fired his pistol shot, Coligny was gasping his life out. The actual murderer was a German mercenary nicknamed "The Bohemian," who cut Coligny down while he was at his prayers and then threw him through the window to the Duke of Guise, waiting below. The body fell on its face and Guise casually put a foot under it and rolled it over; curiously, someone was to do exactly the same thing to his own murdered corpse twenty years later. Coligny's face was bloody, the features obscured, so an attendant wiped it clean with an ironically compassionate gesture and Guise nodded satisfaction. "It is the Admiral." Some said he then kicked the corpse in the face before turning away.

Dawn. In Marguerite's room the Huguenot gentlemen were at last taking their leave, having resolved nothing. Navarre announced his intention of having a game of tennis while waiting for the king to awake, and he left with his cousin Condé. The room was empty and quiet and Marguerite, believing that whatever danger her sister had been alluding to was now past, ordered her nurse to lock the door so that she could get some sleep. She was still sunk in that sleep of utter fatigue when there came a tremendous knocking and pounding at the door and a man's voice, shrill with fear, screaming, "Navarre! Navarre!" The nurse thought that it was Marguerite's husband and hastily opened the door. A man dashed in, streaming blood from two great wounds in his arm and closely pursued by four archers of the palace guard. As Marguerite struggled up out of sleep, he threw himself upon her; she hurled herself out of bed and the two of them tumbled to the floor, for he was grasping her convulsively. "This man was a total stranger to me, and I did not know whether he came there to rape me, or whether the archers were against me, or him. We were both of us screaming, and one was just as much alarmed as the other. At last God willed that Monsieur de Nançay, captain of the guard, should come upon the scene who, perceiving me in this plight, could not refrain from laughing in spite of the compassion he felt for me."[27]

It says much for Marguerite's own warm and compassionate nature that, after having been wakened in such a fashion, she not only begged the life of the man—a Huguenot in her husband's entourage—but bandaged up his wounds and put him in her own bed. Sleep was now out of the question. She changed her bloodstained nightgown for a clean one and Nançay then told her what was happening. Her husband and Condé were under arrest, most of the Huguenots who had been in her bedroom were now all dead, and mass killing had started in the city. He advised her to go to her sister Claude's room and offered to escort her there. Outside Claude's apartment, "a gentleman named Bourse was run through by a pike within three paces of me, as he was flying from the archers that pursued him." The thrust was so violent that the pike completely penetrated the man's body and nearly wounded Marguerite. "I fell to one side, half-fainting, into Monsieur de Nançay's arms, thinking that this thrust was about to impale us both"

Later in the morning Marguerite was able to save the lives of two more men—Miossans, her husband's first gentleman, and his valet—who appealed to her for help, she, in turn, pleading with the king and her mother. But by midmorning there could have been very few Huguenots still alive in the palace. Most of the victims were taken down to the great courtyard, where they were butchered, stripped and their bodies thrown onto a huge and growing heap. Shortly after daybreak the king appeared on a balcony, watching the bloody business, ignoring the appeals of men for whom he was the feudal chief. He was now firmly in the grip of his obsession: at one stage he grasped an arquebus, ran to an outside window and fired blindly into the terrified groups outside the palace. Later, he would feel the most terrible remorse, but now he was behaving in the same way that he behaved at stag hunts. Far more incredible was the behavior of the Flying Squadron. They too gathered in the courtyard, watching with a bright interest as men who had perhaps been their lovers were skewered and thrown onto the bloody pile. At their pretty request, the Swiss butchers removed one of these naked, bleeding corpses so that the young ladies could inspect it at close quarters: it had been the Sieur de Beauvois, who was currently being divorced for nonconsummation of marriage.

There were a few who shared Marguerite's compassion. When Charles's gentle wife, Elizabeth of Austria, was told the reason for the cries and screams, she threw up her hands in horror, praying heaven's forgiveness on her lunatic husband. And curiously, Catherine's youngest child, the eighteen-year-old Alençon, had from the beginning rejected the idea of a pogrom with contempt and disgust. His reaction had been so hostile that Catherine had deliberately excluded him from the conferences, just as Marguerite had been excluded. Later, Catherine tried to justify herself by reading to him that portion of Coligny's will in which the admiral had warned the king against making his brothers too powerful. "You see how much he loved you," she said. "I don't know whether he loved me or not," Alençon replied. "But that proves that he loved the king." But Elizabeth, Alençon and Marguerite were rarities: on that August Sunday morning in the Louvre, every man who could wield a weapon became an executioner, encouraged by his womenfolk.

Noon. In the city itself the last pretense that this was a limited police operation had long since gone. Coligny's body still lay in the dust outside his lodgings, where it would remain for another day; somebody had hacked the head off, and the crowds came to it as to a kind of grisly shrine, feasting their eyes upon it, kicking it, hacking off another lump of flesh. Later, it was dragged away, passing from group to group, losing what remained of its humanity until at last it was gibbeted on Montfaucon, that cathedral of the macabre with its thirty-foot-high columns and dozens of swinging, rotting corpses, that stood outside the town.

Mass slaughter began. Paris had been crowded for the wedding with ambassadors and observers from every independent European state, literate men who recorded what they saw for the benefit of their distant governments and so made their contribution to a new portrait of hell. Their reactions varied not so much according to their religion as according to their nationality: the English feared that the Catholic rage would be turned upon them, but even the Catholic Venetians and Viennese were appalled, while the Spaniards exulted. "As I write, they are killing them all, they are stripping them naked, dragging them through the streets, plundering the houses and not even sparing the children," Cuniga, the Spanish ambassador, wrote. "Blessed be God who has converted the French princes to his cause. May he inspire their hearts to continue as they have begun." He went

to a lot of trouble to collate eyewitness reports, sketch in little vignettes of pain and terror, to please his master. And when Philip at
least read the report, he laughed from pure pleasure, the first spontaneous chuckle his courtiers had ever heard him emit. And certainly
there was detail and cause enough to delight the most blood-hungry
of fanatics. There was the old cobbler, a Huguenot, who lived apart
from his Catholic wife: the hunters pursued him to her very door and
there had their pleasure of him while she looked calmly on. There
was the funny story of the Count of La Rochefoucauld, who died
laughing, in a manner of speaking. He woke up to find his bed
surrounded by masked men and thought that it was his friend the
king playing a prank on him—he was joking with them up to the
moment the knives went in. There was the oddly pernickety monster
who butchered the parents in their home, then carefully gathered
their babies into a basket, took them down to the Seine and tipped
them in like so much vermin. Learning, too, received its lethal ac-
colade: a Catholic professor at the Sorbonne halooed the mob onto
a Protestant rival and later successfully occupied his chair. There was
a kind of hierarchy of cruelty: a butcher called Perou boasted of
having dispatched 180 Huguenots, a threadmaker called Cruce
capped that with a claim of 400. One of the survivors of the massacre
described Cruce: "I remember having seen this Cruce many times,
and always with horror. The man, whose face resembled that of a
hangman, used to roll up his sleeve and show his naked arm and say
that on St. Bartholomew's Day this arm had butchered more than
400 gentlemen." A Piedmontese adventurer, Hannibal de Cocconas,
actually went to the trouble of purchasing 50 victims from their
captors so that he could kill them at his leisure. A group of ten-year-
old boys was seen dragging a dead baby around by a rope tied to its
neck. Pregnant women seemed to arouse paroxysms of cruelty in the
mob: rarely were the butchers content to kill the mother alone—the
child in her womb had to be ripped, stabbed, bludgeoned before the
body was tipped into the river. The Seine became a bloody sewer,
choked with bodies that the current thrust against the piles of the
bridges.

At 5 P.M. there was an impressive royal proclamation ordering an end to the carnage. It might, perhaps, have ended the massacre had there not been a miracle. During the night a seemingly dead may tree in the churchyard of the Innocents put out an unseasonable spray of white flowers, an indubitable sign that heaven was showing its direct approval of the flowering of true religion. The mob went to its work again, spurred on by the friars, and so continued until the Thursday, when the city had calmed sufficiently to allow the royal family to go in solemn procession to Notre Dame, and there render thanks for the preservation of the king and his mother from the fury of the Huguenots.

†

VI

The Brothers

When Henri of Navarre left his bedroom to look for the king, shortly before dawn on Saint Bartholomew's day, it is highly doubtful if he expected to achieve very much. Behind an amiable grin, scruffy appearance, lecherous tastes and drunken habits he concealed a very subtle, very shrewd brain which told him that nobody was going to take him—the nineteen-year-old heir of a tiny vassal state—very seriously. He expected to lodge a protest, no more, saving his face as titular leader of the Huguenots while not committing himself in a confused and dangerous situation. But whatever he intended, his next moves were quite involuntary; almost immediately after leaving the protection of his room, he and Condé were pounced upon by the palace guard and hustled off to Charles. By now they were aware that something terrible was happening, and when they were brought into the presence of the king, they knew that they were staring into the face of death itself, that a wrong move—a wrong word, even—could bring their lives to an abrupt end. Charles was now very far gone in his self-lacerating, autohypnotic state of rage, a state in which he might, indifferently, disembowel a donkey or impale a man. With spittle flying from his mouth, he screamed that he knew all about their plots, but was giving them a final chance: "Death, Mass or the

Bastille," he bellowed, and gave them twenty-four hours to choose. Henry did not need twenty-four minutes to decide: as a child he had had his faith changed for him; now he made his own choice, the first of a dizzying series of changes which he would make in the firm conviction that a live renegade could be more effective than a dead martyr. Condé stuck out for longer, defying Charles even when the king took a dagger to his throat. But he, too, yielded in the end.

That was the first, outright, attack upon Henri of Navarre, leader of the Huguenots; the second came about a week later when the massacres were ending. As Marguerite noted, "Those who had commenced these proceedings, realising that they had failed in their principal object—for their animosity had been directed less against the Huguenots than against the princes of the blood—were out of patience at the thought that the King my husband and the Prince of Condé should have been spared. And recognising that, as the King of Navarre was my husband no one would lift a hand against him, they started upon another attack." Marguerite was summoned to her mother's room and there was asked outright whether her marriage had been consummated: if not, they could begin to have it dissolved, for the dispensation had not yet arrived from Rome. There was a bitter irony in the situation; she was being offered the chance of escape from a marriage she hated—but at the price of again becoming the pawn of her mother and brothers. She had very little status indeed; her husband was utterly helpless, owing his very life to her brother's forbearance; they had no separate household. But still she was Queen of Navarre, and a married woman had certain useful privileges denied an unmarried girl. There was, too, a stubbornness about her and something about which her pliant mother knew little or nothing—a sense of loyalty: "I strongly suspected that they only wanted to separate me from my husband in order to do him some evil turn." If Guise had still been free, her answer might have been different; as it was, she temporized, answering the direct question with an elegant little fiction. "I begged her to believe that I was not qualified to answer her question (and indeed I was in the same condition as that Roman lady whose husband reproached her because she had not told him his breath was unpleasant, and who replied that she fancied all men were alike, never having approached any other man but him) but I said that, whichever way it was, as she had placed me in this position I would rather abide in it."[28] Her daughter's claim to be ignorant of the facts of life, in a court where copulation was a major pastime, must have appealed to Catherine's bawdy sense of humor. But she accepted the answer at its face value, being herself uncertain as to what to do about Henri of Navarre. And Henri, wisely proving himself to be an indefatigible mass-goer, earned the grudging praise of Rome and, ultimately, the dispensation which bound him eternally to his wife.

The court of France was again founded upon the one religion, purged finally of the contagion of Huguenotery. But the court was not France, and in the matter of the Massacre of Saint Bartholomew, Catherine for once acted not as the ruler of a vast country but as a member of the aristocracy in a city-state. In the confined space of Florence, it would have been perfectly feasible to suppress a movement by lopping off a few heads and expelling a few more: in France, extreme violence merely forced the opposition to formulate its objectives. The massacre had spread from Paris to the provinces, partly by contagion, partly by royal edict. Some of the provincial governors joyfully anticipated the edicts. Some protested, as did Orthez, Governor of Bayonne: "Sire, I have communicated your majesties orders to your faithful inhabitants and to the troops in the garrisons. I found there good citizens and brave soldiers—but not one executioner."[29] In Lyons, the citizens butchered Protestants under the benign gaze of a cardinal; in Auvergne the governor refused to take any action unless the king was present in person. No man could possibly know the number of dead throughout the country; in Paris the gravediggers were given a bonus for burying 1,100 bodies, but two or three times that number might have floated downstream. In England it was believed that 100,000 of their co-religionists had perished. But whether 2,000 or 20,000 Huguenots perished in the last days of August 1572, the core of Protestantism remained not merely unharmed, but actually flourished, putting out vigorous new shoots.

After Coligny had been murdered, Chancery clerks had descended upon his lodgings, ransacking it for papers. Over the next few days they collated the information and built up a terrifying picture of what it was Catherine had sought to destroy. The vice-chancellor, Birague, passed on the information to his fellow Italian, the Venetian ambassador, and the ambassador, with the Venetian appetite for statistics and passion for economic summaries, made a neat précis of the whole for his own government. The Huguenots, in effect, formed a state within a state. They had divided France into twenty-four "churches"; above these, for administrative purposes, was a council which, in turn, deferred either to the late Queen of Navarre or to Coligny, "and whatever these two approved and commanded was done." What particularly impressed the Venetian was the financial provisions: the churches contributed 800,000 francs annually to a central fund, "paid by everyone indifferently, even by the people and hirelings, everyone voluntarily taxing himself more or less according to the amount he could carry, and paying with a promptness and zeal which were marvellous." Out of the 800,000, 100,000 francs were paid to the Queen of Navarre—and would have been paid to her son and heir but for his apostasy; "40,000 to the Admiral for his provision and upkeep; 10,000 to Monsieur de la Rochefoucauld"; and various provisions to other officials, mostly soldiers. "And there was such union and intelligence among them, and such obedience to their chiefs that they say the like could not be found among the Turks. Vice-Chancellor Birague tells me that the Admiral could more easily have put together in an emergency seven or eight thousand cavalry and twenty-five or thirty thousand infantry in four weeks than the king could have done in four months."

All that the massacre had succeeded in doing was to remove the aristocratic leaders, together with their immediate followers and some few hundreds or thousands of urban proletariat. The movement was, if anything, strengthened by being democratized. But the massacre had created another and even more unexpected reaction: it had utterly alienated the moderates, the Politiques as they called themselves, such as the Montmorencys, Catholics who, on being forced to chose between country and religion, slowly, reluctantly, but in increasing numbers, began to choose country. A Catholic was now by no means automatically a loyalist even though the contrary was still true.

War, in the form of rebellion by the Huguenot cities of the south and west, again descended on the country. The heart of the resistance was La Rochelle, the great seaport on the Atlantic coast with its convenient lines of communication with Protestant England. Elizabeth of England proved to be considerably more generous with prayers and promises than provisions and gunpowder, but the defenders held on in good heart, partly encouraged by a miraculous draught of shellfish, partly by the dissension among the royal commanders. For the bitter hatred between the king and his brother Anjou had boiled up yet again, this time rendered more complex by the presence of the third brother, Alençon, who hated, and was hated by, the other two with a fine impartiality.

Saint Bartholomew's Day had left no member of the royal family untouched, unchanged. Marguerite it had hardened in some subtle, indefinable manner. Those moments when she realized that her mother was prepared to gamble with her life for a political purpose; those moments when, in the nightmare condition of half-waking, half-sleeping, she had wrestled, shrieking, with a fear-stricken man had left their mark. Outwardly she was still respectful to "the king my brother and the queen my mother"; inwardly, she had determined never again to be manipulated. Henceforward, she took an ever more positive role—subtly, deviously, avoiding head-on clashes with her formidable mother, but making her mark at last.

The king was going through some personal hell. Officially, he had taken on himself all responsibility for the massacre, proclaiming that he had been forced into it to forestall a Huguenot plot. In private, he seemed to be literally haunted, babbling of blood and ghosts to his old nurse, who was powerless to comfort him. His relationship with his mother detriorated. She, at least, had come triumphantly out of the massacre, looking ten years younger, as an ambassador noted. But her influence over her son was weakening. Once, when he was cursing his hounds and huntsman for some fault in his usual sulfu-rous manner, she chided him. "Hé, my son, it would be better for you to curse those who are killing your people at Rochelle." He turned savagely upon her. "Hé! My God! Who but you is the cause of all this. God's death, you are the cause of it all." She sighed and confided to her ladies that she always knew that she had to deal with a lunatic but now there was no holding him. The tuberculosis that would shortly kill him was far advanced, but he threw himself into official work with a kind of desperation, using an energy for state affairs that once he had used only for hunting. There was a new grimness about him; a courtier warned Walsingham to approach the king with care, for "he is not the gentle man you once knew." The massacre had left a scar even on the gay, effervescent Anjou: it was about now that he made a dramatic change in the whole basic pattern of his life, turning aside from his homosexual playthings to take as mistress the light-hearted wife of Condé, plunging as deeply, as genuinely in love with her as his brother was in love with that other little Huguenot, Marie Touchet.

But it was in Alençon—the nineteen-year-old François, Duke of Alençon, youngest member of the royal brood—that the massacre made the greatest change, if for wholly different reasons. In his feverish brain a thought had been lodged, planted there by skilled intriguers but cherished by him, nourished by his fantasies until it was now a thing of monstrous and dizzy growth: Coligny, leader of the Huguenots, commander of the state within a state, was dead. Why should he not be succeeded by Alençon? It could be the first stepping stone to a royal throne—not in France, perhaps, but in the Netherlands, or England, or wherever a Protestant with royal blood would be welcomed.

Few people had much good to say for Alençon: even Marguer-ite, who became his firm champion, ally and protectress, remarked in an unguarded moment that if the world had been empty of treachery her younger brother could easily refill it. His elder brothers, united for once, joined in mocking him. His baptismal name of Hercule gave them a weapon against him, for he was a stunted little man; his soaring ambitions, so out of place in a youngest son, aroused their savage scorn even while it gave them occasional twinges of alarm. For Alençon had more than his share of the family emotionalism and instability. He pestered his mother with his real and fancied wrongs: Charles was the king, Anjou was her favored son, laden with honors. Did not the same blood course through his veins? Why should he not be given command of an army, a navy? Why could he not have his own appanage where he, too, could be lordly? And his mother listened and sighed again, sometimes driving him from her with her cruel tongue but more often trying to explain and soothe and encourage. It was as much motherly love, a sense of responsibility for this unprepossessing duckling among her swans, as it was a sense of statesmanship that led her to encourage him in his preposterous wooing of Elizabeth of England as a kind of comic successor to his brothers. And in England, Elizabeth's courtiers watched her reactions to Mounseer's long-distance courtship with increasing dubiousness and unease, reading between the lines of Walsingham's dispatches describing this potential king of England: his pockmarks are not very thick; he is quite straight; he is tall enough. Alençon, unwisely perhaps, sent ahead as emissary his follower and personal friend, the dashing Hyacinth La Mole, who won Gloriana's heart by proxy, for if the servant was so charming, what would the master be like? But even when she met her suitor at last and took in the enormous, swollen nose, the swarthy, pockmarked skin, the diminutive stature, she liked him. He was, after all, the only one among her royal lovers to dare press his suit in person, to look at the raddled face, the towering red wig, the blackened teeth, and proclaim undying love. She called him her little frog, thus bequeathing a useful word to the vocabulary of English xenophobic insult, listened to his elegant nonsense—for he also had his share of the Valois loquacity—and seemed perfectly prepared to marry someone young enough to be her son.

Catherine would have gladly assented to the marriage on almost any terms if only to get Alençon off her hands and away from his mocking brothers. But in June 1573 there came a distraction: the nobles of Poland, who had been well furnished with French gold, had elected the Duke of Anjou to be their king. It had been touch and go: Saint Bartholomew's day had not helped the negotiations and, in order not to antagonize the powerful minority of Polish Protestants, it would now be necessary to raise the siege of La Rochelle. The queen mother was only too glad of the excuse: the treasury was almost bankrupt with moneylenders demanding a ruinous 15 per cent; the winter had been hard and prolonged, with a consequent hoarding of food and soaring of prices; the army was hungry, under-paid, and undermanned, for mercenaries declined to fight for love of King Charles and Holy Church alone. The Rochellois had proved courageous, skilled and stubborn: twenty thousand royalist dead lay on the field to prove that, including among them the Duke of Guise's brother. A month after Anjou had been elected king, the Huguenots presented their terms. Catherine protested: they could not have de-manded more if their army had been triumphant in Paris, she de-clared. Nevertheless, she signed. After two and a half years of in-trigue, after a massacre designed to eliminate the problem once and for all, after yet another civil war, the Huguenots gained terms that were even more generous than the Peace of Saint Germain.

In August the Polish noblemen arrived in Paris to offer the crown formally to Anjou. Paris thrilled at their barbarically splendid appearance—nearly two thousand enormous men, heavily bearded, dressed in long, sweeping robes in defiance of the August heat, clank-ing with weapons and jewels, their very horses laden with silver and jeweled mountings. And, for their part, the Poles found their newly elected king not a little disconcerting—a scented, willowy young man with sweeping eyelashes and graceful, virtually feminine gestures. Nevertheless, "he has manners serious rather than otherwise," one of them remarked. And as for his sister. . . . It was then that Marguerite appeared in that dress of rose-colored velvet which left Brantôme almost incoherent with admiration. The queen mother was giving a splendid fete in the Tuileries, and Marguerite, with her scruffy young husband, was among those to receive the Poles, dazzling them with her beauty and elegance.

It was almost exactly a year since the massacre in Paris, but there were no discordant voices to interrupt the balls and the fetes and the ballets that marked this, the newest triumph of the Valois. Nevertheless, they ended, somehow, on a flat note. The new King Henri of Poland seemed loathe to pick up his scepter. He was reluctant to leave his beautiful young mistress and the heady pleasures of heterosexual love, but he was even more reluctant to leave his brothers. Charles was now obviously dying, and Anjou wanted to be on the spot to pick up the crown before his other brother, Alençon, could move in and do so. In his dilemma, Anjou turned to the same person he had turned to, for similar reasons, four years earlier. "He tried by every means to make me forget the evil effects of his ingratitude and to restore our friendship to what it had been during our childish years," Marguerite recorded with the equivalent of a cold smile. Again, it is likely that she was entirely correct in assuming that Anjou wanted to ingratiate himself with her simply in order to have a friend at court while he was absent. But he already had a formidable ally in his mother, and it is just as likely that the young man, adrift in a confused sea of emotions, bound for a remote and barbaric country, was reaching out with something like desperation to the person he had once loved and who had once loved him. But whatever the cause for his action, Marguerite brushed aside the hesitant approach, a gesture she was bitterly to regret.

Anjou at last left in November, pursued by his brother's curses and threats. Charles was perfectly well aware why he was lingering and literally ordered him out of the country. But Anjou had barely crossed the border when a preposterous new rival arose to plague the king: precisely as Anjou had foreseen, Alençon now tried to take Anjou's place. He went again to his mother. Nostradamus's prophecies were working out to the letter: three of her sons had now been kings. But what about the fourth? What about him? He demanded that he should be given at least the lieutenant-generalship of the country, vacant now that Anjou was absent. Catherine brusquely refused, determined to guard her beloved son's every right. "You will not be absent long," she had whispered as they parted, and she had no intention of helping Alençon to become a rival. Weeping with anger and self-pity, Alençon took himself off to Marguerite—and so began the most curious and puzzling alliance in her complicated life.

Marguerite referred to the beginning of the alliance in her usual cool and elegant manner. "My brother of Alençon employed every possible means to make himself agreeable to me so that I should swear the same friendship with him as I had done with King Charles for until then, in consequence of his having been always brought up away from court, we had scarcely seen anything of each other and were not at all intimate. I was influenced at last by all the submission, obedience and affection he manifested towards me and made up my mind to love him and to embrace his interests, though always with the understanding that this should be in no wise prejudicial to my good brother King Charles, whom I honoured above all things."[30] The passage was an excellent example of Marguerite's style—the way in which she used half-truths to cover whole fictions, the way in which unpleasant details were glossed or ignored. Skillfully, she projected yet another idealized picture of herself, on this occasion the sophisticated woman at the center of affairs, hinting at her influence over the king even while proclaiming her total loyalty to him, graciously deciding to take her vulnerable young brother under her protection. It is impossible to fault the details; she was undoubtedly loyal to the king—certainly, no one suffered more from his death. He was indeed very fond of her. She did indeed prove a most valuable ally for Alençon. But at no stage does the reader obtain even a passing glimpse of her real reason for teaming up with Alençon. She was far less interested in helping the little frog—as even his mother called him—than in striking through him at the brother she hated, Henri, Duke of Anjou.

Over the next ten years, from that early spring of 1574 until Alençon's death in 1584, the two of them were to be permanently and closely associated. On more than one occasion Marguerite's championing of Alençon drew down trouble upon her head; conversely, Alençon contributed nothing whatsoever to her well-being. The alliance went far beyond a purely political relationship, and in the hothouse atmosphere of the Valois court it came to be assumed that the tie between them was sexual. There was indeed a hidden sexual tie, but it linked her not with the grotesque Alençon but with the dashing Anjou, her alter ego who had betrayed her either physically or spiritually with Du Guast, the first of his many partners. Not a single line of Marguerite's carefully edited memoirs even hints at such a relationship. It is only when the memoirs are taken as a whole that a pattern becomes visible—the near worship that she accorded him before the Du Guast episode and the steady, unrelenting hostility thereafter, the extremes in both instances bearing the hallmark of sexual love and rejection rather than an ordinary quarrel between brother and sister. Anjou's actions, too, argue some such cause and effect. He was neither a cruel nor a particularly suspicious man— ultimately, he was to fall beneath an assassin's dagger because he was not suspicious enough. But the equally unrelenting hostility with which he pursued his sister when he at last came to the throne, doing all in his power to insult and humiliate her, was not the reaction of an exasperated brother trying to control a wayward sister. Rather, it was the unwinking hatred of the one-time lover, a lover, moreover, who has had his generous attempts at reconciliation contemptuously brushed aside.

The king had virtually kicked his brother out of the country to take up the crown of Poland, rejoicing openly once Anjou was beyond the French frontier. But within a matter of weeks of his departure, Charles was regretting his absence and admitting that he had been mistaken in bringing it about. Anjou had acted as a kind of lightning conductor for the endless plots dreamed up by dissidents and malcontents. It was known that he was permanently at loggerheads with the king and the discontented therefore felt it safe to unburden themselves to him and even try to draw him into opposition. But he was also well aware that it would be only a matter of time before he, too, ascended the throne, and he was far too intelligent to take part in activities designed to trim or weaken the power of the monarchy for the sake of short-term advantage. Alençon, less intelligent than Anjou, had no such additional restraint, for there was no real likelihood of his ever succeeding to the throne. He was fully prepared to destroy what he could not control—a tendency of which his mother was very well aware. She made certain, therefore, that her troublesome youngest son was never very far out of her sight. François, Duke of Alençon, Son of France, was, in fact, as much a prisoner as Henri, King of Navarre.

Five days after Anjou left France, Navarre's gentleman in waiting, Miossans, hesitantly approached Marguerite. She had saved his life on Saint Bartholomew's Day and now, out of a muddled sense of loyalty to his master and a real sense of gratitude to Marguerite, he disclosed a plot to her. There was a Huguenot move afoot to bring about the escape both of Navarre and of Alençon in order to put them at the head of a Protestant army. Marguerite was in a dilemma. She had no love for her young husband, but she could have nothing but sympathy for him arising out of the daily irritations, the constant petty insults to which he was subjected. He was not too badly treated by either the king or Catherine, but the courtiers, ever alert to the most subtle changes of official status, combined to harry and mock him; the Duke of Guise, in particular, was abrasively contemptuous of the "kinglet" who had robbed him of the richest matrimonial prize in France. Navarre took the insults with the same grin, the same shock-headed insouciance with which he accepted everything that came his way, but Marguerite and a tiny handful of friends were aware of how he chafed, how the insults bit home. It was the most natural thing in the world for him to wish to escape this petty domestic hell for his own domains.

In theory, too, she should have been actually prepared to help Alençon, or at the very least not to hinder him, her natural ally. Her reaction was the exact opposite: she went to the king and Catherine and, after obtaining their solemn promise that they would not punish her husband and brother, she betrayed the plot. The king and the queen mother honored their promise on this occasion, merely ensuring that the watch on the two young men was discreetly increased. Marguerite gave as the reason for her betrayal the fact that both men were very young and easily influenced by bad characters; she might, perhaps, have been moved by a true sense of statesmanship, and did her best to scotch a conspiracy that might have wrecked the country. But the fact that it could only have been a matter of days before she became involved in the nationwide conspiracy of the Politiques—a conspiracy which directly threatened the throne and ended with axe and block and hangman's rope—argues forcefully that she betrayed the first plot because of its ineptitude.

"Most of the quarrels at court were caused by love affairs. Women had their fingers in everything, making trouble both for themselves and for their lovers," one of the conspirators, the Viscount of Turenne, noted sourly. He had rather an exaggerated belief in the powers and influences of a group of bored young women, whiling away the tedium of the hours with a hothouse gallantry. But there was little doubt that, in the matter of the Politique plot, most of the threads did indeed seem to pass through Marguerite's hand, and from thence through the hands of her first lover, the splendidly named Joseph Boniface Hyacinth, Lord of La Mole, her brother Alençon's firm friend and confidant.

La Mole effortlessly enjoyed the best of two distinct and usually mutually hostile worlds: he was a highly successful lady's man who also held the amused respect of his own sex. Some of them hated him: that was only natural, for his sexual successes were phenomenal and transcended such sober, cramping limitations as marriage vows. He was forty-four years old when he entered Marguerite's orbit— virtually an old man in that court of twenty year olds. Nevertheless, he led them all—the handsomest in face, the most elegant in figure, the best dancer, the most persuasive and honey-tongued, the man who had sweet-talked Elizabeth of England into accepting his master before she had set eyes on him. In his preoccupation with copulation as an index of social success and happiness, he was very much a man of his day and class—but so too was he in his preoccupation with religion. The king, who watched his antics with a mixture of disapproval and amusement, remarked that it was possible to follow the course of La Mole's debauchs by the frequency with which he attended mass.

Some time in the winter of 1573 the king must have noticed

La Mole attending mass with even greater frequency and devotion, for late on a December might a little party gathered at the foot of one of the lesser used staircases in the Louvre. The party consisted of the king, the Duke of Guise, two or three swordsmen and a man who toyed with a length of silken rope. They were awaiting La Mole, at that moment closeted with Guise's sister, the Duchess of Nevers. La Mole owed his life to the fact that, instead of descending the staircase and proceeding to his master's apartment, he ascended and entered the bedroom of his current mistress, Marguerite. Foiled, the party with the professional strangler returned to their own quarters.

In the vast soundbox that was the Louvre, La Mole must have heard within hours that the king had intended to strangle him for debauching a Daughter of France. And that, in turn, could only have strengthened his resolve to aid the conspiracy which had for object the release and aggrandizement of his master Alençon. It was enormous and elaborately detailed, each section of the country being placed under the control of one of the surviving Huguenot lords. Montgomery—whose accidental killing of Henri II on the tourney ground so long ago had precipitated all these horrors—had escaped to England and planned to descend on the Normandy coast with a Protestant army. Turenne, who was later to express his disenchantment with amorous politics, was to open the gates of his own city of Sedan to a Huguenot army. La Noue, once a most faithful servant of the crown, was to occupy the fortresses of Poitou; Louis of Nassau, to invade France from the Netherlands. Finally, the Lord of Guitry, a tough veteran of the wars, was to undertake the most dangerous and difficult task of all—the leadership of a commando force of a few hundred men who would overwhelm the palace guard and rescue both Navarre and Alençon.

It was the reliable, confident Guitry who ruined the plans, and that by the simplest of all mistakes—timing. The court was at the unfortified château of Saint-Germain at the time, an ideal situation for the work in hand. Guitry, at the head of his fast-moving squadron, appeared near Saint-Germain ten days before he was expected, thus throwing out of gear the complex interlocking parts of the conspiracy. There was no general rising to back him up and distract the royal defenders; worse, neither Navarre nor Alençon was able to join him.

Catherine became aware of the presence of several hundred Huguenot soldiers at 9 P.M. on February 23; by 2 A.M., the court was galloping in panic-stricken haste for the safety of Paris. What exactly happened in the château during those five hours was never wholly clear to those outside the royal family. Some said that it was La Mole alone who had betrayed the plot, aware that it had gone awry and anxious to save his neck. Others claimed that it was on Marguerite's advice that he had gone to the queen mother. Others again insisted that Catherine, with her highly developed nose for intrigues, scented the plot and ordered Marguerite to extract its details from her infatuated lover. Alençon was then hauled before his mother and broke down, bursting into tears, admitting everything. The usually imperturbable Catherine was terrified, convinced that a Bartholomew's Day massacre of Catholics was planned, and ordered an immediate retreat to Paris. The king was carried from his bed to a litter, groaning with pain, crying out, "They might at least have waited until I was dead." Navarre and Alençon were hustled off in the queen mother's own coach—"they were not treated this time with quite so much tenderness as upon the former occasion," Marguerite remarked demurely. The rest of the court grabbed what transport they could find in the darkness of a February morning. The cardinals of Bourbon, Lorraine and Guise and the Chancellor Birague had to make do with horses, "clinging to their saddlebows with both hands, as frightened of their mounts as of their enemies."

The third attempt against the throne took place a little over six weeks later. Again La Mole was at the center; again Marguerite was involved in some enigmatic manner, coming into the open with a brilliant defense of her husband but otherwise skillfully avoiding compromising herself, even to the extent of allowing her lover to perish under the axe without protest. La Mole was certainly a devoted servant to his master; certainly also he was a remarkably inefficient conspirator, drawing together a number of bizarre characters

who would have attracted attention as individuals and virtually proclaimed their sinister purpose as a group. He had as lieutenant the
bloodstained Hannibal de Cocconas, who had earned the contempt
of Catholics, as well as the hatred of Protestants, for his cruelty on
Saint Bartholomew's Day, and the group included Cosmo Ruggieri,
the queen mother's astrologer and magician, a fellow occultist called
Grantrye who claimed to possess the Philosopher's stone, the Viscount of Turenne and a number of discontented Catholics who had
little faith in the conspiracy but joined it for lack of a more positive
course of action.

Montgomery landed in Normandy on March 11, and it was
arranged that the escape of Navarre and Alençon would take place
on April 10. Inevitably, someone in that motley collection of plotters
said too much to the wrong person at the wrong time, and the queen
mother, whose every faculty was now alert to the possibility of
treachery, pounced. Unerring, she picked on Alençon as the weak
link. Again, he was brought before her and subjected to one of those
terrifying interviews which could melt the bones of far braver men.
Alençon caved in immediately, again taking refuge in tears and shift-
ing the blame to his fellow conspirators. La Mole and Cocconas were
brought in, then the Catholic moderates, the marshals Montmorency
and Cossé. A routine search of La Mole's room produced a wax figure
of the king, pierced with pins. Catherine's alarm and anger reached
new heights; the king was slipping fast into his grave, and if he
should die while her beloved Anjou was still in Poland, there was
every possibility that Alençon could usurp the throne. She, who
believed quite matter-of-factly in the influence of the stars, accepted
the sinister significance of the wax mannikin without question. The
call went out to find Ruggieri. "It is a certain fact that he constructed
the thing which my son Alençon possessed on his person and I was
told that he has made a waxen figure, the heart of which is pierced
with pricks, and that this figure was found among La Mole's chattels.
And that also in his lodgings at Paris he has many evil possessions
—books and papers and the like. Pray tell me everything that Cosmo
may confess." Immediately after Ruggieri was arrested, she was writ-

ing, "No sooner was Cosmo taken than he asked if the king vomited, if he still lost blood and had pains in the head. We must know the exact truth about the King's illness and Cosmo must be forced to break the spell. If he has worked magic to make my son Alençon love La Mole he must be forced to undo that charm also."[31]

The royal officers worked swiftly and well: among the major figures only Turenne and Navarre's cousin, the Prince of Condé, succeeded in escaping. But the trials presented an embarassment. It was unthinkable that not only Henri of Bourbon but also his cousin Alençon, through whose veins ran the sacred blood, should stand trial for treason. Well might Cocconas scream out under torture, "The great ones escape while we humble ones pay the price." La Mole shared the rack and the boot and the thumbscrew with him; even Elizabeth of England had been powerless to save this happy-go-lucky adventurer, who had wormed his way into her affections. "It is necessary that he die because he has poisoned the mind of Alençon against his brother, the King," Catherine replied coldly to Elizabeth's request. Alençon, whose fear-stricken confession had brought his loyal servant to the scaffold, pleaded with his mother at least to allow them to die in private. She reluctantly agreed, but somehow the messenger was delayed, and it was under the gaze of thousands of hungry eyes that La Mole and Cocconas mounted the scaffold in the Place de Grève, traditional site for executions. La Mole died first, calling upon God to have mercy on his soul and then, in one of the inconsequential asides that was so much a part of his nature, said, "Remember me to the Queen of Navarre—and the girls!" At the last moment the purely animal fear of dissolution robbed this normally gay and courageous man of self-control so that he trembled violently, unable even to hold the cross that was placed in his hands. Cocconas proved that a bully was not necessarily a coward, kneeling at attention, gazing calmly ahead while the executioner measured the distance with the sword. "He was a gentleman, a valiant man and a brave captain," the king said later. "But a villain—aye, I believe one of the greatest villains in my realm." The heads lay where they had fallen for some hours and then mysteriously disappeared. It was said that Marguerite and the Duchess of Nevers, Cocconas's mistress, had paid a heavy price for them and had wept over them that night and then had them embalmed and placed in jeweled caskets.

And now the baleful gaze of the queen mother turned upon Henri of Navarre: it had, perhaps, been a mistake to omit his name from the killing list on the Eve of Saint Bartholomew. The future Bourbon king was to face many dangers on and off the battlefield over the next twenty years, but arguably he stood in the greatest peril of his life in the few days after the uncovering of the Politiques' plot. It would be bad politics to execute a cousin of the Valois—but a pinch of something strong would have the same effect without the embarrassment. "Cooks, rather than soldiers, are going to win these wars for us," a member of her staff was heard to murmur on discovery of another case of poisoning. But she put the temptation from her and handed Navarre over to a commission, composed of members of the Parlement of Paris, for an examination into his crime.

The immediate danger presented by the queen mother's uncontrolled anger was past. But Navarre was still in an extremely unenviable position, a vassal king under suspicion of treason and *lèse majesté*. He turned now to the only friend he had at court, the wife for whom he had no love and who had no love for him. And Marguerite's reaction was extraordinary—in its range and application of intellect, in its steadfast loyalty. She had every justification for washing her hands of a husband who betrayed her as lightly as she now cuckolded him, a husband who, on the face of it, had engaged in a conspiracy against her family. She nevertheless undertook his defense, drawing up for him a document whose elegance of style and forcefulness and clarity of argument would have done ample justice to any professional lawyer. She did not attempt to excuse or deny his involvement in the conspiracy; rather, she sought to explain it. Speaking in Navarre's person, she went back over the events of the previous nine months, detailing all that had happened to him since the massacre, how he had been humiliated and insulted by the very menials of the court, the threats that had been uttered against him by both the queen mother and the Duke of Guise. And finally she painted a moving portrait of the exile, of the open-air man cooped up month after month in an urban court, of his longing for the free hills and valleys of his homeland. His crime had been simply to want to escape and to return to that which he loved.

Marguerite gave no reason as to why she should have undertaken her husband's defense. In part it may have risen from that streak of stubbornness that made her refuse to divorce him simply at her mother's request. But in part, too, it probably arose from a sense of responsibility. She had been unable to save La Mole—no one on earth could have saved La Mole. But she could save her husband, and did so. The informal trial came to no particular verdict; Navarre was simply transferred with Alençon to the fortresslike château of Vincennes. Even now Marguerite tried to help them, again showing her courage and loyalty. She was allowed to enter and leave Vincennes freely in her own coach with a single lady-in-waiting. She proposed that one of them should change places with the lady-in-waiting; the disguise could easily enough be made by dressing the man in a voluminous traveling cloak and the mask which a lady of quality wore to protect her face from sun and wind while traveling. It might very well have worked—but neither man would consent to be the one left behind, and with a sigh she was forced to abandon the attempt. Altogether, Marguerite came out of the conspiracy of the Politiques as a far braver, more intelligent and determined person than most of the male conspirators.

The king's poignant cry that his brother and cousin might at least have waited until his death was a prosaic truth and no melodramatic utterance. In these last few weeks tuberculosis had flared in his weakening body: his skin broke out in a bloody sweat, his days and nights alike were made hideous with waking nightmares. Yet his mind remained clear enough, and, when he had become convinced that his death was now only a matter of time, he began to clear up what affairs of state he could from his sickbed. A few hours before the end, he summoned Henri of Navarre to him. He looked at him steadily and then said, "You are losing a good friend in me. If I had believed only half of what I had been told you would not be here now."[32] Shortly afterward, his mother bustled in with wonderful news: Montgomery, the slayer of his father, had been captured and would be led to the block. He looked at her with utter indifference and then turned away. His last words were "My mother," or, "And my mother," but whether uttered as prayer or as curse no one knew.

Marguerite was shattered. "He was the sole comfort and support of my life, a brother from whom I received nothing but goodwill and who, during all the persecutions which I endured at Angers from my brother of Anjou, had always helped, warned advised. In short, I lost in him all that it was possible for me to lose."

And in Poland, the brother whom she hated, and who now regarded her with a venom as deadly, prepared to hasten home and take up the crown of France.

†

VII

The Isle of
Hermaphrodites

Marguerite met her brother, the new King Henri, at Lyons on September 6. Three months had passed since Henri, learning that at last he was King of France, had scampered from Poland, pursued to the border by indignant and reproachful Poles. His mother had urged him to hasten home and pick up the scepter in his distracted land, and he might perhaps have intended to do so had he not come by way of Venice. But that beautiful and seductive city, so exactly matching his own extravagant and fantastic character, trapped and held him throughout the summer. And even before he entered his kingdom he began that course of prodigality, of frantic spending and waste, that was to be a characteristic of his reign. The Venetians, accustomed though they were to high spenders, marveled at this elegant young man who tossed golden coins around as though they were so much chaff, ignorant of the fact that, in France, his mother was already resorting to dubious methods to replenish his apparently bottomless purse. Half Italian himself, the Italian city wholly enchanted him, and in its turn the Venetian government feted and courted the new ruler of the great Kingdom of France, serenading him upon the gorgeous state barge, the *Bucentaur,* banqueting him among the marble splendors of the Doge's Palace, providing unobtrusive bodyguards for him as he slipped, in a fondly imagined anonymity, through the Venetian crowds. Always he had this passion for traveling incognito, and he indulged it to the full in Venice that summer, here emptying his purse for a jeweled bauble in a goldsmith's shop, or throwing sweetmeats to the clamoring, thronging children of Venice; there reverently watching the fabled old man Titian at work or playing the tourist among the mosaic marvels of the floating city, for he had a swift and discerning eye for such things. Arguably, this was the happiest period in his life, the brief period when he was able to enjoy all the privileges of kingship with none of its crushing burdens. "I owe this all to my mother," he said. "Would that she were here to share it with me."

But as soon as he had crossed the Mont Cenis, France again took him under its spell, and he declared that there was no other country in the world to compare with it. At Lyons his mother clutched him in a fierce and passionate embrace as though they had been separated for decades instead of scarcely eight months. Then, standing back, she ordered his brother Alençon and his cousin Navarre to approach and, with a dramatic gesture, offered them to him as though she were offering victims to a Roman emperor at his triumph. The young men shuffled forward, Alençon sullen, frowning, but also very frightened, Navarre with his habitual grin, sheepish, placatory. In the euphoria of return, of the consciousness of almost unlimited power over these two, Henri forgave them, embraced them both with the ready tears standing in his eyes. Henceforth there was to be nothing but love between monarch and subjects —even if one of those subjects was his sister. For now Marguerite came up to greet him. The last time they had met, she had coldly rejected his hesitant overture of friendship, and now, as she curtseyed, she was suddenly afflicted by an uncontrollable trembling, a portent, she afterward believed, of all the evils that were to come to her through this brother. But now he was all kindliness and courtesy, raising her up and kissing her, apparently oblivious of that terrified shivering.

At twenty-three, Henri de Valois had much to commend him,

much that was potentially noble. Buried within his fantastic personality was that same disconcerting streak of earnestness which all the Valois brothers possessed, even the otherwise worthless Alençon. In Henri, it found expression predominantly in religion. He could laugh about it: when old Marshal Tavannes was heard to grumble that the new king was like a monk, Henri marched off to the stables, mounted the wildest and most intractable stallion, urged it to a tremendous jump and gaily called out to the spectators, "Ask the Maréchal if he has ever seen a monk do that." But the emotion was very real. At one of the intellectual gatherings which he favored, he congratulated a theologian who had proved, by logic alone, the existence of God. The man preened himself and, scenting more largess, asked leave to return on the morrow when he would prove, just as logically and conclusively, that God did not exist. Angrily, Henri ordered him from his presence and forbade him ever to enter the palace again. Despite his taste for the bizarre and the outré, he had the good sense—or the good fortune—to marry a virtuous woman, the sweet and gentle Louise de Vaudemont, whose respectful love for him became outright adoration when he later refused to divorce her for her apparent barrenness. He brought to the business of kingship a genuine if somewhat naïve and tactless intention of reforming, of sweeping away old and corrupt customs. Fastidious almost to obsession, he loathed being touched and insisted on his right to privacy. Offended courtiers found that they were no longer admitted to his toilet as a matter of right; offended subjects found that they were kept away from his dining table by a velvet rope so that they could witness the repast of the majesty of France only at a distance. This, perhaps, was merely an irritation, but he created positive enemies in the matter of petitions. Traditionally, all petitions to the king were passed on to the appropriate officer of State, who granted, or refused, each petition according to the size of the bribe that accompanied it. This was to cease, Henri decreed: henceforth he, personally, would read each petition and make his decision purely on its merit. At a stroke he enraged those officers who had come to regard their bribes as a legitimate source of income and also all those men whose petitions

were refused and who had cause now personally to hate their monarch instead of a corrupt official. Henri never lacked moral courage
and was prepared to defy even the gloomy Philip of Spain for purely
altruistic reasons. When a storm wrecked a number of Spanish gal-
leys on the French coast, Philip arrogantly demanded the return of
the wretched slave crews. Henri refused outright: "the soil of France
liberated all those who touched it."

Altogether, France might have had reason to be grateful for
this new king who could bring style and humanity back into the
business of government. But Henri had had far too much far too
quickly, growing up in a wholly undisciplined court, his only mentor
the mother who worshipped him above all human beings. In a few
brief years he would be burnt out physically, thereby achieving at
least the appearance of austerity and sobriety. But now he was still
excitedly, even hysterically, experimenting, rather like a child seeking to convince himself that the limited world of the senses was
capable of infinite permutations. The offense he created sprang from
innocent enough causes at first. Shocked ambassadors reported to
their governments how the King of France received them with a
basketful of tiny puppies suspended from his neck. Was he mad?
Was it a deliberate and stupid insult? It was neither. Louise, his
queen, delighted in the little animals; at least a hundred lapdogs
cavorted around the palace. Henri had the basket made so that,
during their long drives together, he and the queen could take a
selection of their pets. The ambassadors happened to be received just
before the royal couple left, that was all. These long, incognito drives
were another cause for alarm and offense. On one occasion the coach
broke down miles from Paris; hours later the royal couple arrived at
the palace, footsore, weary, but cheerful, to find the place in an
uproar, the guard under arms and everyone convinced that the king
had been assassinated or abducted.

His preoccupation with costume and personal appearance set
the standard for a display of extravagance that was remarkable even
for a court of France. The Venetian ambassador, citizen of a city that
was not exactly renowned for austerity, was startled enough to re-

port, "No man is considered to be of any standing unless he possesses some twenty-five or thirty suits of clothing so that he can wear a different suit every day." On the day of Henri's coronation, the ceremony had to be postponed hour after hour as he adjusted, readjusted and readjusted again the set of his jewels and the hang of his robes. Habitually he saw to his wife's toilet, dressing her hair with his own hands, even starching her ruffs for her. His passion for theatricals, combined with his genuine religious bent, produced endless spectacular processions in which the entire court had to take part, all persons dressed in suitably gorgeous costumes for the occasion.

Physically, Henri still retained the Valois good looks. He was losing his hair and, at about this period, adopted the turban which, with his dark complexion and exotic earrings, was to give him a curiously oriental appearance. But, in the first months of his reign, the pen portraits of him that the resident ambassadors produced for their governments are of an attractive enough human being. "Above middle height and slender . . . his eyes are fine and gentle . . . he is delicate in appearance . . . possesses intelligence and good sense though something lacking in health . . . a touch of the solemn about him but if you come closer to him you would find him more courteous and easy than other folk . . . has eschewed all wine for his health's sake but is gay enough." Such were the opinions of the new king held by men whose profession it was to judge character coldly and precisely. His idiosyncracies, though perhaps deplorable in a monarch, were harmless enough, and he might very well have grown out of them had there not occurred, shortly after his coronation, an event which nudged his delicately balanced intelligence irrevocably to one side. In 1575 his mistress, the Princess of Condé, died suddenly of a puerperal fever.

The Princess of Condé had no obvious physical or spiritual advantages over Henri's attractive and loving wife. Nevertheless, like his forebears and successors, he had to have his *maîtresse en titre,* and her death, for some unknown, deep-seated reason, destroyed within him the fragile barrier between eccentricity and outright perversion. His reaction to her death was extreme to the point of parody: his mourning costume was of the conventional black but it was liberally covered with a jangling, clattering collection of ivory or silver skulls. The more sycophantic courtiers copied the fashion, but the truly ambitious man who wanted to attract his monarch's attention soon had to do more than merely substitute death's heads for jewels. Henri entered the ranks of the Blancs Battus, that extraordinary society of flagellants who belabored each other's backs and buttocks with vicious whips in the name of penitence and religion. Stripped to the waist, the anointed King of France shuffled in endless processions, alternately praying and flaying the man ahead while the man behind did the same thing to him. There was no compulsion to join the flagellants, but it was highly politic to do so. One of the less enthusiastic members was the Cardinal of Lorraine; as high priest of France, he was able to avoid actually being whipped, but despite his cautious, lackluster approach, he killed himself in the cause of Guise policy. Shuffling barefoot and bareheaded through the bitter autumn weather and clad in flimsy garments of penance, he caught a cold. On the night that he died, a freak storm sprang up—God welcoming a faithful son, declared the Catholics; the Devil claiming his own, according to the Huguenots.

The malign change in Henri's character accelerated. The preoccupation with costume and personal appearance turned into exhibitionism and then, almost inevitably, into transvestism, as his quiescent homosexuality burst into bizarre flowering. Painted and scented, he dressed in sweeping skirts and décolletage: "one does not know whether we have a female king or a male queen," Aubigné snarled. He was a Huguenot and a supporter of Navarre, and his opinions of the king were therefore suspect; but the Catholic monarchist L'Estoile, secretary to that king, was as venomous and considerably more detailed. It was L'Estoile who first sketched in the picture of those extraordinary companions of the king, the *mignons,* who became the very badge and emblem of the corrupt court. A young man, Henri naturally wanted young men around him, but swiftly the usual crowd of hangers-on and rowdy young noblemen to be expected at any court developed into a very curious assembly, the masculine counterpart of the queen mother's Flying Squadron—with one, very important, difference. "There is beginning to be a lot of talk about these *mignons,*" L'Estoile noted. "The people hate and scorn them as much for their effeminate and immodest appearance as for their haughty manners, but most of all because of the excessive liberalities of the King towards them. Popular opinion is that they are the cause of his ruin. These fine *mignons* wear their hair long, curled and re-curled artificially, on top of which they wear little bonnets of velvet like the whores in the brothels. Their shirts are long and loose; they wear enormous ruffs so that their heads look like St John's on a platter. Their occupations are gambling, blaspheming, jumping, dancing, quarrelling, fornicating and following the king around. They do everything to please him, giving no thought to honour or to God, contenting themselves with the trace of their master."[33]

Such was the fairly straightforward description by a sober Catholic chronicler. The Huguenot writer Thomas Artus elaborated the picture into an hilarious satire, *The Isle of Hermaphrodites,* which became as popular with Catholics as with Protestants. Artus pretended that he arrived at the Louvre and was astonished to find that it was not a royal palace but a vast hairdressing salon. Wandering through the rooms, he encounters the *mignons* enduring the agonies of the morning toilet, and his description is probably not far from accurate. "I beheld a single *mignon* surrounded by several attendants. One was holding before him a mirror: another had a large box of cypress-wood filled with powder . . . a third individual tore superfluous hairs from his master's eyebrows, using a fine instrument. . . . Another then came and, kneeling, opened the patient's mouth by gently pulling his beard. Then wetting his finger, he rubbed a white powder on the gums and from a little box he took some false teeth and fastened in wherever there was space." The attendants then painted and perfumed the victim, inserted his legs into silk stockings, crammed his feet into tiny shoes, forced him into a doublet that almost choked him, girded him round with gloves, mirror, rings, chains and a fan, then sent him tottering off to the *lever.* The royal bedroom was part church, part boudoir. The king was lying on an enormous bed, equipped with crimson pillows, known as the Altar of Antinous, and the *mignons* gathered round and "invoked their god by names which cannot be reproduced in our tongue, as all the terms used by the Hermaphrodites are what grammarians call of the neuter gender."[34]

The *mignons* were to prove Marguerite's most formidable enemies, forming not so much a barrier as a malign distorting agency between herself and the king, source of all power. Neither Artus nor L'Etoile was wholly accurate in the picture painted of these epicene courtiers. The public did indeed loathe them; whenever they appeared, mincing along in a cloud of perfume, they were followed by long drawn-out derisory whistles and cries of "Calfhead"—the enormous cartwheel ruff they affected was supposed to give the wearer the appearance of a boiled calf'shead on a plate. But while they were undoubtedly effeminate in appearance and habits, they possessed an almost lunatic courage, a total disregard to personal safety, coupled with a fanatical loyalty to Henri. Inured though Paris was to violence and sudden, brutal death, people still talked of the Duel of the *Mignons* when six of these ferocious fops hacked and stabbed and gouged at each other until only one remained alive.

Such was one pole of the court. At the other was the queen mother, surrounded with her own highly specialized courtiers. She was now grown enormously stout—the Huguenots christened their bulkiest cannon *La reine Mère,* to her considerable amusement—but despite her girth she was as active as ever, prepared to cross France from Atlantic to Mediterranean and back again on behalf of her turbulent family. She resented the *mignons* almost as deeply, almost as bitterly as did Marguerite, for they kept her from her beloved son. "Tell me how your affairs go," she pleaded in one of her curiously touching letters. "I don't ask this because I want to control them but because, if they go well, my heart can be at ease, and if they go badly I can perhaps help you. For you are my all and whether or not you love me I don't think that you trust me as once you did. I have no wish to live any longer. I have no care for life since your father died, excepting as I might serve you and God."[35] She must have been feeling liverish after one of her intemperate meals when she wrote that letter, for she was, in fact, enjoying life to the full. The Venetian ambassador reported that she was sometimes discovered weeping in the privacy of her own apartments, but the face she wore in public was one of confidence and zest. And neither was such an appearance a mere façade: her moral shallowness and sheer animal vitality enabled her to live wholly in the present, forgetting past failures and deceits, contrasting strongly with her sickly sons, who seemed to go through life carrying a double burden of guilt and ill health. Despite her bulk and the dowdy clothes which seemed so incongruous among the peacock glitter of the court, she was to be seen, night after night, in the feverish balls and dances in the palace. By day she rode to the hunt, sitting astride like a man, coming up late for the kill, perhaps, for her mounts were chosen for stamina rather than speed, but taking part with gusto in the gargantuan alfresco feasts that marked the conclusion of a successful hunt. She should have been popular, this stout woman with the jolly laugh and liking for crude jokes. She was tolerant enough. Once she and her young son-in-law Navarre unwittingly eavesdropped on a couple of peasants who were tearing the royal family's reputation to shreds—the queen mother's in particular. Navarre, the later champion of the common man, wanted to hang them on the spot. Catherine prevented him, calling out to the terrified men, "Heh! What harm has the queen mother ever done you?" When a copy of a Huguenot lampoon, *The Life of St. Catherine*, fell into her hands, she read it with interest, laughed and said that she could have given the writer much more interesting material if he had only had the courage to ask her.

But, far from being popular, she was actively hated. In part, the hatred sprang from the fact that most Frenchmen were now convinced that she was a necromancer. Even those in her intimate family circle believed that she had occult powers. In the most matter-of-fact manner Marguerite tells the story of how her mother not merely foresaw but actually seems to have lived through the battle of Jarnac the night before it was fought. She was in a delirium of fever at the time, and the watchers by her bed heard her crying out as she tossed and turned, " 'Behold, they take to flight! . . . My son has gained the victory! Ah God, raise up my son, he is on the ground! Look at the Prince of Condé, lying dead in that hedge.' . . . All those who were present fancied that she was raving and that, knowing that my brother of Anjou was about to engage in battle she had only this one thought in mind. On the following evening, however, when Monsieur de Losses brought her the news, she said to him, 'You are troublesome to have awakened me for this. I knew all about it. Did I not behold it the day before yesterday?' Then it was that they realised that what they had taken for the delirium of fever was an especial warning, such as God gives to illustrious and exceptional persons."

It is in the same unemotional, unquestioning tone that Marguerite recorded how her mother saw—or claimed that she saw—a blue flame shortly before the death of any of her children. And the chronicler L'Etoile, equally impressed with her abilities, gives a chilling air of verisimilitude to his account of her vision on the night that her great enemy, the Cardinal of Lorraine, died. She was at supper, gaily celebrating his death, and was on the point of raising her glass to toast her good fortune when she suddenly began to tremble so violently as to spill the wine. "Jesus, there is the Cardinal. I see him. I see him before me, passing on the way to Paradise. He is soaring up."[36] Even the most sceptical are left with the distinct impression that she did indeed see something moving between herself and the wall. The faculty, whatever it was, could leave her prostrate with the most abject of superstitious fears. In November of 1577 a comet appeared in the east, rising after sunset and setting at about 10 P.M. "The crazy astrologers said that it presaged the death of a queen or great lady in some terrible manner," L'Etoile scoffed. Catherine did no scoffing. During the forty days that the comet appeared, she was in an ecstasy of terror, awaiting the death that the heavens themselves had signaled.

Catherine's occultism did not prevent her paying the most minute attention to the humdrum details of everyday life. She was a good administrator, but even she could not keep pace with the fantastic demand for money in a court which regarded gold and silver as so much tow to be burned. Her son gave a banquet in which he decreed that the men should be waited on by the ladies of the court, all of whom were to be dressed like men in suits of green silk: that little proviso cost the Exchequer some 60,000 francs. Catherine was Florentine enough to deplore the waste of money on mere show and passing fashion, but the court of France was a wheel which, turning faster and faster to destruction, forced all others to run to keep pace. She herself gave a banquet at Chenonceaux which cost 100,000 francs—"borrowed from the Italians," L'Etoile sourly noted. "At this splendid affair the ladies of the court appeared half naked." It was very largely Italian money which allowed the frenetic dance to continue, Italian money which paid for the suits of cloth of gold or silver, the rare foods and wines—but Italian money borrowed at crippling rates of interest, sometimes as much as 40 per cent. Hatred of Italians found an obvious object in Catherine herself and in her intimate counselors, the Chancellor Birague, the Count of Retz, Nevers, Gondi —the little handful of men who had come with her into France all those years ago and had prospered with her.

> *When these cowardly rascals came to France,*
> *They were thin as sardines and empty, save of evils.*
> *But by their fat pickings and not by chance,*
> *They've become as rich and fat as boll weevils.* [37]

So the vicious lampoons sped around the town, not so much attacking the Italians as castigating Frenchmen for lacking the courage and sense to pluck the leeches from their body. But despite the conduit that brought gold—at a price—from Florence to Paris, there was never enough, and the most extreme measures were adopted to raise more. In May of 1575, only two months after Henri's coronation marked the beginning of a new regime, Paris seethed with the news that France's most sacred relic, the fragment of the True Cross, had disappeared from its reliquary in the Sainte Chapelle. "It is believed that the Queen Mother has taken it—the people have such a horror of her that there is no terrible thing they will not put at her door. The common opinion is that it has been sent to Italy as collateral for a large loan of money."[38] A year later Henri announced that he had obtained another fragment "and that everyone should go and adore it during Holy Week as usual," but the more sophisticated Parisians somewhat doubted the genuineness of the new relic. An ingenious new tax on taverns and innkeepers brought a growl of mutiny. But the victims paid up, adding another 100,000 francs a year to the Exchequer: "It is one of the new devices of the Italians to raise money which is dissipated as soon as it is raised." The sale of offices, always the stand-by of a bankrupt government, began to threaten the very machinery of administration. Hitherto, it had been possible to keep some control on the sale of offices by keeping some control on the buyer. Now it became the practice for very wealthy men to offer a large lump sum for a number of offices which they would then resell at their leisure and at a vastly increased profit. Minor offices were therefore sold and resold until the government had only the haziest idea as to who now actually owned and operated them. "The most abominable of these traffics is the sale of benefices, the great majority being held by women or married men, even to infants still at the breast so that it would seem that they come into the world bearing a cross and mitre. In short it is not possible to imagine a crab more twisted and contradictory than the government of France."[39]

Despite the fact that Marguerite kept a sharp eye and a suspicious ear open for every vice and foible of her brother's, she was too much of a Valois to see anything at all remarkable in the parade of conspicuous and prodigal waste. As to the rest of her family, money to her was a natural product which was simply harvested in the quantities required whenever it was needed: time and again she was to be brought to the edge of penury, as the Valois estimated penury, due to her magnificent disregard for the humdrum virtue of account-ancy. Brantôme proudly tells of the occasion when she gave her sister-in-law, the queen, "a fan made of mother of pearl enriched with precious stones and pearls of price, so beautiful and rich that it was called a masterpiece and valued at more than fifteen thousand crowns." It was a New Year's gift, and Louise reciprocated with a gift valued at one hundred crowns. Marguerite's was a particularly rich gift considering that Henri and her mother still kept her in a deliberate state of financial subjection; she had not yet received the lands and revenues due her on her marriage, and her husband, young Navarre, was still a virtual prisoner in the royal palaces. Money came to the young King and Queen of Navarre according to the whim of the young King of France. And that whim was singularly ungenerous, for Marguerite and her brother were again luxuriating in the emotion of mutual hatred.

Marguerite blamed it all on the *mignons,* in particular, on the red-headed Louis du Guast, her brother's first homosexual companion, who, she believed, was directly responsible for breaking up her own first love affair with Guise. Du Guast tried to assure her that he was by no means her enemy. While Henri was still in Poland, du Guast waited on her with some business of his master's. She received him, spitting with rage, swearing that it was his safe conduct alone which prevented her from teaching him "to speak about a princess like myself, the sister of your kings, your masters and sovereigns." Du Guast "very humbly" denied that he had ever spoken of her other than with the utmost respect, but she cut him short and dismissed him "with an assurance that she would ever be his cruel enemy—a promise which she kept until his death." She made a very great mistake, for du Guast's influence over the king was now paramount. And neither was that influence by any means malign. Brantôme, who had been present at that interview between his adored princess and the powerful courtier, admitted that du Guast was one of the very few people who could argue Henri into a more sober, more responsible line of conduct; his assassination at an early period opened the way for the wholly corrupting influence of the *mignons.* This crewcut courtier with the sidelong, arrogant glance might be a homosexual but it was in the classic manner of Alcibiades, not in the enervating, hothouse manner of the *mignons.*

Du Guast was an honest man, according to the very devious standards of the court, but he would have had to have been an

unusually noble man to ignore the threat made by the king's beautiful, influential and wholly unscrupulous sister. He struck back
swiftly—or, at least, Marguerite believed that he did—in the curious
affair of the empty coach. They were all still in Lyons—indeed, it
could only have been a matter of a few days after Henri's arrival—
when Marguerite and five of her friends and ladies-in-waiting suddenly decided to visit a nunnery in the town. The six young women
seated themselves in Marguerite's coach and they were just leaving
the palace when two of the king's equerries "made their appearance
and jumped up on the step of the coach where, holding on as best
they could and playing the buffoon, being of a ribald humour, they
declared that they too meant to go and see these pretty nuns. The
presence of these two, who were confidential servants of the king
was, I believe, a provision of God to save me from the calumny of
which I was accused."[40]

The gay little party rattled through Lyons; when it arrived at
the convent, everyone went inside, leaving the coach empty and
unattended outside. It was a distinctive vehicle, gilt, with upholstery
of yellow velvet and silver, and when, a short while afterward, the
king, with Navarre, and a party of his bravoes, rode through the
square, it immediately attracted the royal attention. It so happened
that one of the houses in the square belonged to a certain Bide, a
notorious gallant, and Henri immediately jumped to the conclusion
that Marguerite was having an affair with Bide. He nudged Navarre.
"Look, there is your wife's chariot outside Bide's lodgings. I'll wager
that she is inside." He then sent one of his companions to make
inquiry. The man, naturally, found nothing but, wishing to curry
favor with the king, said on his return, "The birds have been there
but they are now flown."

Marguerite knew nothing about the incident until she returned to the palace, when her husband met her with a broad grin,
to tell her that the queen mother wanted to see her at once and that
she would certainly return "in a fine rage." Marguerite demanded to
be told what was the matter; he refused to tell her but, growing
suddenly serious, assured her that he did not believe the story, which

was simply a means to set them against each other. Puzzled, she went in search of her mother. Outside the queen mother's apartments she met the Duke of Guise, who came forward and detained her for a moment. "I've been waiting for you here to warn you that the queen credits you with a most dangerous form of benevolence." He then went on to describe the entire incident to her, having learned it from a member of the party. Guise was probably motivated by nothing more than a desire to warn somebody for whom he felt a very real affection, but Marguerite, hypersensitive to anything that concerned him, simply believed that he was crowing over her troubles, "hoping no doubt to gather up some spars from the wreckage." Icily, she thanked him and swept on into the queen mother's apartments but her increasing anxiety was hardly alleviated when one of her mother's ladies tried to prevent her going in. "Good heavens, madam, the queen your mother is in a terrible rage with you. I don't advise you to present yourself before her." Inwardly quaking now, but outwardly confident, Marguerite swept on her regal way to be brought up short by the queen herself, "who opened fire as soon as she saw me." Catherine de Médicis in a rage was formidable, for that baleful glare from the protuberant pale eyes seemed to strike down through every defense. Her twenty-year-old daughter, whose conscience was by no means wholly clear although in this particular matter she was innocent enough, fell to pieces before the vehement bombardment. She tried to explain the circumstances, demanded to be told the name of the informant. Catherine pretended that it was one of her own lackeys who had seen the empty carriage, uneasily aware, perhaps, that the role of informer hardly befitted the King of France, and when Marguerite refused to be taken in, she angrily ordered the girl from her presence. Seething with rage, Marguerite sought out her husband, who again reassured her that he had no belief in the story and warned her again that the object was to create trouble between them.

The affair collapsed in an anticlimax with an odd little sequel. The two equerries who had lightheartedly accompanied Marguerite's party told Henri of his mistake—and he promptly went to confess it to the queen mother and asked her to try and make his peace with his sister. Marguerite inevitably thought that his request came from nothing more than the fact that he was aware "that I might know better how to revenge myself than he had known how to offend me." To the unbiased outsider it seems at least as likely that Henri, having made a genuine mistake, was making an honest effort to apologize and reconcile himself with his sister. Marguerite spurned her mother's attempt at peace-making, and even when Henri came personally to make his apologies, haughtily stood on her dignity. It was the last attempt at apology or reconciliation he ever made; the trivial affair of the empty carriage proved to be the opening shot of a battle between them that ended only with his death.

Navarre, for all his insouciance, was keeping a very watchful eye on his beautiful young wife. The sexual side of their marriage was now totally broken down, each indifferent to the infidelities of the other, but, apart from the genuine mutual liking that survived the debacle, Navarre was vividly aware that he owed even the limited freedom and safety that he enjoyed to Marguerite. And she, partly from a desire to irritate and spite that omnipotent brother of hers and his too complaisant mother but partly, too, as an outpouring of her warm and generous nature, remained loyal to him. There thus came into existence, in the heart of the royal, Catholic court, a most curious alliance between the young King of Navarre, still regarded as the leader of all Huguenots despite his apparent apostasy, the deeply Catholic but smouldering sister of the King of France and the weathercock brother of that king, young Alençon, who would have turned Moslem if it had served his ravening ambition.

It is to Louis du Guast's credit that he saw the danger of the alliance and energetically set to work to break it up, using a means that would have been impossibly bizarre in almost any other context but that of the Valois court. Among the members of the queen mother's Flying Squadron was a certain Madame de Sauves, a lady of uncertain age but possessed of an extraordinary sexual attraction. She possessed, too, an extraordinarily docile husband, for though the Baron de Sauves occupied the important position of secretary of state, he might have been nothing more than a legal fiction for all the part that he played in his wife's prolonged and convoluted affairs. Charlotte de Sauves was not particularly beautiful—the mean twist of her mouth and heavy-lidded, treacherous eyes effectively canceled any claim to formal beauty. But the sexual aura that surrounded her, the purely animal magnetism that emanated from her was something far stronger than mere beauty, for it outlasted the ravages of time itself: the Duke of Guise was to spend his last night on earth in her bed in a little over twelve years' time, and Marguerite, highly favored though she was in that particular field, paid her the compliment of hating and fearing her.

In 1576, when the court was still at Lyons, Charlotte de Sauves was already the mistress of Navarre. She was also the mistress of quite a number of other men, including du Guast himself, Guise and Souvre, one of the king's more heterodox *mignons*. It was du Guast who suggested that she should, in effect, abandon her amateur status, enlarge her role and enter politics by seducing young Alençon, thereby creating jealousy between him and his ally Navarre. It speaks much for the lady's very real skill that she was able to achieve exactly what du Guast asked of her. Hitherto, the relationship between her various lovers had been either indifference or perfect amiability; it would, after all, have been difficult for any one man seriously to resent the caresses lavished upon another when Charlotte broadcast those caresses with such a free and open hand. But, within a very short time, she was able to insert a wedge in the alliance of Navarre and Alençon.

Marguerite watched her technique with a reluctant but very real admiration for its professional expertise: "she worked up the love of my brother and of my husband the king (which had previously been somewhat careless and lukewarm like that of very young people) to such a pitch of violence that, forgetful of every other ambition and object in life, the sole idea in their minds seemed to be the pursuit of this woman." Both men were perfectly well aware that the object of their feverish desire would have slept with the meanest pageboy if there was financial or political profit to be made from it. Both were perfectly aware that they shared her with every other gallant in the court who showed any desire to enter her bed. Nevertheless, her skill was such—Marguerite actually compared her to Circe—that Navarre and Alençon hated each other exclusively for the favor each enjoyed from her. Tightlipped, Marguerite followed the antics of her husband and brother, the allies she had counted upon in her feud with the king, and in her irritation and anxiety made a move which she, of all people, should have known to be worse than useless: she warned the lovers against their mistress. Her brother promptly repeated the warnings to Charlotte, and from that moment on Marguerite had a direct enemy. Until now, Madame de Sauves had been interested simply in separating the two young men. Now, correctly identifying Marguerite as the true center of opposition, she went over to the attack, employing a dizzingly devious twist on even that free and easy morality that the court adopted for day to day living. She told Navarre that his wife, through jealousy, was encouraging his brother's suit. It had a twofold effect, for while increasing Navarre's hatred for his rival, it turned his tolerance toward his wife into a furious rage. Madame de Sauves swiftly followed up her advantage. Navarre normally left her very late at night, but at least spent the mornings with his wife, for his mistress had to attend the queen mother's levee. Now, however, Charlotte ordered him to accompany her to the levee on pain of loss of favor. Yawning, heavy-headed from the previous evening's excesses of wine and sex, Navarre nevertheless would drag himself out of bed and after a very sketchy toilet, shamble into the queen mother's apartment in the wake of his crisply dressed mistress. The casual, amiable conversation that had enabled husband and wife to keep some form of contact now ended, for Navarre was in his mistress's company from shortly after dawn until midnight. Days could now pass before Marguerite exchanged a single word with her husband and even then it would be in the midst of a crowd. It would seem that the alliance, as well as the marriage, was at an end.

It was at this dreary period of anticlimax, when, beaten at her own game by a thorough professional, Marguerite was somewhat anxiously reappraising her role and tactics, that there flashed across her sky the comet known as Bussy-d'Amboise. Primly, she referred to him in her memoirs simply as her brother's most loyal servant, but the warmth with which she spoke of him, years after he had taken his beauty and arrogance and corruption and courage to the grave, told clearly enough of the very special relationship he enjoyed with her, a relationship which even managed to push into the background the ceaseless, dull pain that was her relationship with the Duke of Guise. Bussy, entering his late twenties when he first came into contact with Marguerite, summed up in his own person all that was contradictory in the Valois court—the physical elegance and the moral squalor; the rootless, purposeless day-to-day drift and the lunatic courage that impelled a man to hazard his life on the drop of a handkerchief. During the Massacre of Saint Bartholomew he had taken the opportunity to murder a cousin with whom he was involved in a lawsuit, but though people might deplore such excesses of spirit, they shook their heads with a half-smiling reproach, for he had a seemingly limitless charm. The craggy Calvinist Agrippa d'Aubigné held up his hands in horror at the man's morals but grudgingly allowed his brilliance; the Catholic L'Estoile agreed that he was "highhanded, of invincible courage, proud and bold, as brave as any captain in France of his age," but that all these high qualities were marred because he was "vicious and scornful of God—which was eventually his undoing as usually happens to men of blood." Bussy-d'Amboise was untroubled with false modesty: after reading Plutarch's *Lives,* he announced, "There is nothing here that I could not do under the same circumstances." Women adored him, men liked him unless they were fearing for their lives or their womenfolk. It could also have been predicted, with near-actuarial certainty, that his merry life would be a short one.

Originally, Bussy had been a member of Henri's entourage even before Henri had become the king. He had loyally followed his royal master into the barbaric exile of the Polish adventure, had taken part in the escape and eventually the triumphant return. It was therefore all the more bitter for Henri to see this brave, gay and devoted soldier suddenly desert him for the opposition grouped round Marguerite. Nobody outside the circle ever knew the true reason for the switch. Bussy may have become disgusted with Henri's grovelling homosexuality, although this was unlikely, for he seems to have been sexually ambidextrous, like so many in that court. He may have thought that life with the hungrily ambitious Alençon promised more fun. He may have been drawn across the divide by the very powerful attraction of the Queen of Navarre. It was inevitable that two such people, in the limited area of the court, should be drawn to each other, but whether they became lovers before, or after, they became political allies was uncertain. Du Guast rapidly learned of the affair and as rapidly passed it on to the king. Furious with rage at Bussy's desertion and wounded, too, in his ambivalent regard for his sister, Henri rushed to his mother with the latest news of Marguerite's indiscretions.

He received a very cold reception. Catherine was quite sensitive over the fool she had made of herself in the matter of the carriage in Lyons and said as much. "At Lyons you made me offer her a very serious insult which I fear she will remember as long as she lives. What is there to complain of? Bussi sees my daughter in front of you, in front of her husband, in front of all her husband's servants and in front of everybody else. She does not see him in secret or behind closed doors. Bussi is a person of quality and the first gentleman-in-waiting upon your brother," she said indignantly and then lapsed into a plaintive nostalgia. "In our day we spoke freely to everybody, and all the gallant gentlemen who served the king your father were constantly in the chamber of your aunt—Madame Marguerite—and no one thought anything of it. Nor was there any reason why they should! My daughter is unfortunate to have been born in such times. I cannot think who the mischief makers are who put such ideas in your head."

Catherine's reaction was the exact opposite of what Henri had expected and he could only stammer lamely in reply that he was but repeating what others had told him. Then he should have known better, Catherine snapped back. "There are people around whose only desire is to set you at loggerheads with your family."

Or so, at least, Marguerite reported the conversation, a good ten years after both mother and son had died. After the disconcerted Henri had withdrawn, Marguerite continued, her mother called her in and, with something like a sigh, told her everything, ending with the remark, "You are born in an evil day." Catherine again lapsed into nostalgia with an old crony, Madame de Dampierre, "conversing with her about the pleasant liberty of action which they enjoyed in their time without being, like us, subjected to slander."[41] Despite the literary polishings and elaborations, the whole conversation has the feel of truth, not least that rather touching little vignette of two stout, elderly ladies reminiscing about the golden age of their youth while the twenty-year-old princess looked on part impatiently, part enviously.

There was a determined and elaborate attempt to murder Bussy in the street not long afterward. Marguerite was convinced that du Guast was to blame, but although he undoubtedly planned it, equally doubtless the king was deeply involved, for the palace guard were employed. Nobody thought it worthy of particular note that the only way the King of France could remove an enemy was by way of a common street brawl. The attempt failed partly because it was bungled—two or three hundred guardsmen stumbling around in the dark were not the ideal instrument for an assassination—but partly, too, through a simple mistake in identification. Bussy had recently been wounded in the right arm and had it in a sling made from a pretty dove-colored scarf that Marguerite had given him. An unfortunate member of his party also had his arm tied in a light-colored scarf and it was he who was cut down while Bussy made his escape.

But though the attempt was a failure, it brought to flashpoint the hatred between the royal brothers. One of the members of Bussy's party ran, streaming with blood, to the palace. "They're killing Bussy, they're killing Bussy," he shouted as he stumbled up the stairs. Marguerite leaped out of bed—not to go to Bussy's assistance but to stop her brother, who had dashed from his own bedroom. Alençon was almost hysterical with rage, swearing that he would kill du Guast, kill the king, kill anybody who had dared lay hands on his faithful Bussy. Marguerite desperately tried to hold him back, crying out for her mother, and it was Catherine who stopped the half-mad boy, her ponderous presence and ice-cold voice penetrating even his disordered mind. Together, mother and sister got him back to his room where Catherine ordered the guards to restrain him until the morning. Morning brought Bussy to the palace "with as gallant and gay a demeanour as if this assault upon him had merely been a passage of arms for his amusement," the admiring Marguerite noted; but the affair had not yet ended. During the morning Alençon and the king had a furious exchange, Alençon demanding revenge on du Guast, the king hinting very plainly that Bussy was yet another of their sister's disreputable lovers. They would have come to blows if Catherine had not intervened and persuaded Alençon to send Bussy away. The two of them had a hurried consultation in private and Alençon then agreed, if sullenly, and Bussy left Paris for the nearby town of Dreux.

Du Guast had not yet finished with Marguerite, although, in the labyrinthine intrigues of the Valois court he was able to keep his activities concealed from all but those immediately involved—in particular, from the baleful eyes of the queen mother, who would have reacted violently and implacably against an outsider interfering in the family's business. Marguerite and her husband were briefly reconciled through a somewhat curious circumstance. Navarre collapsed unconscious one night, "the result, I believe of his amourous excesses for I never knew him to be subject to anything of the kind before." Marguerite nursed him through what seems to have been a very serious illness; certainly he believed that she had saved his life. In consequence, the old easy friendship came to life again and, with it, the alliance between Navarre and Alençon because, says Marguerite, "I acted as a kind of unguent—such as exists in all natural objects— but which is most observable in the case of serpents that have been cut in half and which joins and cements their severed parts." But her knowledge of du Guast's capabilities was about as accurate as her knowledge of natural history. Madame de Sauves, alone, was apparently no longer sufficient to drive a wedge in the three-cornered alliance. Du Guast, like a skillful chess player, worked several moves ahead to obtain a goal: he put pressure upon the king to put pressure upon Navarre to order Marguerite to send her favorite maid, Torigny, away from court. It was a mean but effective move, for Torigny was not only Marguerite's confidante but also the means whereby she kept in contact with her exiled lover Bussy. Navarre acted reluctantly. He had not the slightest desire to interfere in his wife's domestic arrangements and was totally indifferent to the fact that Torigny was helping to make him a cuckold. But his brother-in-law the King of France could make life very unpleasant for him and, after Marguerite had at first indignantly refused, he ordered her outright to send the girl away. And despite the fact that his wife was not only a Daughter of France but also a highly intelligent and strong-willed young woman, she was nevertheless his wife, and the whole force of custom and morality dictated that when the husband commanded, the wife obeyed. She therefore sent the girl away; but her rage was such as to shatter the frail reconciliation. As she put the position herself, "Du Guast and Madame de Sauve had estranged him from me upon one side and I withdrew myself from him upon the other we ended by no longer sleeping together or even speaking to one another." More than two years were to pass before they were again on speaking terms, and that was to take place at the other end of France.

†

VIII

The Prisoner

"This court is the strangest you've ever seen. We are nearly always ready to cut each other's throats—most of us carry daggers and even shirts of mail under our coats. The King is in as great a danger as myself, and loves me you can guess how much. I'm only waiting for the moment when I can have a go at them for they all want to kill me and I intend to get my blow in first."[42] So young Navarre wrote to a close friend. If the letter had been intercepted he might have had excellent grounds for worrying about his future, but so good was the façade he had erected as the drunken buffoon lurching from bed to wine bottle and back again that few paid much attention to him. Catherine occasionally suspected that there was more to the young Béarnais than a seemingly limitless appetite for women and alcohol but he gave her nothing specific to go on. Marguerite, more than anyone else in the court, had a very shrewd idea of what lay behind the grin and the provincial accent, but he had always kept his inner core hidden from her, and now, since their quarrel, she could only guess at his plans. And those plans did not, at that stage, include her. Henri of Navarre was to go down in history with an awesome reputation as a lover, numbering his women by the score, yet it is to be doubted if he had a truly meaningful relationship with one of them.

146

There was, at the center of his being, a coldness which enabled him to switch off an affair apparently at will no matter how deeply he and the woman might have been mutually involved. Marguerite, for whom he had felt nothing sexually from the beginning, was now cut out from his mind as though she were nothing more than a palace flunky, for she had no immediate role to play in his life.

Nevertheless, he had need of Marguerite's brother Alençon, their common danger overcoming the rather theatrical role of jealous lovers for which they had been cast by Charlotte de Sauves. Marguerite was aware that they were in frequent and close consultation; what she did not know then was that they were discussing the possibility of escape. Obviously, she would be the scapegoat for any successful attempt, but neither of the men thought to warn her, much less include her in their plans. They did express to each other the pious hope that "no one would dare to offer me an affront once it became known that they were at large," but that was the most they did for the young woman who had been their most loyal ally. They decided that Alençon should escape first and Navarre should follow a day or so afterward upon pretense of going on a hunting expedition. Alençon did indeed escape, with ludicrous ease, on the evening of September 15, 1576, but the escape triggered off such an explosion of royal rage as to prevent Navarre's attempt and, incidentally, put Marguerite in fear of her life.

Alençon's absence was not noticed until about 9 P.M. when the family gathered for supper as usual. The king and the queen mother expressed surprise but in reply to their questions Marguerite could say only that she had not seen him since dinnertime. Messengers were sent up to his room, to see if he were indisposed; they returned with the information that he was nowhere to be found in his apartments. Henri, becoming alarmed, ordered the search to be widened, first among the women's quarters, then in every part of the palace, and finally Paris itself was combed without success. It was at this point that Henri dissolved into an hysterical rage, screaming out that he wanted his brother back dead or alive, swearing that he had escaped to stir up rebellion, ordering all within earshot to go out and arrest the traitor and bring him in immediately. A few could not escape the direct order and trailed out with a marked lack of enthusiasm. Most of the nobles refused such a dangerous commission outright, being reluctant to "pinch their fingers between two stones," as Marguerite put it neatly; it was an indiscreet man who interfered in a royal quarrel.

Henri's rage undoubtedly had a personal element but, as head of State, he also had excellent reasons for fearing the trouble that his feckless brother could stir up. Outside the scented, overheated, claustrophobic world of the court, the specter of civil war was again rising. The Prince of Condé, Navarre's cousin, was negotiating with a huge force of German mercenaries, the dreaded Reiters. They were Protestants—but were far more interested in obtaining a legal entry into the fat land of France than worrying about minute theological issues. The Politiques, the moderate Catholics, now utterly disgusted with the conditions at the Catholic court, were raising their own army under Damville, the dead Coligny's kinsman. The country was fragmenting and it needed only a semi-legal center of opposition to provide the force that could polarize the factions. François, Duke of Alençon, next in line to the throne of France, provided just such a catalyst. After he had escaped from Paris he went on to Dreux, where Bussy-d'Amboise was awaiting him, and from there he issued the usual pompous proclamation. He was fighting not for himself but for France, for liberty, for the preservation of the laws and statutes of the realm. The king shook his head sardonically when he read the proclamation. "I know just what these things are worth. Plenty of them involved me when I was with the late admiral and the Huguenots. He will start out by thinking that he's in command but bit by bit they will make him their servant"[43]

The day after Alençon's escape Marguerite fell ill—afflicted with a most painful neuralgia that was caused, she said, through weeping the entire night. The sickness was probably fortunate, for it confined her to her room during the first furious outburst of Henri's rage: unable to lay hands on Alençon, his tortured and chaotic mind turned toward Alençon's vulnerable ally, the sister who somehow always seemed to be involved in some action against him, the king. Marguerite learned afterward that "he inflamed himself against me to such an extent that, had he not been restrained by the queen my mother, I believe that his rage would have led him to perpetrate some cruelty to endanger my life."

Catherine, not for the first or the last time, was placed on the rack by her children. No matter that it was Henri she really loved, that Marguerite and Alençon seemed able to arouse in her only irritation, the three together were the family, the sacred physical expression of the Medici and Valois spirit. And now Alençon was busy stirring up trouble which could destroy the whole structure of the monarchy; the king seemed to be going the way of his dead brother, and Marguerite was, after all, the Queen of Navarre, and if harm came to her then the scandal would have endless repercussions. She took the king on one side and in that liquid, vehement Tuscan which came to her lips in moments of emotional crisis urged him to calmness and outlined a plan to him. She, personally, would leave right away and go in pursuit of his rebellious brother and bring him back. Henri agreed, if sullenly, but insisted that one precaution should be taken before the queen mother left on her journey. And so it was that a day or so later when Marguerite was moving feebly around her room, still weak and unsteady from the effect of her illness, her mother appeared in the doorway. The girl should have still been in bed, for she could scarcely stand, but so alarming were the rumors that had come to her, so torturing was the uncertainty that she had to get up and find out what was really happening. The queen mother took in her half-dressed state and then helped her back to the bed, gently enough: "There's no need to be in such a hurry to get dressed—and please, don't be angry at what I have to tell you." She was in an unusually hesitant, unusually placatory mood as she told Marguerite what had been decided. She was to consider herself under arrest, confined to her room until such time as the king ordered her release. Despite her weakness Marguerite protested bitterly: she had broken no law, done nothing wrong; the king was a tyrant and bully. Catherine could only shake her head, distress on the froglike face. Marguerite was not to blame the king. It was the Council who had decided that she represented a real danger in that she would act as a spy for her brother—and probably her husband as well. She would be well treated, with all the privileges and honor of her rank —but she was not to leave the room. "Please God it will not last long. And don't be annoyed, either, if I don't visit you as often as I should. I dare not arouse the king's suspicions. Meanwhile, I'll do my very best to bring about a reconciliation between your brothers." The queen mother then withdrew hastily and, shortly afterward, Marguerite heard in the passage outside the tramp and shuffle of the guards who thereafter maintained their position, day and night, outside the door.[44] So began a period of captivity that would extend throughout the autumn, through the winter and well into the following spring. Confinement to quarters was a fairly common fate among the courtiers of a wholly autocratic monarch; sooner or later some unfortunate would attract the royal ire or transgress some rule of the complex court etiquette and find himself or herself in temporary disgrace. But such confinements usually meant little more than keeping out of the public eye. Henri subjected his sister, however, to what was in effect solitary confinement. She was allowed her servants— it was quite unthinkable that a Valois should pick up clothes, serve food, sweep and dust for herself. But, with one exception, not a single equal passed through Marguerite's door during the months of imprisonment. The exception was a gentleman in her husband's staff, a certain Louis de Crillon who, "braving all prohibitions and loss of favour, came to see me five or six times in my room, astonishing so much thereby the Cerberus that had been posted at my door, that they did not venture either to address him or to deny him entrance." In keeping with her usual discretion in these matters, Marguerite did not see fit to remark that Crillon was an intimate friend of Bussy-d'Amboise—whose life he had actually saved in Poland—and now displayed this signal loyalty to keep his friend informed as to Marguerite's condition.

Among all the hundreds who thronged the palace, men and women from the lowest to the highest levels of society, some of whom Marguerite regarded as close and personal friends—not one other risked the royal displeasure to bring some comfort to the prisoner. She did not bear them any malice, for she, better than others, knew that a courtier was the most sensitive of plants, shrinking back from the slightest change of temperature. But the experience changed her in a subtle but very real manner. Looking back upon it years later she declared that she was "indebted to the sadness and solitude of my first captivity." It was then that she developed her passion for reading, the voracious intellectual hunger which could keep her up throughout the night until she had read the book at a single sitting. She was allowed armsful of books from the Royal Library, one of the greatest in Europe, and by the end of her captivity had laid the foundations for a wide, if highly individualistic, learning. She also became deeply religious—religious not in the ceremonial, liturgical sense which passed for religion among most of her aquaintances but as a result of intellectual effort, her powerful if still untuned mind probing out in "the study of that grand book of universal nature in which so many of the Creator's wonderful works are revealed, following this chain of Homer, this delectable encyclopaedia which has its origins in God Himself." Not the least of Marguerite's misfortunes was that she should have been born a woman in a country where law and tradition alike excluded her from the highest office. A mind that could have been harnessed to real problems of state was condemned to occupy itself with intrigue and frivolity.

News continued to reach her from the outside world via smuggled letters, via the rather distorted word of mouth of her servants. She learned of the particularly vicious little piece of revenge that du Guast—or Henri—had tried to wreak on her through the person of her favorite maid Torigny. A detachment of du Guast's soldiers had arrived at the house in the country where the girl had taken refuge and, in the king's name, demanded that she return with them to Paris. Their intention, in fact, was to drown her in a nearby river, but, just as they were leaving the house with their prisoner, a party of Alençon's soldiers fell upon them and saved the girl. It was the last piece of spite in which du Guast was enabled to indulge, for the next she heard of him was that he was dead—murdered.

She was overjoyed. "I am sorry that I'm not well enough to celebrate it with the joy it deserves," she said; yet, curiously,, she was completely misinformed regarding the way he died, believing it was from natural—if horrific—causes, "his body having been undermined by every sort of abomination and given over to the corruption which erelong overtook it."[45] Most people believed that she had a direct hand in his death and an elaborate story made the rounds as to how she had sought out his assassin and, with her limitless charm, seduced him and ordered him to kill her great enemy. Du Guast, in fact, was murdered as a result of one of the feline intrigues which was strangling the court. His murderer was a swashbuckling bravo, the Baron de Viteaux, who had killed a male lover of du Guast's in a duel and was expelled from Paris by the king on du Guast's urgent request. Viteaux sneaked back to Paris and waited his chance. It was long in coming, for Louis du Guast was a highly skilled survivor and never moved out of the palace, day or night, without a bodyguard of at least a score of men. It was his misfortune, however, to fall in love with a woman who had a rather unusually high regard for her own reputation; she objected strongly to the bodyguard lounging about her house and announcing to all the world with their presence that she was entertaining their master, and du Guast got into the fatal habit of dismissing them when he visited her house at night. Viteaux, with two hired thugs, simply followed him one night, entered the house and found him, improbably enough, reading in bed. He was murdered out of hand, his assassins escaping without trouble.

But the murder of du Guast was, after all, only a domestic scandal of a kind that was becoming more and more common. The king wept bitter tears, swore hideous revenge but could do nothing but bury his favorite with fantastic display. The hunt for du Guast's murderer led back not only to Viteaux but to a far more influential figure, the king's own brother, who had his own reason for hating the favorite. And there was nothing that Henri could do to revenge the murder, for Alençon was suddenly a very important and powerful young man indeed, the rallying point for every discontented Frenchman, be he Calvinist or Catholic. Open war had broken out; the Duke of Guise had halted the vanguard of German mercenaries in a terrible battle—in which, incidentally, he gained a severe wound that afterward entitled him to bear his heroic father's nickname of Scarface. But elsewhere Huguenots and Politiques were alike arising and massing under the banner of the young man who was also entitled to bear the fleur-de-lys. Catherine caught up with Alençon at Chambord and, swallowing the rage and indignation that must have been consuming her, tried to point out to him that his posturing was endangering the entire structure of the state. Deep inside himself, a cold little voice must have told Alençon that his motley followers were using him, that it was purely his position as a breakaway member of the royal family that gave him his brief but heady power. But loftily he brushed aside his mother's complaints and arguments; as the representative of the true spirit of France, he demanded immense concessions of land, and title and revenue, for it seemed that the true spirit of France was best honored by increasing the wealth and power of the Duke of Alençon. Then he demanded his sister's release.

The demand was very much an afterthought and later poor Marguerite tried to embellish the unsightly fact, turning the blusterings of a braggart boy into the considered policy of a statesman: "Had it not been for the love of his country he would have waged so terrible a war that the people would have borne the consequence of their prince's resentment." But being restrained by the force of his natural affection, he merely said that if the family continued to ill-treat Marguerite he would be extremely annoyed. Catherine might be uncertain as to the degree of his attachment to his sister but there was no doubt but that he intended to exploit his sudden eminence for his own benefit. Wearily, the aging woman climbed back into her carriage and took the long tedious road to Paris where her other son, the anointed king, was impatiently awaiting her. And when at last they did meet, she could give him no comfort, no other advice but to comply with his brother's demands.

Marguerite benefited temporarily from the situation. She was still not allowed to leave the palace but, after the weeks of solitude, it was a delight simply to move among people again, to go from room to room, to talk to friends—if with a certain malicious amusement at their embarrassed protestations of goodwill. But then, like the repetition of a nightmare, the whole sequence happened again. On February 3, her husband escaped, "without even saying goodbye to me," she said sadly: within hours she was back in confinement with a guard again outside her door.

It was not altogether Navarre's fault that he left without taking his wife into his confidence. True, he was still besotted with Madame de Sauves, entering the marital bedchamber long after Marguerite was asleep and leaving it before she was fully awake, so that their opportunity for private conversation was almost nonexistent. But his escape was the result of a sudden decision. He had, for nearly three years, put up with a humiliating situation with the best grace he could, but now that young Alençon was usurping his position as leader of all Huguenots, there was an additional bitterness in his imprisonment, an additional and powerful incentive to escape. He and his close friend, Agrippa d'Aubigné, began to make plans. Left to himself Navarre might have had the good sense to bring Marguerite into the planning. But Aubigné loathed his friend's wife: in later years it was to be his brilliant but vicious satires which launched her into history with such a grotesquely evil reputation. But though Marguerite remained in ignorance of their plans, the probability is that Navarre took the bewitching Charlotte de Sauves into his bedtime confidence; certainly somebody betrayed them to the king.

On the evening of February 3, Navarre was returning from the hunt when Agrippa d'Aubigné came galloping through the dusk to break the news with his somewhat flowery brand of speech: "Sire, we are betrayed. The road to Paris leads to dishonour and death, those to life and glory lie in the opposite direction." "You talk too much. The matter is decided," Navarre snapped back, and jerked his horse's head round. The handful of king's men with him looked at the suddenly grim and desperate young man and his equally menacing companion and wisely drew back. They rode all through the night—"very dark and cold it was" Aubigné remembered—and legend later declared that not a single word passed Navarre's lips until they had crossed the Loire.[46] But though this was unlikely, it was probably after the river crossing that he drew rein and looked back toward Paris and said, "God be praised who has delivered me. They killed the Queen my mother in Paris and murdered the Admiral and all my friends and would have done the same to me had not God protected me. I'll never return there unless they drag me back." That single brief speech ended the tradition of the feckless buffoon, but even so, he could not help adding "in his usual joking manner that he regretted only two things he had to leave behind in Paris—the Mass and his wife. He could manage without the first but not without the second, and he wished her in his arms."[47] Considering how he had treated Marguerite over the past few months, this last remark sounds like a vicious little sneer; but he was sincere enough. After he had safely arrived in Navarre, his counselors persuaded him to write to his wife, the woman who was, after all, sister to the King of France and daughter to the formidable queen mother. He did so willingly enough and Marguerite was probably right in putting down his changed attitude toward her to the fact that he was away from the influence of Charlotte de Sauves.

After the king's first hysterical reaction, when he had to be restrained from physically assaulting his sister, Marguerite was left severely alone in her room. The heavy hours again passed with stifling slowness, the days again became chasms of boredom, the library again provided a bridge to sanity. But while she read and sewed a little, and tried her hand at Latin epigrams and yawned much and wept sometimes, in the world outside events were tumbling to a conclusion that would, as by-product, not only free her but give her a voice in high affairs. The main body of the Reiters had erupted across the frontier into Burgundy, plundering and murdering in the comfortable knowledge that they had been summoned by a Prince of the Blood. And at about the time that, leisurely, they joined Alençon's main force west of Paris, to the south Navarre, easily shedding his temporary Catholicism, led a resurgent Huguenot force against the crown. In Paris, the king sat powerless. The money that should have been used for defense had been frittered away on cloth of gold and silk and rare wines and vast gifts to the *mignons,* and the troops, unpaid, moved sullenly or openly went over to the enemy. Their aristocratic leaders, still reluctant to commit themselves in a struggle between two royal brothers, hung back until one of those brothers should emerge as definite victor.

It was the queen mother who solved the problem, although the price she paid was heavy enough. Sullenly the king agreed that she should try and use her influence with the rebellious Alençon, and once again her Master of Horse brought out the great clumsy coach while the Captain of the Guard rounded up a mounted escort from the handful of men who still remained loyal. Once again the heavy, aging woman exchanged the comfort and safety of her palace for days spent in the lurching, heaving vehicle that France now knew so very well. She had wanted to bring Marguerite with her. The girl could drive her wild with frustration and irritation but Catherine nevertheless had a very high opinion of her daughter's intelligence and persuasiveness, particularly where Alençon was concerned. But the king totally refused to allow her release; it was bad enough that his mother should be personally paying court to his hated brother, without climbing down on the matter of Marguerite's punishment.

But Alençon refused to discuss any treaty until she was released. Six months earlier he had contented himself with words, but now that Marguerite's husband, too, was on the loose, building up his own following and challenging the champion of liberty and order, it was obviously worthwhile to ensure the loyalty of their common ally. Resignedly, Catherine turned her coach around and lumbered back to Paris, and in a few sharp words made Henri understand just how perilous was his position. He scarcely needed the lecture, for he was quite intelligent enough to see how matters had deteriorated over the past few weeks. "See what happens in civil wars," he cried when told how a simple captain in Provence had set himself up as an independent leader. "Once on a time even a Constable or a Prince of the Blood could not have formed an independent party but now a mere valet can get away with it." And, with a feeble flash of his old wit, he announced that he was studying grammar "to learn to decline."[48] The Parisians looked on contemptuously as he made the rounds of the city churches with his wife and her lapdogs, lavishly giving alms, veering between a facile optimisim and a black despair. He was putty in his mother's hands and not merely agreed that Marguerite should be freed but actually visited her in person and pleaded with her to act as intermediary. Marguerite accepted the charge with a fine condescension and drove out of Paris, on a May morning in 1576, with her mother. The spring-green landscape seemed enamel bright to eyes whose horizon had been the gray walls of the Louvre for nearly seven months, the spicy air intoxicating after the mingled smell of stale sweat and perfume and wood smoke that somehow characterized the Louvre in winter. All around her were the painted beauties of her mother's Flying Squadron, twittering prettily after watching their mouths so long in her presence. Her star was in the ascendant and the courtiers, male and female alike, squabbled to come within speaking distance of her as her litter advanced through the soft spring air. She enjoyed the conversation, the air of gaiety and festivity, but she enjoyed, perhaps more, the irony for her wit ever had a cutting edge.

Their destination was Beaulieu, the enormous Romanesque abbey not far from the pretty little town of Loches. And toward Beaulieu, over the next few days, advanced other cavalcades, most of them composed of armored men, all of them grim, suspicious, their nerves at hair trigger—Politiques and Huguenots and Guisard Catholics, meeting yet again for a conference in which few really believed, trying yet again to repair the cracks in their disintegrating country with paper promises and parchment oaths. And swaggering, strutting among them—François, Duke of Alençon, at the intoxicating peak of his twisted career. His opponent was no Catholic or Politique or Huguenot but the aging woman who heaved her massive body out of the carriage and, breathing heavily, gained the ground—the mother who had denied him the toys he demanded, and now had no choice but to yield to the most outrageous of demands, for to refuse to do so was to split her own self into two parts and watch them war upon each other. So François, Duke of Alençon, who already could style himself Monsieur, being heir to the throne, now picked up his hated brother's former title of Duke of Anjou and with it, as appanage to support his splendor, the provinces of Anjou and Touraine and Berry as well as an additional revenue from the privy purse of 400,000 golden crowns each year. The booty would not content him for long but, for the moment, he was satiated, leaving his mother free to make what terms she could with his supporters. And those terms were harsh for her; it was a Huguenot dagger that Alençon held at the throat of the monarchy, and the only way to blunt it was to wrap it round with concessions. Eight cities were ceded to the Huguenots, together with total freedom of worship through all France, save only Paris. The crown officially deplored the Massacre of Saint Bartholomew and made reparation to the families of those who had suffered. France itself was apportioned among the leaders of the parties so that Navarre was assigned all the province of Guyenne, the Politiques established in Languedoc. And who was to pay the Reiters, the German horde which had been conjured into France to frighten the king? Who else but the king, and this Catherine pledged to do, even though she knew it would mean pawning the crown jewels, for there was no other way to raise the enormous sum of two million livres that they were owed. And having made this most disastrous of all French treaties, she summoned her two sons and her daughter to a great banquet in Tours to celebrate the abdication of the monarchy of France. The king protested vehemently and was backed up by an unexpected ally—the Duke of Guise—but the queen mother ignored his objections. Later, the Huguenots claimed that it was all a trick, that she had deliberately inflated their demands and yielded to them knowing that Catholic France would react violently. But whether or not she was able to instill such Machiavellian precepts into her son, he agreed to meet his brother in a public reconciliation, dressing carefully for the occasion in an extraordinary costume made of cloth of gold. His brother, the new Duke of Anjou, very nearly outclassed him even in this field by turning up in a suit of blue and silver brocade smothered in pearls and diamonds, power seemingly best expressed by narcissism.

Marguerite had played little direct part in the negotiations.

Her brother had offered to include a demand for her own appanage as part of his package deal and she had been strongly tempted to accept—after four years of marriage she had still not received her portion, was still dependent upon the casual beneficence of the king or her mother. But Catherine argued forcefully that it was better that the king should dower her voluntarily than that he should be, in effect, forced to yield to blackmail, and Marguerite accepted the argument reluctantly. She agreed, even more reluctantly, to return to Paris with her mother. She wanted to stay free of Paris, to turn her back on the humiliation and boredom of the past dark months and continue on to the south, to her husband. By now she realized that there was little chance of their marriage being anything more than a mutual convenience but, at its lowest level, it did offer her a means of breaking free of the shackles imposed by her mother and brother. She was, after all, Queen of Navarre, and although Navarre was small enough and poor enough in the scale of nation states, it was better to be the first lady in Nérac or Pau than of uncertain status in the Louvre. But again her mother persuaded her against her deepest inclination. Catherine appeared almost agitated. At first she attempted to argue that, because Navarre had abjured Catholicism, it was unfitting that Marguerite should join him and so countenance his apostasy. But when the girl remained stubborn, instead of losing her temper and ordering her outright to obey, "with tears in her eyes she declared that, if I did not return with her I should be the ruin of her because the king would imagine that she had induced me to join my husband and that she had promised to bring me back with her." Age was beginning to soften the tough fibers of Catherine de Medicis spirit and, astonished perhaps at the spectacle of her mother actually pleading with her, Marguerite gave in, if with bad grace.

The party returned to a Paris that was boiling with excitement, seething on the very edge of armed rebellion. The news of the humiliating Peace of Beaulieu was now abroad—the Peace of Monsieur, the wits named it accurately enough—and the total yielding to the Huguenots incensed the fanatically Catholic city. Even the moderates were astounded by the degree of the rebel triumph. "Those of the

Religion have got more without any stroke stricken than, before this time, could ever have been had by all the wars," the English ambassador reported to his sovereign. In the churches the clergy contemptuously refused to sing the Te Deum as ordered while, in the streets, the mob pounced upon any sign of official rejoicing, smashing all windows which loyally displayed illuminations, tearing down placards, scattering bonfires. The king became the target of an hysterically mounting rage and contempt: "Henri, by the grace of his mother, imaginary King of France and Poland, despoiler of the churches, Concierge of the Louvre, master of the wardrobe, hairdresser to the court, merchant of justice, habitué of the sewers. . . ." And in their rage and despair and baffled sense of shame, aristocracy and plebeians alike began to look beyond the discredited Valois, beyond the mired throne for a champion. Carefully directed rumors began to circulate about the existence of a document which proved that the Valois were bastards, illegitimate usurpers, that the true and honorable and legal line of descent from the mighty Charlemagne ran through the House of Lorraine, and that therefore the people's hero, the Duke of Guise—the man who, like his father, had gained a terrible wound in the defense of Catholicism—was the true inheritor of the throne. And in Peronne, a city in the very heart of Catholic France which had been given, with incredible stupidity, to the Huguenots, debate and despair suddenly bred action. The Catholic League of the Holy Trinity came into being, a league ostensibly devoted to Henri III but which carried a poisonous sting in its tail, for its whole purpose was to restore the power and universality of the Catholic Church in France, and whosoever hindered such a holy object, whatsoever his rank, was to be swept aside. There was, at the moment, no head of the League, but when he was indeed chosen, all others would swear absolute and undeviating loyalty to him, a loyalty qualified by no other loyalty or duty. And in all France there was only one super-Catholic with a stature great enough to fit that role, a man whose lineage was suddenly proved to be older by far than that of the upstart Valois, the man popularly called Le Balefré, or Scarface—Henri de Lorraine, Duke of Guise.

†

IX

Journey to the Netherlands

Along the uncertain edge of Europe where land and water melted confusingly into each other as though in the primeval stage of separation, the enormous power of Spain encountered the paradox of a yielding barrier. The barrier yielded because it could do nothing else; the cutting edge of the Spanish power was composed of perhaps the most ferocious, the most coldly cruel soldiers which had hit Europe since the Huns, and the dynamic was provided by the wealth of an empire which sprawled across Europe and bestrode the Atlantic. But the barrier held firm because it was composed of the intangible, the stubborn will of a race of stolid, somewhat unimaginative men who had decided to defend a pattern of thought and a way of life regardless of the physical price. They had already paid very heavily. In 1576, at about the time that Alençon adopted the farcical role of Huguenot champion, the Spaniards had fallen upon Antwerp and, in the name of booty pure and simple, had added that city to the bloodstained roll of European massacres. Eight thousand citizens were murdered and the life of one of Europe's richest cities brought to a sudden halt. But though the awful sack was to sear itself upon the Netherlands' consciousness as the Spanish Fury, it was only an extreme form of the alien pressure that was slowly turning a people

into a nation. The Religion had found as fruitful a soil in the Netherlands as it had in France, but under that relentless pressure Catholic
and Huguenot discovered that they were fellow citizens before they
were hostile Christians and looked for help wherever it might be
found or whoever might give it, whether a Protestant Tudor or a
Catholic Valois. So it was that, in the spring of 1577, the French agent
in Flanders, Mondoucet, arrived in Paris with an interesting proposi-
tion. Would the Crown of France consider the possibility of extend-
ing sovereignty over its small neighbor and so protect it from the
terrible Iberian power?

Mondoucet came at a good moment for, despite the heavy
price that Catherine had paid for peace, her children were viciously
squabbling among themselves again. There had been a brief honey-
moon after the Peace of Monsieur: inevitably civil war had broken
out yet again and Alençon proved his worth—if proof were needed
—by turning on the people upon whose backs he had ridden to power
and rending them, personally conducting the onslaught upon the
Huguenot city of Issoire as though it were a holy crusade. The king
had sardonically approved his action, for no Huguenot would ever
again trust the word of the new Duke of Anjou and it would be a
foolish Catholic indeed who put any credence in the honor or promises of such a man. But nevertheless, Alençon's apostasy meant that
his ravening ambition again had no object, and therefore was dangerous to all those within his orbit. And at the same time Marguerite was
proving obstreperous about being united with her husband. For several weeks after her return to Paris, Henri had been able to stall her
with vague replies and indefinite promises until, with the outbreak
of civil war, he refused her outright. "I gave you to a Catholic, not
a Huguenot. It would be impossible to allow you—a Catholic and my
sister—into their hands as a kind of hostage." Not even Catherine
knew whether his refusal arose out of simple malice for his sister or
from the real, if perverted political objective of holding her as a
hostage against Navarre's own actions. Marguerite grew increasingly
impatient, increasingly abrasive and at last burst out that she would
join her husband, with or without royal permission. "If you do that,"
Henri snarled back, "be certain that you will have both myself and

the queen my mother as your bitter enemies."[49]

It was at this crisis, with Alençon restive in his brother's shadow, hungrily seeking he knew not what, and with Marguerite resentful and bewildered and beginning to be a little afraid, that Mondoucet arrived with his plans for a French expedition to Flanders. He received a very short, very cold answer from the king: Henri had no intention of going to the aid of the Flemings, be they Catholic or Huguenot, and embroiling himself with Philip of Spain. Mondoucet looked elsewhere. The unemployed, crudely ambitious Alençon was the obvious instrument, but though he eagerly assented to a plan that might put a crown upon his head, there seemed to be no way to avoid his brother's flat prohibition of any such adventure. But Mondoucet, the perfect courtier, finely tuned in to every nuance of the court, was already aware of Marguerite's dilemma and now discreetly he suggested to Alençon that if his beautiful and talented sister could find a pretext for visiting Flanders, she would not only escape from a court she hated but could prepare a way for Alençon by presenting their brother with a *fait accompli.*

The vision of a gold crown took on reality before Alençon's eyes—Marguerite as his ambassadress, charming, persuading, beguiling the already restive Flemings in his favor. . . . Yet how could she escape from a court where she was under permanent surveillance? And how would the Flemings receive a fugitive as a royal emissary? They would have to do no such thing, Mondoucet assured him. As it happened, a party of ladies was about to set out to take the waters at Spa. Their journey, naturally, would take them through the most important cities of Flanders. "If, sir, the Queen of Navarre could only feign some manner of indisposition for which the waters of Spa would be beneficial," she could join the party with perfect propriety. Alençon leaped at the idea and, hastening to Marguerite, somewhat ungallantly reminded her that she suffered with erysipelas brought on, even at this early period of her life, by the washes and bleaches with which she sought to maintain her complexion. It provided her with the perfect excuse for going to Spa—via Flanders. Marguerite agreed and went in search of her mother.

It was no easy matter to outmaneuver and deceive Catherine

de Médicis, and the girl wisely decided to take her partly into her confidence, disguising the truth with part of the truth. She was in an impossible situation now that civil war had broken out again, she argued forcefully, for she was the wife of the rebel Huguenot whom her Catholic brother had sworn to destroy. Her marriage vows bound her to Navarre; family loyalty and her own religion drew her to her brother. She had to escape the conflict of loyalties which was tearing her apart. And Catherine, regarding this beautiful, troublesome, unhappy child of hers, automatically looking for the true motive behind the torrent of words, could do nothing but agree. Marguerite was indeed in an impossible situation—but nothing could be done about it, for had not the king her brother specifically forbidden her to leave the court? But not, surely, for reasons of health, Marguerite retorted and, drawing up her sleeve, displayed the angry red rash of the erysipelas which, over the years, was to take so much of her beauty. The Spa waters could perhaps cure her, and give her a perfectly reasonable excuse to leave Paris. Catherine pondered: visiting Spa was becoming quite the fashionable thing in court circles, and the party which would be going into Belgium was of irreproachable respectability, for it was led by the elderly Princess de La Roche-sur-Yon. The proprieties would be observed and she, the queen mother, would be relived for a few weeks at least of the endless, bitter squabbling between her son and daughter. She agreed and undertook to obtain the king's permission for the journey.

In this manner began what was perhaps the happiest period in the life of Marguerite de Valois. The entire journey to Spa and back again took scarcely four months and the return journey was to be of very great physical danger to her. Nevertheless, the record of her brief Flanders expedition was to occupy nearly a quarter of her memoirs, written in her sprightliest, most vivid style, as though the writer were looking back down the long, dark tunnel of memory upon that springtime cavalcade as upon a Paradise lost. For a brief period she was free of the importunities of husband and brothers and mother. For a brief period she was able to direct her powerful mind and magnetic personality toward something other than a palace in-

trigue or a boudoir affair. And for the first—and indeed only—time
in her life, she traveled outside France, so that everything she saw
came as a delightful or grotesque surprise.

It was on May 28 that the party left Chenonceaux for Flanders. It was a large, predominantly feminine party, although among
the masculine escort were the Cardinal of Lenoncourt and the Bishop
of Langres, also intent upon mixing politics with mineral waters.
There were ten young ladies on horseback, another twenty or so in
six chariots and three litters, including Marguerite's own. She was
extremely proud of this extraordinary vehicle, which attracted much
attention. It was "fashioned with pillars, lined inside with rose coloured Spanish velvet embroidered in gold and having shot-silk
hangings ornamented with sundry devices. The sides were of glass,
each pane of which was covered with designs so that there were as
many as forty different ones altogether, which had mottoes in Spanish and Italian concerning the influences of the sun." Traveling
slowly through the beautiful early summer, feted at every town
where they stopped—for the king, to save his face perhaps, had
specifically ordered that she be accorded all the honors of her rank
—the party reached Cambrai in mid-July. The city was virtually a
sovereign state, ruled by its pro-Spanish bishop under Spanish protection, and its enormous new citadel spelled out the fact that it was
a major key to Flanders. It was Marguerite's first foreign town and
she was delighted with it. "I found it much pleasanter than our own
French towns because, although it was not built of such good
material as they are, the streets and squares are so much better
planned and proportioned." The bishop—the "Spanishified Flem-
ing," as she called him contemptuously—met her at the frontier of
his miniature state, entertained her at supper and then took himself
off to bed without joining in the dancing, one of the very few people
in Flanders who remained impervious to her. She expected little else
from this coldly formal man and, at that same banquet, she made a
conquest which more than compensated for the bishop's indifference. During the ball a good-looking young man "who possessed no
share of that ingrained rusticity which seems to be natural to the

Flemings" acted as host in the place of the bishop. He was the Sieur d'Inchy, governor of the citadel, who fell so hopelessly and totally for the beautiful French princess as to act as her escort about the town, "imprudently, as I thought, considering that he had charge of the citadel." Cautiously she sounded him as to his possible reaction to the coming of Alençon; cautiously he made it known that his loyalties were by no means wholly wrapped up in the Bishop of Cambrai and his Spanish friends. Modestly she recorded how the lovesick young man "took so much pleasure in my conversation" that he could not bear to be parted from her and received permission from the bishop to accompany her on her journey through Flanders, during which time she was able to win him over wholly to her brother's cause.

From Cambrai the party moved on to Valenciennes, where the French members where astonished and delighted by the clocks and fountains, "they being unused to behold clocks which discoursed delightful vocal music." The following day they were at Mons, and it was here that Marguerite met the Lalains and began a friendship that not only meant much to one of her warm and affectionate nature but was to have great political significance to her. The Count of Lalain claimed to be a distant relative of her husband and was predisposed to welcome her even before he had met her and come under her personal spell. A Catholic, he had refused to throw in his lot with his Huguenot neighbors—but just as stubbornly he had refused to have anything to do with the alien Spaniards. The martyred Egmont, beheaded by order of Philip of Spain in Brussels some eight years earlier, had been a kinsman of his, and family loyalty no less than patriotism fed his hatred, so that no Spaniard dared to cross the frontiers of his territory. The Spanish governor in Flanders had power enough to compel the recalcitrant Lalain—but to do so was to alienate all Catholic Flanders. Lalain was therefore in the neutral area between two opposing forces, yet he knew well enough that only a slight shift in the balance of those forces was necessary to overwhelm him. Marguerite as a beautiful and charming woman would have been welcomed, but Marguerite as the unofficial emissary from his

great Catholic neighbor must have appeared to Lalain like an angel
of deliverance. Nothing was said at first, for among the webs of plots
and counterplots which smothered the Netherlands, an indiscreet
word could have disastrous results, and neither was as yet wholly
certain of the other. But over the next eight days, political interests
were strengthened by personal affection.

Over the years, Marguerite de Valois was to gain a remarkably
unsavory reputation. Much of it was salacious rumor of the kind
inevitably produced about any beautiful woman who insisted on
behaving unconventionally. Much of it was propaganda—peculiarly
vicious propaganda, designed to discredit her for purely political
reasons. But much of it, too, was entirely justified; she enjoyed sex
and did not much care who knew it. Her generous sensuality il-
luminated her beauty, drawing men of all conditions and degree
toward her, and she yielded to their pleas and cries on some purely
personal code of morality. But, unlike the majority of such sex god-
desses, she also attracted and enjoyed the warm friendship of members of her own sex, and on the day that she entered the home of the
Count of Lalain, she made one such friend, the count's beautiful
young wife Margaret.

The countess was about Marguerite's own age, a charming,
lighthearted girl with an engaging sense of responsibility and a streak
of unconventionality which immediately endeared her to her guest.
Indeed, at the great state banquet on that very first night, she provided an exquisite little tableau which Marguerite recorded with
something between amusement and wistfulness. Unlike the majority
of women of her class, the countess was breast-feeding her baby, and
during the banquet, while she was engaged in a lively conversation
with her guest, a nurse brought the child to her and laid it on the table
between them. She was dressed elaborately in cloth of gold and
silver, heavily worked with jewels and embroiders, "a dress appropriate to the office of wet nurse," Marguerite remarked with gentle
irony, but quite casually unbuttoned herself and gave the heavily
swaddled infant her breast. "This, in another, might have been ac-
counted bad manners but she did it, as she did everything, with such

grace and ingenuousness as to give only pleasure to the assembled guests."

It was later on that same evening, after the tables had been cleared and the dancing begun, that Marguerite found herself momentarily alone with her hostess and took the opportunity to hint at the reason for her presence. The girl eagerly responded, speaking openly and confidently of the political situation. "This country was formerly French—which is the reason why lawyers still plead here in that language—and most of us still have a great affection to France. There was a time when this country was devoted to the House of Austria but this affection was rooted out of us. at the deaths of Egmont and Horne and Montigny and of the other noblemen who were defeated and nothing can be more odious to us now than the rule of these Spaniards. If only it would please God to will that your brother the King of France should desire to reconquer this country that is his by ancient right, we should all receive him with open arms."[50]

This was almost exactly what Marguerite wanted to hear—almost, but not quite. Carefully she pointed out that the King of France himself could not undertake an expedition but that an ideal champion was even now awaiting the call. And with all the vivacity at her command, while the dancers whirled and bowed and curtseyed to the plangent Flemish music, she painted the Duke of Alençon's portrait in colors which would have much astonished those who knew the feckless, faithless, rootless young man—"bred to the profession of arms . . . of an amiable disposition . . . never ungrateful, ever anxious to acknowledge a service, loves and honours the gallant and the brave." The girl, listening wide-eyed to this fervent eulogy, had no difficulty in believing that such an accomplished and magnetic a person as her guest should have a paladin for a brother—and neither did she have any difficulty in obtaining from that eloquent guest permission to report the conversation to her husband. And now that the ice was broken, Lalain hastened to open negotiations with this most influential ally. He and his wife waited upon Marguerite the following morning when, unequivocally, he endorsed everything that the countess had said the previous evening, promised the fullest possible support to Alençon and told Marguerite what she knew already—that the key to Flanders lay in the hands of the lovelorn governor of the citadel of Cambrai. The next week passed for her in a heady admixture of political intrigue and social gaiety. Originally, she had intended merely to remain overnight, but so warm and pressing were her host and hostess that each evening saw her intention of departing weaken, "and indeed it was only by sheer force that I was enabled to leave at the end of eight days" with the promise of passing a much longer visit on the return journey.

The next point of call was Namur, where the Spanish Governor of Flanders was expecting her. It promised to be a potentially embarassing visit, but not one which she could very well avoid without raising deep suspicions. Lalain with all his nobleman rode with his guest far beyond the actual boundaries of his own territories, even entering the hated Spanish domain and not drawing rein until there appeared, in the distance, the governor's cavalcade. Then, reluctantly, Lalain turned back, leaving his charge in the delighted hands of the Sieur d'Inchy, who, as officer of the pro-Spanish Bishop of Cambrai, had no inhibition in meeting the Spanish governor. The two parties approached each other down the long, dusty road until at last Don John of Austria, Governor of Flanders, looked for the second time upon Marguerite de Valois, and she, for the first time, consciously looked at the legendary hero of Lepanto.

Don John was then just thirty-two years of age. His father was Charles V, Emperor of Germany, King of Spain, Dominator of Asia, Africa and Europe; his mother was Barbara Blomberg, the redoubtable washerwoman of Ratisbon, the termagant who terrified the Duke of Alva, a man not obviously lacking in physical or moral courage. It was Don John who ended the scandal of her tumultuous, fantastically extravagant career in the Netherlands, persuading—or threatening—her so that at last she left for Spain, taking her revenge by yelling to the world that it was not the emperor who had been his father. And certainly it seemed impossible that he and the ice-cold, pedantic bureaucrat, Philip of Spain, could have been sired by the same man. Yet Philip had gone out of his way to acknowledge the relationship, and after his bastard half-brother had brought off that stupendous triumph at Lepanto, he had sent him to Flanders as his personal representative. Don John had crossed Europe disguised as a Moorish slave, so dangerous was the situation in the Low Countries, but arriving at Paris he had not been able to resist the temptation of seeing the fabled princess dancing. He dismounted—an unusually handsome man, rather slightly built with fair hair and beard, richly but soberly dressed—and walked across to her sumptuous litter. She looked out at him impassively, shrewdly noting that "none of his followers were of any particular name or mark—mostly small gentry, of mean appearance, none of the Flemish nobility being amongst them." But he was the governor-general, a handsome man of high chivalry, and she opened a window of her litter and saluted him "in the French manner"—offering him her cheek to kiss. He then remounted and rode by her side to Namur, conversing amiably as they went.

Despite the fact that it was nearly midnight when they entered Namur, the city was a blaze of light from countless torches in the streets, shops and even private houses, a graceful compliment that Don John had ordered for his visitor and one which was efficiently carried out—"the Spaniards being excellent managers in this respect," as Marguerite admitted. She was further surprised to find, in the handsome apartments that had been set aside for her use, "the most beautiful, costly, and superb hangings that I think I have ever seen," a prodigal display of priceless tapestries of velvet and satin worked with gold, fit more for a king than a young bachelor prince, as one of her party observed. A member of Don John's staff explained: they were the gift of Ali Pasha, commander in chief of the Turkish fleet at Lepanto. Don John had captured his children and had later not only returned them without a ransom but loaded with rich gifts, and the Turk, not to be outdone in magnificence by a Roumi, had sent this incredible collection to his victor. The suite that now housed Marguerite was the prince's own, and throughout her stay in Namur she was surrounded by this very tangible evidence of the potentialities of the courteous young man who was her host.

It was highly unlikely that Don John had been wholly taken in by the story that the sister of the King of France was journeying through Flanders simply to take the waters at Spa. True, King Henri had gone to considerable trouble to obtain passports from the governor-general, but it was common knowledge that he and his sister were now permanently at each other's throats. She had, moreover, spent far longer with the Lalains at Mons than was strictly necessary. But Don John kept up the fiction that Marguerite's presence was for purely social reasons. It was neither particularly difficult nor unpleasant for him to act as escort and squire to the Valois princess, even though he was on his guard. She had, in addition, a particular attraction for him, "for he told me frequently that he observed a strong resemblance between me and the queen his 'Signora'—by which he meant my sister the late Queen of Spain—whom he had greatly honoured." The two days which her party spent in Namur, waiting for the boats that would take them up the Meuse, were passed in the manner in which she delighted, with music and wine and dancing and elegant flirtations at boat parties, at alfresco banquets, at formal balls, with the son of the great emperor constantly at her side. She was just twenty-four, at the height of her astonishing beauty, vivacious, utterly confident of her ability to control her life, surrounded by brilliant men who, even if they were opposed to her, nevertheless fell victim to a matchless charm, planning, manipulating in the midst of laughter and song and the richest luxuries of a civilization at its peak. July 1577 was probably the high water mark of her life: all that came after was a long defeat.

And it was as though fate had decided that she should receive some warning, for, within minutes of embarking at the quay, tragedy struck the party that had known only gaiety since leaving Chenonceaux two months earlier. Mademoiselle de Tournon, a sprightly and popular girl who was Marguerite's favorite lady-in-waiting, was seized by a singularly agonizing heart attack. For some undisclosed reason, Marguerite refused to turn back to Namur—she seems to have thought that Mademoiselle de Tournon was simply suffering

from unrequited love—and the party had the nerve-wracking experience of proceeding up the Meuse to the accompaniment of the
wretched young girl's terrible screams. But even this was not all that
that day had in store for them. Shortly before they arrived at Huy,
their next point of call, a sudden freak flood rushed down upon them.
The party barely had time to disembark before the quay disappeared
under the deluge and, just as they were, without baggage or change
of clothes, ladies, gentlemen and servants alike fled for the high
ground on which the town was built. Marguerite spent that night in
the upper story of a sturdy house, watching as the black water rose
to the upper windows. Overnight, the flood fell as unpredictably as
it had risen, the more impressionable members of her party whispering about divine warnings and casting anxious glances at their outwardly unperturbed mistress.

And so at last to Liège, nearly three months after setting out.
The city was, like Cambrai, a sovereign state under its prince-bishop,
but, unlike the Bishop of Cambrai, Gerard Grosbek, Bishop of Liège,
was not only anti-Spanish and pro-French but was captivated by his
guest and took little trouble to disguise his feelings. And she, ever a
Valois, wholeheartedly approved of him and his aristocratic chapter,
"all the sons of dukes, counts, and great German nobles," the splendid city itself, "larger than Lyons and very well built with every one
of the canon's houses resembling a noble palace," and the noble
company which flocked into Liège as soon as they heard of her
arrival. The bishop established her in "the finest of his palaces, pos-
sessing beautiful fountains, gardens and galleries, all richly painted,
gilt and ornamented inside with marble," and to this court of love
there came daily lovesick noble swains from miles around to walk
with her in the gardens while she took the waters. Spa itself was a
primitive little village some seven or eight miles distant, without
accommodation for anyone of her standing, and the doctors gravely
agreed that the virtue of the water would not be impaired if it was
transported overnight, before sunrise. "I was extremely glad to hear
this as it ensured our remaining in more commodius quarters and in
such agreeable company." And so passed six carefree weeks, the

normal period for taking the waters. She noted with delight how the waters were indeed beneficial, curing the painful and disfiguring outbreak on her arm. There were endless balls and more water parties and artless alfresco meals that had taken as long to prepare as any banquet and visits to fashionable churches. And conferences. Not all the beautifully dressed ladies and gentlemen who waited upon the Princess of France were wholly occupied with dalliance or the display of wardrobes. In the privacy of her rooms, or while strolling in the gardens sipping the distinctly unpleasant mineral waters—"it is necessary that these should be taken while walking about"—she received news of the outside world and what allies her brother might rely upon and, as important, who were likely to prove his enemies. Mademoiselle de Tournon died and Marguerite cried a little, but life went on with its trumpet notes of excitement and its gay, vivid sparkle.

And suddenly the sparkle was gone, for just about the time that she and her chaperone, the Princess de La Roche-sur-Yon, were reluctantly thinking of the return journey, she received two visitors in quick succession. The first was a woman, a Madame d'Aurec whom she had met in Namur and who now brought most alarming news: Don John, the chivalrous Christian knight, had seized the citadel of Namur and had kept Madame d'Aurec as hostage for her husband's behavior. The whole country between Liège and Namur had burst into flames, with Catholic fighting Protestant or combining to fight Spaniard, and the Spaniards, led by Don John, apparently bent on final conquest. There could be no return through that road. Barely had she assimilated this alarming piece of news when the second messenger arrived—a certain Monsieur Lescar, one of her brother's men. He brought with him the first certain news she had received from France. Her brother, after his brief moment of glory, was again in royal disfavor, for it seemed that the king was now utterly in the hands of his *mignons*, each of whom hated the noble Alençon. But far worse was the fact that Henri had learned of the true reason for her journey to Flanders and was so beside himself with rage that he had betrayed her both to the Spaniards and the Huguenots. One or the other of them would almost certainly seize her before she could get to the safety of her own town of La Fère some four or five days' journey away.

But still she had her entourage, the gay, gallant company who had danced and laughed and banqueted with her across half France and deep into Flanders into this trap. She gathered them around her and found, as in some waking nightmare, that there were monsters behind the gay masks, that those who were not now openly Spanish in sympathy were equally openly Huguenot—even such as the Cardinal of Lenoncourt. Once, perhaps, she might have thrown herself upon the mercies of the Huguenots, but ever since her brother had betrayed them, washing out his alliance with the blood of Issoire, they hated her as deeply as they hated him. She turned to Madame la Princesse de La Roche-sur-Yon, but all that that elderly aristocrat could do was to burst into tears, urge Marguerite to commend herself to God and say that, if necessary, she would consent to traveling by long stages in order to get out of Flanders as quickly as possible. The Bishop of Liège was considerably more helpful, offering to lend her horses and provisions. She accepted the offer gratefully and dispatched Mondoucet, the agent who had started all this, to the Prince of Orange for the necessary passports.

Mondoucet never returned; what Marguerite did not realize was that he was Huguenot in sympathies and now wisely decided that, in these times of trouble, his place was far away from the beleaguered Catholic princess. For three days she waited in growing desperation before deciding to risk the journey without passports. The Cardinal of Lenoncourt and her first equerry, the Chevalier Salviati, urged her to wait for the passports, but by now Marguerite had a shrewd idea that both were prepared to betray her to the Huguenots. They would leave on the following morning, she decreed, but immediately there was another obstacle. Salviati put pressure on her treasurer, who announced that there was not sufficient money to pay the very large sums which they owed in Liège. On their eventual safe arrival at La Fère, Marguerite took the trouble to check the books and found that there was more than enough for at least another six weeks, but in the panic-stricken atmosphere in Liège, it did not occur to her to doubt her official's word. It seemed that she was trapped in Liège.

It was the Princess de La Roche-sur-Yon who saved her, by lending her the necessary money. Marguerite was touched and grateful for the tardy generosity, but it was at least as likely that the princess possessed a lively regard for her own skin. She perhaps could not really believe that a Daughter of France could be literally penniless and it was only when circumstances made it evident that that Daughter really was bankrupt, and that they ran the danger of leaving their bones in Flanders as a result, that she came forward with her loan. Even in her extreme need and danger, Marguerite could not resist the grand gesture, presenting the bishop with a great diamond worth three thousand crowns and scattering gold rings and gold chains among his servants. It was beneath the dignity of a Valois to pay for services with sordid specie.

And so at last they left Liège, a party split into mutually suspicious fragments and held together only by the fact that it was passing through a confused countryside which was likely to be hostile to any foreigner, whatever his or her supposed political or religious loyalties. The bishop had lent Marguerite his grand master to act as her escort through his territories, but swiftly it became obvious that the episcopal authority stopped at the boundaries of Liège. Huy was like a disturbed ant's nest. The citizens resented the fact that the bishop was cagily sitting on the fence, and paid not the slightest attention to the remonstrances of his grand master. Shortly after their arrival there was a tremendous uproar; the citizens—"rough and unreasoning persons of mean condition"—feared a Spanish onslaught and rushed around the town dragging up cannon, ringing the alarms bells, barricading the streets in such a manner that the members of the party were unable to communicate with each other. No one was actually molested when they rode out on the following morning, but it was an ominous curtain-raiser for a far more alarming experience.

The party retraced its steps only as far as Huy, supposedly

under the control of the friendly Bishop of Liège, but beyond they would have to travel in a wide circle to avoid Don John's headquarters at Namur. Consequently, it was late at night when the main body arrived at Dinant, the next point of call, after a hard day's traveling —only to find that the advance party of cooks and stewards who should already have chosen the lodgings for the night and had a meal prepared were standing helplessly in the road outside. Beyond them was a hastily erected barricade guarded by a mob which broke into threatening yells as soon as the cavalcade approached. The official in charge of the advance party approached Marguerite's litter. Everyone was drunk, he explained. The inhabitants of Dinant had that day elected their burgomasters and, in accordance with Flemish custom, had combined the elections with a prolonged drinking bout. There was probably not a sober adult male in the town, and it was impossible to get any sense out of them. In their fuddled, bellicose state they had mistaken Marguerite's impressive entourage for an invading force and had sounded the call to arms.

She reacted promptly and with remarkable courage. A retreat would not only condemn them to a night in the open but would very likely precipitate an attack upon the rear. She therefore ordered her litter to be carried up to the very edge of the barricade and, standing up in the litter, removed her traveling mask and imperiously beckoned to one of the better dressed men in the mob. He came forward —probably a little dazed—and leaning out of the litter toward him, she begged him, with that wholly unopposable charm, to calm his fellow citizens so that she could speak to them. Obediently, he bellowed for silence and gradually the yelling died away until at last she could make herself heard. She threw herself on their mercy—the helpless girl, traveling in strange lands far from home as night was falling; would they not grant asylum to at least her and her women and one or two of the gentlemen? The rest of the party could stay in the suburbs for the night. After some confused arguing it was agreed, the barricades were dragged aside and the women, with a few of the older men, allowed in.

Dinant was built into the side of a steep hill; most of its streets were therefore short and narrow so that, on an occasion such as this, they were solidly crowded. It was particularly unfortunate that, just as soon as Marguerite and her companions had passed the barricade, the crowd recognized the Bishop of Liège's grand master as a man who had waged war upon them some years before. "Thereupon they commenced hurling insults at him, and desired to set upon him— nothwithstanding that he was a venerable old man of eighty with a white beard reaching down to his girdle," Marguerite remarked indignantly. She kept the old man close to her as they forced their way through the drunken, excited crowd and, reaching her lodgings, insisted that he should come in with her. The news spread that the hated grand master was in the town and the crowd outside the house grew larger, noisier and ever more hostile. Soon some of the more drunken began to fire arquebuses at the house, and Marguerite sent for the landlord. Would he go to the window and try to get some of the more responsible citizens to come into the house? It speaks much for her powers of persuasion that the man opened the heavy shutters and, despite the shower of missiles, shouted out the names of the new burgomasters. Eventually they fought their way through the crowd, reeled up the stairs and presented themselves before the indignant princess, "so drunk that they did not know what they were saying." By now Marguerite was far more angry than frightened. Bitterly she told them that she had had no idea that they would object to the presence of the grand master: haughtily, she reminded them of her high status and how unwise it was to offend a person like herself, a person royal born who was also the friend of all the principal figures in their land, such as the Count of Lalain.

Throughout the diatribe the burgomasters listened half owlishly, half insolently, but at the mention of the name of Lalain an astonishing change came over them. Was she really a friend of Monsieur le Comte de Lalain? they demanded eagerly. "Yes, and not only his friend but his kinswoman," Marguerite replied. It was a fortunate accident that led her to use the name of Lalain, the local leader of the anti-Spanish Catholics and therefore the hero of the Dinanters. The burgomasters were now as courteous as they had been insolent, apologizing for their conduct, granting free passage to the grand master and passing the news on to the crowd outside. The yelling and cursing changed to cheering and then eventually to a blissful silence as the mob dispersed to the taverns again and then to bed.

Upon the following morning, just as Marguerite was about to leave for mass, a dumpy little man with an ingratiating expression was brought in to her. He was a Frenchman, Dubois by name, and she recognized him as the agent or ambassador to the court of Don John. The fact that the man was not only openly pro-Spanish but was also an agent of her hated brother was enough to put her on her guard, and she became even more suspicious of his proposal. He had been charged by the king her brother to see her safely out of Flanders, he said smoothly. Don John, at his personal request, had gallantly placed a troop at the disposal of the distressed princess and offered her the protection and hospitality of Namur. Where was the troop now? Marguerite demanded. Outside the city, Dubois replied, awaiting only permission to enter and escort her safely to Namur. And who was the commander? A Monsieur de Barlemont, a powerful pro-Spanish Catholic.

Giving no hint of her suspicions, Marguerite dismissed the little man and sought the advice of the Cardinal of Lenoncourt, and together they came to the conclusion that there were two hooks concealed in the bait—the capture of Marguerite and of Dinant simultaneously. Cooler consideration might have shown Marguerite that, no matter how much her brother hated her, it was highly unlikely that he would connive at any plot which would place her, a Daughter of France, in the hands of the Spanish Governor-General of Flanders or that such a man as Don John would offer her harm if indeed she fell into his hands. But the circumstances hardly allowed of cool consideration and she was, in any case, almost certainly justified in her suspicion that the "escort" was rather more interested in occupying Dinant than in escorting her. And if that happened she would be damned throughout Flanders as pro-Spanish. Lenoncourt, the pro-Huguenot, had his own compelling reasons for not wishing to fall into Spanish hands and it was therefore agreed that he should talk to Dubois and so keep him out of the way while Marguerite took the burgomasters of Dinant into her confidence.

Despite their debauchery of the night before, the city fathers were clear-headed enough to appreciate the threat to Dinant; but they were still so demoralized as virtually to leave the defense of the town in her very capable hands. Briskly, she ordered them to bring out the militia, bring up the artillery and then admit Barlemont, alone, into the town, his troops being ordered to withdraw under threat of the cannons. This was done, Barlemont joined Dubois, and they both tried to persuade her to accompany them back to Namur. Graciously she assented to the proposal and after a hasty dinner she and all her party, together with Dubois and Barlemont, began to walk casually down toward the river gate of the city. Accompanying them were perhaps three hundred citizens, all armed but giving the impression of merely escorting the princess out of courtesy on her departure.

About halfway to the river gate Barlemont noticed that they were walking away from the Namur road, where his troops were waiting, and interrupted Marguerite's vivacious chatter to draw her attention to the fact. She smiled brilliantly, answered vaguely and slightly quickened her pace, while the Dinanters began to crowd around the two men, still in a perfectly courteous if clumsy manner, eventually cutting them off from the French party. Hastily now the French made for the quayside, where a boat was waiting, and embarked, reaching the other side of the river in safety while Dubois and Barlemont called out their reproaches from the bank. The litters and horses still had to be ferried over, and this was done while the citizens still hemmed in the two infuriated men. But now there was the width of the Meuse between Marguerite and her potential captors, and long before they could organize their own river crossing, she and all her party were far on their way.

During her conference with the burgomasters she had learned which of the castles and towns that lay on her route were occupied by friends and had decided to spend that night in the castle of Fleurines, whose lord she had met while staying with the Lalains.

Unfortunately Barlemont was also aware that Fleurines promised the most obvious asylum, and after leaving Dinant picked up her track as night was falling. The princess's party found the outer gates of Fleurines wide open and thankfully entered just as their pursuers came into sight on high ground about half a mile distant. To their consternation, however, they had no sooner entered the outer court-yard when the great drawbridge of the castle was immediately raised, leaving them with nothing but the ramshackle outer gate between themselves and Barlemont's troop. What had happened was that the Lord of Fleurines was absent and his wife, disliking equally the appearance of Marguerite's cavalcade and the armed troop that was pursuing it, firmly locked both out and kept the drawbridge up despite the desperate entreaties of the French. But the growing dark-ness came to their aid. Barlemont had seen them enter the outer courtyard but was now unable to see them milling round unhappily before the drawbridge, and so assumed, reasonably enough, that they were safe within the keep. Accordingly he bivouacked for the night, waiting until the French resumed their journey in the morning.

Marguerite settled down to a cold, uncomfortable and appre-hensive night in her litter, but help was even then on its way. News had come to Lalain of her hazardous journey and he had promptly dispatched the Lord of Fleurines with a powerful escort for her. Fleurines, clattering into the courtyard of his own castle late that night, was astonished and humiliated to find that the lady whom he had been charged to succour had been denied the most elementary right of hospitality by his own wife. Angrily he ordered the draw-bridge to be lowered and ushered his involuntary guest across it with the most elaborate of apologies; angrily he upbraided his wretched wife, awestruck now by the identity of the traveler who had been kept locked out. The incident, however, worked to Marguerite's ad-vantage, for Fleurines, anxious to absolve himself, insisted upon accompanying her to the Flemish border.

There was one more danger that suddenly threatened at this, the very end of the journey, a danger that came from the open treachery of one of her own staff. They were passing through the state of Cambrai when she received warning that a detachment of Huguenot troops was marching to intercept her at the Cambrai-French border. She kept the information to herself and the tiny handful of people whom she felt she could trust and decided to leave before daybreak the following morning. It was at that bleak hour that her chief counselor and first equerry, Salviati, the man who bore the singularly inappropriate title of Chevalier, came out into the open and did all within his power, short of physical violence, to postpone the departure so that she would arrive at the frontier at the same time as the Huguenots. And it was at this point that her nerve broke. Looking back on the incident years later she made it appear as though her subsequent action was the result of a deliberate plan, but there was little doubt but that the days of anxiety, the mounting terror of betrayal and capture, came to a climax in that gray dawn of a September day. She could trust no one, there was no champion now to appear, so, precipitately, she abandoned everything—the mountains of luggage, her clothes, perfumes, cosmetics, books, even that sumptuous litter of which she was so very proud—and took to horseback, "followed by those of my people who were ready first," and galloped through the dark morning until she reached safety in Castelet in France. From there she proceeded, decorously now, to her own château at La Fère and awaited the coming of her brother.

The Flanders expedition had ended in fear and ignominy, yet she had reason to be proud of what she had accomplished during this, the very first of her diplomatic attempts, the first and only time that she traveled outside the protection of the French crown. In Flanders now were solid alliances for her brother which would bear fruit in a very little time, but more important, perhaps, was the self-discovery that she had made—the knowledge that she could react boldly and effectively to sudden danger, that she could manipulate events as well as be manipulated by them. Sadly, she had discovered more depths and vistas of treachery, yet her character now was such as to allow her to chart that discovery as simply another aspect of the human psyche, smiling perhaps a little ironically, a little scornfully, but refusing to let it upset the basic equilibrium which she was gaining, if at very great expense. "Sadness, unlike joy which does not allow us to reflect upon our actions, awakens the soul within us which straightway summons all its energies to cast off evil and cling to good," she noted tranquilly years later.

†

X

The Frog

Alençon joined his sister at La Fère during the first week of October, full
of his woes, eager for sympathy. "Oh my queen, how pleasant it is
to be with you! Good heavens, this place is a paradise whilst that
from which I came is a hell filled with all kinds of dissensions and
torments."[51] The hell from which he came was the luxurious court
of the Louvre, the dissensions and torments very largely of his own
creating. But Marguerite gave him the comfort and flattery his mean
little soul demanded and told him of the great things she had accomplished for him in Flanders. Solid proof came shortly afterward with
the arrival of Lalain's brother, bearing the assurance that all of Artois
and Hainaut would declare for Alençon if and when his Flemish
expedition took place. A messenger from the Sieur d'Inchy also arrived at what was rapidly becoming a council of war, offering d'Inchy's services to the brother of the princess together with the promise
that the vital citadel, key to all Flanders, would assuredly be placed
in his hands. Marguerite had created a path for Alençon: all that he
had to do was follow it and clutch the prize at the end.

The exact relationship of Marguerite with her unsavory
younger brother was a matter of considerable interest to her contemporaries. Her enemies, who provided most of the documentation for

her life and so established her legend, assumed as a matter of course that the relationship was incestuous. But as they assumed, also as a matter of course, that she had committed incest with all her brothers, the dead Charles IX as well as the living Henri III, apparently following her mother's custom, the charge against her bears about as much truth as the portrait she herself paints of the Duke of Alençon. For this was the very key, the very heart of the problem to puzzle contemporary and posterity alike—how could so very shrewd and intelligent a judge of character make such a grotesque error about her brother? Almost the entire weight of contemporary opinion—informed as well as purely hostile, scholarly and legal as well as popular —was solidly against that brother. In part, opinion might have been governed by his repulsive physical appearance—which all court painters discreetly ignored but which the chroniclers dwelt upon at some length in the privacy of their pages. The smallpox which had attacked him as a child had left his face horribly disfigured; in particular, his nose was so swollen and pitted as to give the appearance of being bifurcated, a fact of which his enemies in Flanders later made telling use:

> *Flemings, be not astonished*
> *If on François you see two noses*
> *Because by all use and reason*
> *A double nose best suits a double face.* [52]

This, added to a stunted figure, spindly legs, a hoarse voice and a tendency to burst into tears when frustrated made him a gnomelike figure fit for mocking. But physical disfigurements were commonplace among his contemporaries, for whom smallpox, syphilis and battle wounds were virtually occupational hazards. It was the stunted soul within the stunted body that drew the contempt even of those who sought his political help. "Ferocious without courage, ambitious without talent, bigoted without opinion"—so the terrible charges rang down the centuries. Navarre, an excellent and temperate judge of character, made perhaps the best summing up of the man he came to know so well during their three years' semicaptivity. Navarre's devoted young follower, the Sieur de Rosny, had asked his permission to serve Alençon in Flanders, and he gave it, if rather reluctantly: "I'll be surprised if he does what is expected of him. He has so little courage, a heart so malignant and deceitful, a body so illmade, such want of dexterity in every kind of exercise that I really can't believe that he will ever do anything very great."[54] Rosny rapidly found out the truth of that assessment for himself, for Alençon tricked him out of his reward for his services. He had been promised the estates of an uncle who had disinherited him for his Huguenotery, but when he came to claim them, Alençon coldly answered that they had been given to somebody else—somebody more useful than the young Rosny. "There was something in his answer more disobliging than the refusal itself," Rosny remembered years afterward—yet another implacable enemy whom Alençon had created by his belief in short-term gains and the profound conviction that he, the Son of France, was above all human judgments.

Against this weight of dislike and contempt and disapproval —a weight to which his own mother added her contribution—can be set only the enigmatic record of his sister and the even more enigmatic behavior of the Virgin of England. Elizabeth did indeed seem, at the very least, to be amused by his antics and might even have been stirred to greater depths by his extravagant protestations. There was that poignant little entry in her wardrobe accounts. "Item, one little flower of gold, with a frog thereon and therein Mounseer, his phisnomye, and a little pearl pendant";[55] there was the paleness and the tears and the storm of rage against her servants when it seemed that no marriage was possible between France and England. But to follow Elizabeth in this matter would be to follow a maze in a mist, while Marguerite's record confuses from a very opposite cause—an excess of light, an excess of precision, an excess of enthusiasm. Many of the people whom she immortalized in her memoirs were alive and active while she was writing them. Many of them were still very capable of doing her good—or harm—but the portraits of both friends and enemies were sketched in accurately enough with shade as well as light so that they emerge as credible human beings—far more credible indeed than the confections of her friend and admirer Brantôme. The portrait of Alençon alone blazes out with a more than human nobility: his every action born of the highest possible impulse, totally incapable of a mean thought or deed, generous, chivalrous, courageous, resourceful, greedy only for honor. . . . Such a figure might have fitted happily into one of the rubbishy romances which Cervantes was to belabor with such gusto; in Marguerite's misleadingly demure little work, with its occasional refreshing touch of feminine acerbity, her brother appears simply as a grotesque, a work of pure fancy. Her detractors pounced upon this impossible portrait of a very perfect, gentle knight, proclaiming loudly that here was proof incontrovertible of a guilty love, a love so powerful that it spilled unconsciously into the written word. It proved, if anything at all, the exact opposite, for Marguerite, of all people, was capable of manipulating words so that they disguised her true thought if she felt that this was necessary. The Duke of Guise played a fairly important and continuous role in her memoir, but the reader would never gain, from that source, the knowledge that they had been passionate lovers. Even her relatively unimportant affairs with Bussy and La Mole could not be detected from her writing. Posterity is left to make what it can of her curious, wholly uncharacteristic literary adoration of the Duke of Alençon, guided by nothing more than the suspicion that it was a sustained satire, an exercise in the irony in which she delighted. The suspicion has no more substance than the accusation that the portrait was that of an incestuous lover, but it is inherently more likely; she and her brother might have formed, in childhood, an alliance against the world, but in their maturity he brought her nothing but trouble.

The impromptu conference at La Fère came to a satisfactory close, the Flemings went north to prepare for their champion's coming, Alençon threw himself into the task of collecting a force and Marguerite returned to Paris. She did so with apprehension, but to her surprise and considerable relief, instead of being upbraided and threatened, she was actually welcomed by both her mother and brother. The alarming reports she had received in Flanders had either been grossly exaggerated or Henri was biding his time, for he went out of his way to put his sister at her ease, plying her with questions regarding her travels, affectionately asking after her health, giving no indication at all as to whether he knew the true purpose of her travels. Puzzled, but determined to take full advantage of this most unusual affability, Marguerite not only demanded permission to join her husband but also asked that her long-delayed marriage portion should be paid up. Somewhat to her astonishment, both her mother and brother agreed; not only that, the queen mother herself would be graciously pleased to accompany her daughter south.

But the remarkable harmony in the Valois family scarcely outlasted the first days' balls and banquets. Catherine almost certainly meant what she said, for she had a strong sense of the proprieties and there was, too, an obvious value in establishing her daughter in the rebellious court of Navarre. Henri, too, might very well have intended to keep his promise, but the control of his own court was rapidly slipping out of his hands. It was a common enough situation that was developing, nothing more than the challenge being delivered to the herd bull by an unintimidated rival. If Henri had been more ruthless—or, perhaps, wiser—he would have eliminated his envious, unscrupulous younger brother and so effectively eliminated a focus of discontent; but, as it was, his occasional petulant outbursts only antagonized Alençon while putting him on his guard. Rapidly, the court polarized into two factions. Marguerite, with her finely developed persecution complex, had no difficulty in placing all the blame on one side and identifying the chief persecutor. Du Guast was long since dead but now there was a certain Louis de Maugiron, who had once been a follower of Alençon but quitted him on scenting richer service with the king, "and in consequence imagined that my brother bore him illwill (as it is generally the one who is in the wrong who never forgives) and therefore hated my brother with such an intense hatred that he sought to injure him in every possible way." The young men who surrounded the king were certainly no worse than those who surrounded Alençon, but the effect of their inexperience, flattery and jealousy was to insulate the king from reality so that he lost all sense of scale, the boudoir battles of the court looming as large as the real battles outside. But because he was the king, and this overheated, scented stage was the court of France, the boudoir battles had their effect upon the outside world like some monstrous pantograph.

It was Bussy-d'Amboise who was responsible for the outbreak of open hostilities—the swashbuckling Bussy, who loved fighting and killing as much as he loved drinking and copulating. He and Alençon returned to the court to begin a cautious preparation for the Flemish invasion, but almost immediately the scented, mincing *mignons* attracted his delighted attention and he was off among them, like a dog joyously assailing a pack of sheep. But these were singularly ferocious sheep, hurling themselves into duels with the same alacrity as Bussy and his jeweled thugs. News came to the king's ear of a mass duel that was to take place between Bussy's and Maugiron's men. He forbade it, but he could not detect and so forbid the endless petty insults that kept the whole childish affair on the boil. Bussy eventually overstepped himself at the great Twelfth Night ball. The *mignons* had spent endless painful hours preparing for this, one of the most splendid of the court entertainments, and appeared in a dazzle of cloth of gold and silver, of palest silks and richest satins, all ablaze with jewelry. Bussy appeared in a suit of the soberest, plainest cut possible, announcing that finery was most fitting for servants. Marguerite, eyeing her royal brother's peacock attire, was maliciously amused, but Henri was furious and Alençon, by no means addicted to Puritan costume himself, began to feel that Bussy was becoming too much of a liability. The matter of the Flanders invasion was now out in the open but, so far, Henri had still made no sign of displeasure and even Alençon felt that there was no profit to be gained by deliberately irritating him. Bussy therefore discreetly left the court at his master's most urgent request.

But the brawls, far from ending, became more frequent and ever more vicious. Marguerite assumed that they were all the work of Maugiron, that Henri was wholly at the mercy of his homosexual playmates. But the exact opposite was rather more probable: Henri, knowing that an outright clash with Alençon would merely result in a test of strength he could not afford, was probably using his *mignons* to goad Alençon, partly out of malice, partly in the hope that Alençon would adopt some extreme and indefensible position. And only a few days after Bussy's departure Alençon placed himself in just such a position.

On February 9, 1578, the Marquis of Saint-Luc, one of the most favored *mignons,* was married off to a girl who was as ugly as she was wealthy. The weddings of *mignons* were always celebrated with a prodigal splendor: for days beforehand the court prepared as feverishly for it as for some great state occasion, and on the day itself a kind of bacchanale took place. The more sensible courtiers took themselves off, if they could find an excuse, and Alençon wisely decided to follow suit, begging Marguerite to do the same. Their mother approved. She, too, was growing more than a little weary of the arrogance and endless puerile pranks of her eldest son's favorites and, aware that almost certainly they would make Alençon their chief butt for the day of misrule, she invited both him and Marguerite to spend the day with her in the country. They dined together, a pleasant, friendly family party, and came back to the Louvre in the evening. Catherine had asked—had almost pleaded—that Alençon should at least attend the formal wedding ball that night and so give the king no cause for offense and, reluctantly, he agreed.

It was a mistake. The wedding guests were by now far gone in drunkenness, and the sudden appearance of the king's grotesque-looking brother at the ball spurred them into ecstasies of satire and insult. Marguerite was apparently at the ball—certainly she recorded some of the insults, with what seems an ill-concealed and unsisterly amusement. They called out "that it was a waste of time for him to have changed his dress—that he might just as well have worn his old clothes—that it was a good job that he had arrived at dusk with a face like his—twitting him with his ugliness and meanness of stature."[56] Alençon tried to put a brave face on it, but when even the poor, deformed little bride laughed openly at someone who was as ugly as herself, his nerve broke and, crying with anger, he ran to his mother.

She calmed him and agreed that it was best for him to leave the court for a few days on a hunting expedition. By the time he returned, the festivities would be over and normality would have returned—or what passed for normality at the court of Henri III. She then dispatched one of Alençon's gentlemen to the king, telling him of the arrangement, and Alençon, believing that his brother would almost automatically grant him permission to leave, retired to his own quarters and began to make preparations for departure.

Darkness came over the palace as in room after room, suite after suite, the occupants retired for the evening. But in the great banquet hall the torches blazed on far into the night, the wine continued to make its rounds, the music shrilling, the favored company growing more feverish, responding to that almost hysterical rhythm of pleasure that marked the life-style of this court. And even when at length the revelers reeled away half dazed with wine and heat and noise, a handful of them accompanied the king into his own apartments—"a Jeroboam's council of some five or six young men," Marguerite called them with her lively feeling for a phrase, and represented them as playing upon his fears and jealousy of his brother. Henri knew of Alençon's intention to leave in the morning—had, indeed, specifically given permission. But sometime during those midnight hours he changed his mind. He, personally, was abstemious for reasons of health, but he was highly sensitive to atmosphere—and the atmosphere in his apartments was probably somewhere near hysteria, the product of a day's drinking and debauchery, of the excitement engendered by music and dancing. Suddenly he leaped to his feet, screamed for the palace guard and, dressed just as he was in a nightgown, he ran straight to his mother's room. She was not yet asleep when he burst in with an almost hysterical denunciation of her. "How on earth could you think of giving him permission to leave? Don't you know that, if he goes, the realm will be exposed to peril? This business of hunting is only a pretext. I'm going to arrest him, with all his people."[57]

Catherine, sitting up in alarm, must have been most vividly and unpleasantly reminded of that other midnight occasion when this raving young man's brother, the dead Charles IX, had also burst in on her with an hysterical denunciation of Marguerite. Behind Henri was the Scotsman, Losses, the captain of the king's guard and a strong force of Scottish archers—sufficient, it seemed, to repel a siege. With dread at her heart the elderly woman left her warm bed and, drawing on a dressing gown, shuffled breathlessly down the long cold hall in the wake of her son and his very competent killers. Henri threw himself at Alençon's door, kicking and hammering at it as though he intended to break it down, bellowing that he was the king and demanding entry, while the archers strung their bows and stood back in readiness.

The hideous noise woke Alençon with a start. He had, for once, a clear conscience, and although he would have been less than human had he not felt a twinge of fear on hearing that hate-filled voice outside, he ordered his valet, Cange, to open the door. Henri erupted in, swearing that he would teach his brother to go on plotting against the state and ordering the archers to search the room for papers. They did so very thoroughly indeed, dragging Alençon's attendants outside and searching them personally, tipping the coffers and drawers upside down. Henri searched his brother's bed himself, found nothing, and then noticing that Alençon was clutching something in his hand, demanded that he hand it over. Almost weeping, Alençon refused; Henri, dancing with rage and hatred and triumph, snatched it from him and unfolded it. He began to read it aloud then stopped, embarassed: it was a love letter from Madame de Sauves.

Henri's embarrassment was only momentary. By now he had worked himself up into that Valois rage which was only a hair's breadth from madness. The wretched Alençon stammered his innocence, pathetically demanded from his unhappy, silent mother what, exactly, he was supposed to be accused of. The king refused either to substantiate, apologize for or even withdraw a charge that was born of nothing more than vicious, wine-laden gossip. Instead he whirled on Losses, fiercely placed his brother in the Scotsman's personal charge with orders that he was to be allowed to speak to nobody, and marched out, taking his mother with him.

The time was a little after 1 A.M. For an hour or so thereafter, the frightened Alençon remained silent under the unblinking gaze of the archers. Losses, however, although a foreigner and a mercenary, was as aware as any native aristocrat of the dangers of being caught up in a royal quarrel, and Alençon noted his distress. Nevertheless, he dared not make any comment in front of the ordinary soldiers and simply asked him what had happened to Marguerite, assuming that she too had been arrested. Losses replied that, as far as he knew, nothing had happened to the princess, whereupon Alençon said, "I'm very glad indeed to hear that she is still at liberty. Nevertheless, I'm sure that she loves me so much that she would rather share my captivity than continue in freedom without me." He therefore asked Losses to obtain from the king and queen mother permission for Marguerite to share his captivity. This was granted, very readily granted, and one of the archers was dispatched to arrest her. Throughout this palace drama, Marguerite had been sound asleep in her own suite some little distance from the center of activity, and the first she knew of what had happened was at dawn when she was abruptly awakened by someone drawing the curtains of her bed. Startled, she looked at the man in the gray light of morning. He reassured her—"with the accent peculiar to the Scotch. 'Good day Madam. Monsieur your brother desires that you will come and see him.'

"I gazed at him scarcely awake, fancying that I must be dreaming. Then, recognising him, inquired whether he was not one of the Scottish guard. He replied that he was and I then rejoined, 'What is the matter? Has my brother no other messenger but you to send to me?'"

The archer then told her of all that had happened, and it is at this point, perhaps the only point in her memoirs, that she let her mask slip momentarily and showed her real opinion of her younger brother. The king's rage had been directed, wholly and exclusively, against his brother. Not once had he displayed the slightest interest in the whereabouts or activities of his sister. She had been comfortably, safely asleep in bed only to be dragged out by a foreign soldier at dawn, in order that she might share her brother's captivity, in order that she, too, might become the target for the insults and threats of the king because "she loves me so much that she would rather share my captivity than continue in freedom without me." On which modest remark Marguerite commented, "The firm confidence which my brother had in the depth and strength of my affection inspired me with such especial gratitude that, although he had already placed me under an obligation by his kindnesses, I have always set this one before them all." Considering that she had never gained anything from this brother of hers but danger and insults and imprisonment, and was about to gain more of the same, it is difficult to see anything but the profoundest irony in that remark.

But the mask, if mask there were, was smoothly replaced. Dressing hastily, she followed the archer through the palace to the room where her brother was under detention. It was still barely light, but the passages and staterooms and the antechambers were murmurous with people, some standing in little groups about the hastily lit braziers. Marguerite experienced, for the second time, the effect of a sudden fall from grace. She knew by sight most of the people she passed; some had, successfully, begged favors of her, all usually fawned upon her. But now all ignored her as soon as they saw her walking under guard—turning their backs unobtrusively upon her, letting their eyes slide past hers, feigning deep interest in a conversation—all the tricks of the professional survivors.

She was taken to Alençon's room and they were left to console each other as best they could while a vigorous search was made through the Louvre for all Alençon's staff and friends. None escaped, not even the redoubtable Bussy, whose capture added an element of farce to the whole confused situation. Bussy had slipped back into the palace on the previous afternoon, probably in pursuit of a love affair, and during the hue and cry took refuge with his friend Simier. Henri promptly gave orders to the captain of his personal bodyguard, Nicolas de Gremonville, to arrest the pair of them. Gremonville reluctantly went off to do the royal bidding. A ribald, lecherous, cheerful man, he was a personal friend of Bussy's and probably deliberately omitted looking in the most obvious place in Simier's room—the great four-poster bed with its heavy curtains. He was marching out with the frightened Simier when Bussy's grinning face appeared through the curtains of the bed. "What-ho, father. Aren't you going to arrest me? Surely I'm a better catch than that scoundrel Simier." Gremonville looked at him glumly. "Ah, my son, would to God that I had lost an arm rather than that you should have been here." Bussy leaped out of the bed, mocked the trembling Simier, clapped Gremonville on the shoulder and marched out with him under arrest. Bussy-d'Amboise was himself no tyro in the art of survival. In the few moments behind the curtain he had decided that arrest was inevitable and it was better to be in the custody of a friend than of one of the king's *mignons*.

By midmorning all were either in the Bastille or under heavy guard in the palace. But by midmorning, too, older, soberer and rather more frightened counsels were beginning to be heard. The first that Marguerite learned of the reaction was when the aged scholar Loste was put in charge of her and Alençon. The old man was near tears. "The heart of every true Frenchman must bleed at beholding what we behold today. I have served the king your father too long for me not to sacrifice my life." He had a well-meaning but not very practical plan to bring about Alençon's escape, but Marguerite sensibly dissuaded him and insisted instead that the king should be asked on what charge they would be detained. After some time an elegant young man, Robert de Combaud, arrived and asked them what explanation they were prepared to give the king. They were demanding, not offering, explanations, Marguerite retorted, whereupon Combaud replied loftily, "Gods and kings must not be called to account for their actions, since they did all things for a good and just purpose." Alençon burst out laughing and Marguerite, barely swallowing her anger, insisted again that a formal charge should be made and Combaud took himself off, promising to do what he could.

But meanwhile a far more formidable agent was working on their behalf. For some hours after that midnight visitation the queen mother seems to have been in a state of shock, dumbly aquiescing in whatever her hysterical son demanded. But gradually the powerful mind again took control of the emotions. This was a family matter —but with potentially national repercussions, for in that hostile out- side world were many who would pounce upon the breach and enlarge it, exploding a brotherly squabble into civil war. But if she, personally, were to take Alençon's side and reproach her other son this would give only more fuel to his sullen anger. Urgent summons therefore went out to the Councillors of State, to "the grave princes, and nobles and marshals of France," most of them belonging to her generation and, with her, seeing where this quarrel could lead. And with this massive backing, speaking not as mother but as councillor, she went in search of her son.

Henri was secretly grateful, for in the cold light of day what had begun as personal pique had taken on some very threatening aspects. Yes, he would be glad if his mother were to arrange a recon- ciliation—provided. . . . Provided that in the future Alençon treated him with the respect due to his semidivine office; provided that there were no more plots and conspiracies; provided that Alençon's man Bussy apologize to, and make his peace with, the king's most loyal servant Quélus, for the two had recently quarreled and come almost to a duel, and it was not fitting that such malicious things should be said of a friend of the king. Off trudged Catherine to lecture her second son, eye her daughter dubiously and arrange a grand recon- ciliation scene in her own apartments. Everyone was there: Marguer- ite found that the same people who had been so careful to avoid her that morning were now "gazing at us with tears in their eyes, praising God at beholding that we were delivered out of danger." The two royal brothers kissed and embraced and the king then commanded their followers to do the same. Bussy swaggered up to Quélus and gave him a smacking, exaggerated kiss "à la Pantaloon," and there was an uncertain laugh from the assembled company.

It was now three o'clock in the afternoon. Most of the actors in that drama had been in a high state of tension for over twelve hours; few had eaten more than a hasty bite since the night before and the queen mother now proposed that they should all dine together as a happy family party. She turned to Marguerite and her brother and, as though they were still little children, ordered them to go upstairs and change before dining, for they were still wearing the now disheveled clothes they had hastily put on during the small hours. Alençon went out with a black expression but Marguerite remained behind long enough to hear her mother exchanging a few words with one of her confidants, Michael de Seurre, a man with a sardonic turn of humor whose foible it was to speak his mind. "Well, Monsieur de Seurre, what do you say to all this?" Catherine asked with a touch of coquetry, plainly very satisfied with her diplomacy. Seurre shrugged. "I consider it too much to have been done without premeditation, and too little to profit by," he answered and then, turning to Marguerite, said in a low voice, "I don't think we have reached the last act of this drama. I shall be much surprised if that man [Alençon] allows the matter to stay there."

Seurre was right, and the last act of the drama took place just four days later.

On the morning of February 14, a young pageboy in Marguerite's suite took from his mistress's bedroom the trunk which usually stood at the foot of her bed and carried it away for repair. He brought it back later in the day, opened it to her eager inspection and displayed a length of very stout rope, just long enough to reach from the window of this room on the second floor to the bottom of the dry moat outside. The last act of the drama was about to begin.

Over the previous four days the already brittle relationship between the king and his brother deteriorated further. Alençon was furious at the insult he had received, chafing with impotent hatred, giving Henri now very solid reasons to believe that his brother would do almost anything to injure him. Self-defense alone decreed that Alençon should be kept under surveillance and, ever since the wedding night furor, he had been kept under virtual house arrest in the palace while all his staff, including Bussy, had been expelled from the palace. For the second time, Alençon decided to escape and, naturally, turned to his sister. It was she who thought of using her window as an escape route, such a plan naturally appealing to her rather theatrical sense. But it also had the virtue of simple, direct action involving the minimum number of conspirators and Alençon took up the idea eagerly and impatiently, so eagerly and impatiently as nearly to wreck the whole scheme.

The normal evening practice in the Louvre was for the family to sup together in some state. Music or dancing usually followed supper and it would be very late indeed before the party broke up for bed. Tonight, however, the king was fasting, for he was going through one of his religious phases, and in consequence Marguerite was dining informally with her mother in the queen mother's private apartment. It was perfectly natural that Alençon should have made his own private arrangements for supper, and mother and daughter therefore enjoyed a leisurely and casual meal *à deux*. Catherine enjoyed the company of this witty and accomplished daughter of hers, and the meal drew to a pleasant and friendly close. The queen mother arose and began to walk from the room and Marguerite was about to do the same when, to her dismay, Alençon burst into the room, hurried over to her and, bending close, impatiently whispered to her to hurry up. He could not have looked more guilty, more conspiratorial if he had worn a placard stating the fact. The queen mother's back was toward them and, for a moment, Marguerite hoped that Alençon's stupidity had gone unnoticed. But one of her mother's staff, Odet de Matignon, "a dangerous and cunning Norman," had seen what had happened and, as the company left the dining room, he caught up with Catherine and warned her that Alençon was up to some mischief and was planning to escape. It seems likely that someone—probably Alençon—had talked too much, for Matignon could not have guessed so accurately even if he had overheard the whispered exchange.

Marguerite was close enough to hear Matignon's remark and entered her mother's closet with justifiable apprehension. Immediately, Catherine took her on one side. "Are you aware of what Matignon told me?" she demanded.

"I did not hear what it was, Madam, but I saw that it was something that pained you."

"Yes, it pained me indeed," Catherine returned with heavy

irony. "You know that I have pledged my word to the king that your brother shall not depart and Matignon has just told me that he knows perfectly well that he will not be here tomorrow."[58]

The two of them faced each other—the short, stout veteran of a thousand political battles, the tall, graceful apprentice with a will as strong, and a mind almost as devious as her mother's. Later, Marguerite claimed that the issue presented her with a moral dilemma, forcing her either to lie outright, "a thing I would not have done to escape a thousand deaths," or to give away the escape plot. The dilemma may have existed, or she may very well have realized that Catherine possessed her own methods for detecting an outright lie. She therefore used her favorite technique of using one truth to disguise another, pointing out, accurately, that Matignon hated her brother and would do anything to harm him. Catherine was aware that all was not as it should be, but it was late at night, she was old and tired and, perhaps, more and more heartsick, more and more reluctant to uncover the hatred and deception that lurked at the heart of her family. She left the matter with a warning that might have chilled a less ebullient character than her daughter's. "Consider well what you say. You will be my surety for it—you will answer for it upon your life."

Marguerite almost skipped off to her room, hastily undressed and got into bed, dismissed her ladies-in-waiting, who were almost certainly spies for her mother, and waited with the three personal servants who always slept in her room. Shortly after midnight a discreet tap at the door heralded her brother, his personal servants Simier and Cange, and the pageboy who had smuggled in the rope. The rope was paid out through the window and the three men descended, Alençon first, laughing and joking, then the wretched Simier, who was trembling with fear, having no head for heights, and finally the valet Cange.

So far, everything had gone with ludicrous ease, considering that this was one of the great fortified castles of Europe, but at the very last moment Marguerite received the fright of her life. Just as Cange was sliding down the last few feet, a shadowy figure jumped up from the bottom of the moat and ran at a great speed toward the guardhouse. The identity and purpose of the mysterious stranger was never, in fact, discovered—he was probably involved in one of the endless political or amorous intrigues which riddled the Louvre. But at the time Marguerite was convinced that he was a spy, posted at Matignon's warning, that Alençon was captured and that she, at any moment, would be arrested, for her safety now depended exclusively on Alençon's freedom of action outside. What had been a prank became suddenly infinitely sinister; her mother's ominous words, which she had taken so lightly, now sounded with their full import. Her normally quick mind deserted her and, for some vital moments, she just stood half-stunned. Her maids took matters into their own hands, with results that really did precipitate discovery. Hastily they hauled up the rope and threw it on the fire. The fire blazed up, the chimney caught alight, one of the guards gave the alarm and a de-tachment of archers ran to the room and pounded on the door. Marguerite had by then come to her senses. Although she was con-vinced that that excited knocking on the door heralded the an-nouncement that her brother was, indeed, captured, she jumped into bed and told her women to go to the door and speak softly, as though she were asleep. They did so and the archers explained that they had merely come to extinguish the fire. "My women told them that it was nothing, that they could quite well put it out themselves and that they must take care not to waken me." The door was gently but firmly closed in the face of the men and the immediate danger was past.

The Valois family seemed to specialize in dramatic nocturnal scenes. About two hours afterward, when Marguerite had drifted into a shallow, troubled sleep, there was another authoritative knock at the door. This time it was the Captain of the Guard himself, the Scotsman Losses, come to escort the Queen of Navarre to yet another midnight interview with her royal brother and his mother. While Marguerite was resignedly dressing, one of her women began to scream, crying out that she would never see her mistress again. The Scotsman roughly silenced her, then turned to Marguerite: "If this woman had made such a scene before anyone who was not as devoted to you as I am, it would have got you into trouble. But as it is, fear nothing and give thanks to God, for Monsieur your brother is in safety."

The interview was an anticlimax. Henri was inevitably spitting with rage but his mother was in firm control and she, ever a realist, was perfectly well aware that Alençon temporarily had the whip hand and that Alençon's ally must therefore be treated carefully. She did not fail to upbraid Marguerite bitterly for breaking her pledge. Marguerite retorted that she had done no such thing, that Alençon had deceived her as he had deceived them and that, in any case, her brother's true intention was not to stir up trouble in the country but merely to prepare for his expedition into Flanders. Curiously, the announcement that his unstable brother was preparing to launch an attack upon the possessions of an immensely powerful neighbor "mollified the king" instead of driving him into a royal and entirely legitimate rage. Marguerite may have been right. Aware of the crumbling foundations of his power, Henri may indeed have been glad to hear that his brother's destructive energy was to be directed outside the State. Marguerite was allowed to return to bed and on the following day the queen mother wearily collected her personal belongings and set off yet again in pursuit of her youngest son.

†

XI

Queen of Navarre

"I have been away a month from the Court, running after my son," Catherine wrote to her old friend the Duchess of Nemours. "He often gives me great anxiety lest he should again play the fool. But, God be thanked, I found him so resolved—or so he says—to do nothing to displease his brother or break the peace that if his deeds square with his words, the kingdom and I have cause to be grateful to Providence."[59]

The queen mother's usually highly efficient intelligence service had for once let her down; just a month after she had written that letter, in June of 1578, Alençon marched into Flanders. The old queen gave the equivalent of a shrug. There was nothing now that she could do to stop this lunatic boy; he seemed, indeed, to be meeting an altogether undeserved success—largely because the first few weeks of campaigning took place in those provinces which his sister had already won over to him. Catherine therefore returned to Paris to prepare for her own journey south. The ostensible cause was to deliver Marguerite at last to her husband but behind that ceremonial cover the queen mother would be able to penetrate deep into the rebellious lands of the Huguenots. France was again at peace, but it was the peace of a volcano between eruptions. Her intention was to prevent another eruption. No matter that her ice-cold realism told her that such an intention was now only a pious hope: "It seems to me that one ought to leave everything else, and to invent any kind of means to avoid the storm of war. I am resolved not to return till I see peace. I may return like a wrecked ship without its rigging but, if God give me the grace to fulfill my desires, I hope this kingdom will feel the good of my labours and that enduring peace will reign there."[60] The task that faced her was one that might have daunted a young man, much less an aging, gouty woman. There was the reconciliation to be made with her rebellious son-in-law Navarre; the thousand minor problems of the Catholic minorities in the Protestant provinces —minor, but each could light a flare to set a war alight; and there was perhaps the even trickier problem of the provincial Leagues, those Leagues of theoretically loyal Catholics who still seemed to be look-ing for a leader, somehow overlooking the divinely appointed leader in the Louvre.

Marguerite and her mother left in August in a truly regal cavalcade as befitted the status of two queens. After six years of marriage Marguerite had at last been assigned her dowry lands— Quercy and Agenais, Condomois, Auvergne, and Rouergue, Rieux, Albi and Verdun-sur-Grand—so that now she ranked among the wealthiest and most powerful landowners in France. Her entourage therefore reflected her status, consisting of some three hundred men and women—ladies of honor and maids of honor, councillors, secre-taries, confessors, chaplains, physicians, surgeons, apothecaries, down to her personal cooks, scullions and laundresses. The nobility and their attendants formed a roll call of the French aristocracy. Her chancellor was the fifty-year-old Sieur de Pibrac, who had accom-panied Henri in that semi-exile in Poland and was therefore looked upon as a very safe and solid man. His role in Marguerite's court was to act as spy, but he was to fall in love with this Queen of Navarre, to Henri's intense irritation and his own deep distress. The Cardinal of Bourbon was there, that slow-moving, slow-thinking Red Ass who improbably shared the same blood as Marguerite's volatile hus-band. The Duke of Montpensier had brought his quicksilver wife along; she was sister to Marguerite's one-time lover the Duke of Guise, and the two vivacious young women maintained a kind of amiable guard toward each other. Brantôme came, agog at all this wit and splendor, prepared to admire every man or woman above a certain grade in society but above all noting, in his retentive mind, every action of the Queen of Navarre. There were enemies, too— Matignon, who had more important things to do than flirt and gossip; Madame de Sauves, brought along as a kind of well-matured bait for Henri of Navarre. And if, perhaps, his taste was for younger, fresher fruit, there were the queen mother's maids of honor, Bazerne and Dayelle—the latter with a romantic history to go with her beautiful face, for she had been one of the few Greeks to escape the sack of Cyprus nine years earlier. And there were, inevitably, the rest of the Flying Squadron, for Catherine de Médicis, like a good general, en- sured that she had weapons and tools suitable for all occasions and circumstances.

The enormous, luxurious procession traveled with appropriate leisure, and it was not until the beginning of October that Marguerite crossed the border into her husband's vassal kingdom. It was the farthest south she had yet traveled; it was the first time that she entered the land of which she was titular queen but, judging by her memoirs, it meant far less to her than her journey into the Nether- lands. Her mother had determined that she should travel as queen and be received as queen; Brantôme recorded how she entered Bor- deaux "with all the magnificence that could be desired, dressed in an orange robe, her favourite colour, covered with embroidery and mounted on a white horse." She herself remained coldly indifferent even when, on October 3, she met her husband for the first time since he had escaped nearly three years before.

Her first, spontaneous reaction might very well have been one of surprise, seeing him anew after such a length of time. People tended to think of Navarre as a big man and were apt to be discon- certed by the reality: though broad and powerfully built, he was undeniably short and spent most of his life looking up into people's faces. He had made some attempt at dressing for the occasion but the gaudy court costume looked singularly out of place on him; his usual shabby clothes suited him far better even with their habitual odor of sweat and garlic and strong wine. The eyes above the great fan-shaped beard were alert and direct, the expression on the dark, heavily tanned face simultaneously cheerful and watchful. Henri of Navarre had grown up over these past few months, blooded in the first of the two hundred battles which he was destined to survive, his shoulders already adjusting to the burden they would carry to his grave. He knew perfectly well that the main purpose of the queen mother's visit was to render him impotent in a web of intrigue, but he acted as though the entire occasion was a carnival got up for his especial delight. He embraced his stately wife enthusiastically, saluted his mother-in-law gallantly, passed an appraising eye over her Flying Squadron—an eye which slid over the hopeful Madame de Sauves but rested speculatively upon the lily-fresh Mademoiselle Dayelle—cracked jokes in his broad, Gascon accent, and then was gone in a jingle of harness and clatter of hooves to prepare a fitting reception in his capital at Nérac. The royal entourage followed slowly. Most of Marguerite's new lands were adjacent to her husband's and she took the opportunity now to make herself known. Traveling day after day in wild country at the beginning of winter took its toll, and she fell ill in Toulouse at the end of October. By November 10 she was fit again to travel and graciously spent some time in Pibrac's sumptuous mansion, giving her unfortunate chancellor quite unjustified hopes of favors to come. Catherine too had been criss-crossing the country on her own affairs, and it was not until December 15 that Marguerite joined up with her mother and husband at Nérac.

"I have been so tormented by the brawls of Provence that I have only enough brains left to get angry," Catherine wrote her old "gossip" Madame d'Uzès. Altogether she was to spend eighteen months in the south, eighteen months threading her way through problems of an almost metaphysical dimension—like that of Montpellier, where the Huguenots demanded the nave and tower of the only surviving church while the Catholics demanded it all. She had been threatened, flattered, thanked, deceived, and had done the same in her turn. The Nérac conference was the epitome of all her hopes, all her difficulties, the problem of the distracted kingdom writ small. Striving for balance, all her instincts were nevertheless against these arrogant Protestants and once, driven almost to distraction by their mulish obstinacy, she burst out against them "royally and haughtily, even going so far as to declare that she would have them all hanged as rebels." She had counted upon her daughter as a natural ally, only to find that that exasperating girl had thrown her capricious weight on the side of her husband. Catherine, of all people, should have expected just such a reaction. Marguerite had tasted the delights of intrigue and diplomacy in Flanders and, in addition, now had the opportunity to build her own life, follow her own beliefs instead of being forced to accept those of the court around her. Unblushingly she used the infatuated Pibrac to counter many of her mother's tactics and so gained for her husband—and the Huguenots—far more favorable terms than they might otherwise have obtained. Yet her distaste for them increased, rather than diminished. She and her mother mockingly adopted the stiff, pompous Puritan speech—the "language of Canaan," they called it—and vied with each other to see who could cram the most polysyllables, the greatest number of obscure biblical quotations, into the same sentence.

Bitter though were the undercurrents and deadly the enmities of the conference, to an outsider it must have seemed as though Nérac was given up to one long, romantic dalliance. Catherine, longing to return to her beloved son in Paris, actually accused Navarre of drawing out the conference so that he, and his followers, could enjoy their affairs at leisure. Navarre merely grinned without denying it. During his long absence from his wife he had succumbed, totally and permanently, to that satyriasis which was a mocking reflection of her own instability, taking his bed partners from cottage or from palace with a fine democratic indifference. To do him justice, he never went to bed with a woman without persuading both her and himself that he was deeply, passionately, madly in love with her. He had found a new eternal love among the ranks of Catherine's ladies-in-waiting—not Madame de Sauves, Marguerite noted with malicious pleasure, but the little Greek girl Mademoiselle Dayelle—and in between the battles at the conference table pursued her with his usual verve. Marguerite shrugged: she was engrossed in her affair with the dashing Viscount of Turenne—uninhibited by the fact that he was a Huguenot and a member of her husband's staff. The example set by the king and queen was enthusiastically followed by their courtiers. "Ease hatched vice as heat does serpents," Agrippa d'Aubigné snarled, yet he too was overwhelmed by the perfumed tide, falling willing victim to one of the Flying Squadron. Even the solemn young Rosny took a mistress from among those rosy ranks and, looking back complacently down the years at his dashing young manhood, essayed a frightful pun: in Nérac at that time, nothing was said *"d'armes mais seulement de Dames."*

"I heard M. de Pibrac say on one occasion that these Navarre marriages are fatal because husband and wife are always at variance," Brantôme remarked in his essay on Marguerite, and then went on to give historical justification for Pibrac's statement, tracing the curiously constant inconstancy that did indeed mark Navarre marriages. "They say that the quarrel between Queen Marguerite and her husband came more from the difference in their religion than from anything else for they each loved his and her own, and supported it strongly."[61] Marguerite's Catholicism was the deep instinctive faith of her Italian ancestors, whereas Navarre's Protestantism was purely cerebral; he had shed it once to save his life, he would shed it again to gain a crown. But in Navarre, in these years of struggle when he was still trying to establish himself in a secure base, a public devotion to Huguenotery was vital. He and Marguerite clashed almost as soon as the queen mother had left, taking with her, to Navarre's extreme annoyance, the delicious Mademoiselle Dayelle. The Navarre court accompanied her to the frontier and then returned to Pau, instead of the relatively cosmopolitan Nérac.

Pau was Henri's birthplace, a high, windy place among the foothills of the Pyrenees and the very heart and core of Protestantism in Navarre. Elsewhere in the state Catholic worship was permitted, if under stringent and occasionally humiliating conditions: here, the Béarnais would as soon have tolerated open celebration of the Black Mass. Marguerite insisted on her rights as in the marriage contract and, grudgingly, a tiny little cell of a chapel was set aside for her popish practices in the castle. The chapel could just about hold seven people and, to ensure that the contagion did not spread, the drawbridge of the castle was raised whenever mass was celebrated. The concession caused considerable indignation among the more fanatical Huguenots and the chapel itself exercised a kind of horrific fascination for them. A little group of them was usually to be seen near the door trying to peer in, and their desire for scandal was duly rewarded on Whitsunday. On that day a little group of Catholics from the city had slipped into the castle before the drawbridge was raised and crept into the chapel. The watchers promptly took their news not to the King of Navarre, but to his secretary, a man called Dupin.

They had excellent reason for doing so. Navarre himself would probably have laughed the matter off or given his wife a good-humored and discreet warning. Dupin belonged to a breed of Protestant that was becoming depressingly familiar, a breed for whom Calvinism or Lutheranism or Huguenotery was merely another way of expressing their own narrow, intolerant and intolerable sense of virtue, a breed indifferent to the philosophy behind protest except insofar as it coincided with their constricted and monochromatic universe. The color and gaiety that surrounded the Queen of Navarre was utterly repugnant to the king's secretary, and he grasped the opportunity that would at once punish those who she had led astray and demonstrate just how powerless was this scarlet woman in godly Béarn. Without bothering to tell the king, he summoned the guards, who entered the chapel, beat up the unlicensed worshippers and threw them into prison. Marguerite, in a furious rage, stormed in to see her husband, but even while she was pouring out her vehement protests, Dupin entered the room and actually had the insolence to upbraid her for troubling the king, telling her that she ought to be grateful for the concession that had been granted her, instead of trying to abuse it.

Henri was undoubtedly in something of a quandary. It was,

indeed, a gross insult for a mere secretary to speak of, and to, the Queen of Navarre in such a manner in his presence—but the secretary was also a fanatical Calvinist who could make a great deal of trouble for him. Marguerite burst out, demanding satisfaction; Henri temporized, dismissing the man and assuring his outraged wife that it was all simply an excess of religious zeal. But she refused to let the matter rest there, rightly seeing it as a test case. Over the next few days she demanded again and again that he should dismiss Dupin outright. Henri refused to do so, and when she flared up and told him that he would have to choose between his secretary and his wife, he began to avoid her altogether. Eventually he was forced to give way, but not before she had resorted to the crudest blackmail, hinting heavily that "if the circumstances ever came to the knowledge of the king or the queen my mother," Henri would have cause for regret. She had won the first round, but only by immediately calling on her reserves, and her husband took it very badly indeed.

The court shortly afterward left Pau—"that little Geneva of a Pau"—as Marguerite described it scornfully, and took up permanent residence in Nérac. It was a pretty little town, open and airy after the cramped hill town of Pau, and for Marguerite, exiled among an alien people, it had a personal attraction, for it was here that her great-aunt and namesake, Marguerite, had established her court fifty years before when she, too, had married a Henri of Navarre. The religion which that first Marguerite had embraced as an exhilarating intellectual novelty was now an iron discipline, but in Nérac there still remained traces of her gay and courageous spirit. The gallant company she had drawn together had long since scattered and gone, descended to the grave, but her touch could still be seen in the elegant additions to the massive castle, in the books that were still housed in it and, above all, in the beautiful gardens that she had laid out and which were now in their full maturity. It was in these surroundings that the second Marguerite of Navarre was to spend almost all the time that she remained in her husband's kingdom, leaving, in her turn, a few touches of lightness and color. Looking back on the five years that she spent in Nérac, she remarked complacently that the court she established "was so brilliant that we had no cause to regret that of France." Consciously, perhaps, she modeled herself on her illustrious forebear; she too laid out a garden with avenues of laurel and cypress and a formal park along the cool riverside. She, too, gathered wits and savants and poets around her. The giants were dead; there was no Rabelais now to dedicate a poem to this Queen of Navarre, no Erasmus to make ironic but affectionate greetings, no Calvin to bare a tortuous—and perhaps tortured—mind to an elegant and powerful convert. But there was Brantôme and Ronsard, suffi-cient—if only just sufficient—to provide antidote to the sour pens of the Huguenot writers and give a convincing impression of a gay company gliding through flower-spangled gardens by day, some-times flirting, sometimes deeply debating, and by night whirling in brilliant halls in an endless delight of dance. Certainly it was suffi-cient later to deceive the young English playwright who was looking for a plausible locale for his *Love's Labour's Lost.* Shakespeare's Court of Navarre, however, comes from much the same area as his Coast of Bohemia. The dazzlingly beautiful, witty Princess of France can, perhaps, just be identified with the dazzlingly beautiful, witty Daughter of France known as Marguerite, but it is wholly impossible to see any relationship between Shakespeare's Ferdinand, King of Navarre, who vowed to spurn all women for three years while he studied, and the real, lecherous, bibulous cheerful Henri, King of Navarre, who could no more have given up women for three years than he could have given up oxygen.

For, despite the intellectual atmosphere that Marguerite might have liked to create, the overall impression conveyed by the court was of an almost drugged addiction to sensuality. "One heard of nothing but love affairs and pleasures and pastimes," L'Estoile noted in distant Paris, even though he admitted that life down south seemed "sweet and pleasant."[62] Agrippa d'Aubigné was inevitably more caustic. "She told her husband that a knight without a love affair was a one without a soul. He caressed her servants and she caressed his."[63] Again this very attractive couple, living in close and daily proximity, could strike no sparks in each other. Years later, a vivid if accidental light was thrown upon their relationship with each other by the scurrilous *Divorce satyrique* which purported to be Henri's apologia for divorcing her. In trying to build up a case against her, it demonstrated Henri's curious personal habits and her spontaneous reaction of disgust. He would come home after violent exercise and take her to bed, all sweating and dirty as he was. Not unnaturally, "she complained that my feet and armpits smelt and that my caresses made her sick to the stomach and she would go to the length of changing the sheets, even though we had been between them scarcely a quarter of an hour."[64] It is not difficult to see the basic, instinctive revulsion between a fastidious woman and a man who regarded bathing more than once a year as a thoroughly effete habit. His mistresses accepted the physical unpleasantness for the sake of the social status those caresses conveyed; his wife had to do no such thing, as she made very clear. "On one occasion I wanted Madame de Tirans to eat at her table one day and she placed a basin of water and a napkin before her so that she could wash her feet, inferring that they were smelly."[65] Even his friends and relatives, it seemed, were coldly regarded by the civilized woman from the north. Husband and wife remained allies and even good friends, enjoying each other's ability to play with words, but there was small wonder that each should look elsewhere for deeper satisfaction.

There was no lack of talent for Henri to discover: there was, indeed, a suspicion that Marguerite was copying her mother and creating her own Flying Squadron of beautiful, biddable and quite unscrupulous maids-in-waiting. If so, she lacked her mother's talent for controlling them, for some actually became her rivals in an increasingly bizarre situation. After Mademoiselle Dayelle had departed, Henri had consoled himself with one of his wife's ladies, a Mademoiselle Rebours—"a malicious girl who disliked me and who endeavoured, by every means in her power, to prejudice me in his eyes," Marguerite remarked. Fortunately, the girl fell seriously ill after a few months and the insatiable Henri promptly turned to another of Marguerite's maids, a girl who bore the attractive nickname of Dimples—Fosseuse—from her family name of Fosseux. She was scarcely more than a child, perhaps fourteen, when the royal eyes fell upon her, and for some months Henri restrained himself, if with difficulty, contenting himself with kisses and caresses, taking the child on his knee and feeding her delicacies. During all this time, Fosseuse continued to be entirely respectful toward her mistress. But then the inevitable happened. Henri did not scruple to use the oldest, most effective, if most ignoble of stratagems to get a girl into his bed. He may even have convinced himself that he wanted, that he intended, to marry the girl of the moment—certainly he convinced her. The inexperienced Fosseuse took his passionate declarations at their face value; his wife was indeed barren, unfaithful, and altogether unworthy of him. Why should not she, Françoise de Fosseux, become Queen of Navarre as soon as Henri could arrange the formality of a divorce? Puffed up with conceit, dazzled with dreams of splendor, the wretched child scornfully regarded her mistress, announcing her pity in loud tones, and began her heady planning for the future.

Marguerite was not particularly upset. She knew her husband well enough now to evaluate these springs with which he sought to catch his plump woodcocks. She was glad enough, too, to have him amused and diverted while she pursued her own fancies. But it was at about this time that there crept into her mind the first cold fear of barrenness, almost certainly created by Fosseuse's loud boasts that she, at least, could provide an heir for Navarre. Marguerite was now in her late twenties; at that age her mother, after that terrifying decade of barrenness, was producing a child a year and so securing her position. For no matter how illustrious the wife's family, no matter how close she and her husband might be or how politically vital was their marriage, the failure to provide an heir could undermine and destroy all else. Marguerite declined to go to the extreme lengths to avert barrenness that her mother had done; she was too fastidious, perhaps, too much aware of the inherently ludicrous nature of the "remedies." But she did go to take the waters at Bagneres, supposedly very beneficial for promoting pregnancy, and passed on the news to her mother with a flippancy that disguised her real and deep anxiety. "I am at the baths of Bagneres, where I have come to see if I shall be fortunate enough to increase the number of your servants."[66] Nothing came of it, yet another example of the irony that pervaded her life: she, blessed with so many gifts, was denied the one that might have given some meaning and purpose to her life.

But for the moment, among the sunshine and flowers of Nérac and with her husband still her ally if not her lover, it scarcely seemed to matter. For the first time in her life she had her own money, the revenues from her vast estates flowing in steadily, to be promptly turned into perfume and wine and rare books and banquets and masques. Even these estates could not keep up with her demand: her chancellor, Pibrac, had to sell her large house in Paris to tide her over an emergency. But it seemed to be merely a temporary embarrassment, for were not the vineyards and the cornfields and the olive groves of her lands eternal and inexhaustible? The "sweet and pleasant" life went on unabated, if increasingly on credit, and, though Nérac was delightful, yet it was still a provincial town, and she took care to keep in touch with the wider world through her racy, vivid letters. Her chief correspondent was that Madame d'Uzès who was also her mother's intimate confidante: "Ma Sibille," Marguerite called her, and made of a woman twenty-five years her senior a close friend, opening her heart in a way she rarely did with any other, and was not betrayed. She apologizes for the dullness of her letters, but "Gascony is dull and can therefore produce only dull news." A little later she amends that: "I am, in fact, very happy and content here in Nérac—I say that without dissimulation." The waters had apparently not effected a permanent cure for her erysipelas: she asked Madame d'Uzès to send her a special powder "because I have found nothing better for the blisters to which I am a little subject at the moment."[67] And always she asks for news of the court, of her brothers and friends in Paris. For much had happened over those past few months, the most important being that Alençon and the king had been reconciled and that Bussy, the swaggering, heartless, debonair Bussy-d'Amboise, was dead, hacked and pierced by more than a half dozen swords and daggers.

Bussy owed his theatrical death directly to the man whom he

had served faithfully according to his lights. He had written a light-hearted letter to Alençon boasting, among other things, that "he had cast his nets over the hind of the Grand Huntsman and held her fast in his toils." The Grand Huntsman of the realm was the choleric count of Montsoreau and, normally, Alençon would have been highly amused to hear that this self-satisfied man was about to be cuckolded by his friend. But he and Bussy had recently had a bitter quarrel and Alençon, from malice, perhaps, or simply from a desire to ingratiate himself, showed the letter to his brother. Henri, seizing the chance to revenge himself on the man who had abandoned his service, passed the letter on to Montsoreau and he, in his turn, simply gave his wife the stark alternative of immediate death or her help in trapping Bussy. Montsoreau, too, wanted his revenge, but he had a very healthy respect for Bussy's ability as a swordsman. The unfortunate lady was therefore forced to write to her lover, arranging an assignation, but when Bussy arrived he was met not by the scented and sighing lady of his feverish dreams but by a pack of revengeful males. He died as he had lived, with gaiety and lunatic courage. The sword in his hand was shattered after he had severly wounded some of his assailants, but he seized a bench and continued to fight with that until at last he sank under the sheer weight of numbers.

Marguerite said nothing about his death, either in her memoirs or even in those intimate letters to Madame d'Uzès. The subject was, perhaps, too poignant: Bussy belonged to her youth, to the relatively innocent and hopeful years, and that blood-spattered death drew a thick and lurid line between what was and what might have been. And the blue skies of Nérac, too, were beginning to cloud over, harbinger of the storm that was to burst over her. In the spring of 1580 she had an extraordinary letter from her chancellor, Pibrac, who had gone to Paris on official business. An astrologer had told him that she would die at the hands of her jealous husband before the end of the month, and he wrote, begging her to leave Nérac at once. She was furious, even though she might have admitted to a twinge of alarm, considering her affair with the Viscount of Turenne. Pibrac undoubtedly meant well—he was by now thoroughly besotted with love for her—but his clumsy attempts to help involved her in an increasingly bizarre situation. The King of France learned of her affair with Turenne, probably through Pibrac's indiscretion, and, over-joyed at the opportunity at once to wound his sister and weaken her alliance with her husband, he wrote to Navarre telling him about the affair. Navarre put the letter before her with his habitual broad grin, pretending that he believed not a word of it, and she had no choice but to smile back, inwardly seething, dismissing the matter as her brother's malice even while she promised herself vengeance upon the clumsy Sieur de Pibrac.

In May 1580 war came again to the south.

Afterward, there were to be many and bitter recriminations regarding who was supposed to have started it. Navarre claimed that the Governor of Guyenne, the Marshal Biron, deliberately provoked the Huguenots so that they could be crushed once for all; the marshal claimed that the Huguenots had broken the treaty of Nérac and were persecuting the Catholic minorities in their area. In Paris, the king contemptuously put it down to far more frivolous reasons: it was Marguerite who was the cause of it, he claimed, revenging herself because he had revealed her adultery. One of his *mignons* laughed and said it was a lovers' war, and it was as the *Guerre Amoureuse* that the civil war went down in history. In fact, the true origin of the war was simply spontaneous combustion; the treaty of Nérac had merely damped down, not extinguished, the fire that had been smouldering for a generation.

The Lovers' War brought political and military benefit to no-body, although it enabled Navarre to appear in that heroic role which was to be his greatest asset in the struggle for the heart of France over the coming years. A Gascon, he actually seemed to like fighting, to enjoy the dust and turmoil, the lethal gamble of the nerve-tingling business where fear and excitement were only two words for the same thing. He went over immediately to the offensive with an attack upon Cahors. The city was part of his wife's dowry but the fanatical Catholics who formed the bulk of its population declined to become part of the Huguenot kingdom—a fact that undoubtedly led the king to choose it for Marguerite's appanage. Navarre attacked at midnight with a strong force. The city was a natural fortress, situated on a high bluff so that it was surrounded on three sides by the river Lot, and its citizens resisted vigorously. It took the Huguenots five days and nights of almost continuous fighting to gain the town, fighting in which the King of Navarre lightheartedly took far greater risks than the lowest of his mercenaries. The distinctive white plumes of his helmet formed as excellent a target for arquebus or crossbow as they did a rallying point for his men, but somehow he survived bullets, bolts, halberd and sword thrusts as the invaders inched their way forward house by house and street by street. Marguerite was impressed: "he conducted himself less like a prince of quality than a daring and experienced general," she remarked, but had the political acumen to add the rider that "the taking of this town weakened, rather than strengthened" the Huguenots because it would have required a disproportionately large force to hold down the smouldering Catholics. In Paris, the king immediately assumed that his sister was up to her old tricks of plaguing him—for was not Cahors her own personal appanage? He summoned her unfortunate chancellor Pibrac and in a public audience humiliated and threatened Marguerite in the person of her chief official. Was not Pibrac aware that Cahors had been sacked, its inhabitants massacred, the very goods of the Church exposed for public sale in Nérac? "The officers my sister appointed to the city betrayed it and received the enemy. I won't give her a further chance to injure me. All her lands will be seized and, as far as you are concerned, I forbid you to use her seal or perform any other offices for her."[68]

Pibrac's devotion and legal skill were just sufficient to extricate his mistress from that particular tangle, but she remained in an impossible position, the inevitable scapegoat for the failures and disappointments of either side. She might, perhaps, have been better advised to withdraw altogether and take up residence in some city removed from the battle area, but there was still alive within her the hope and desperate need to create a life for herself free from the pressures of both mother and brother. Her marriage was a failure as a marriage, but it was still the only path open to her and, courageously, she supported her husband not only morally but politically, giving precise instructions to the officers of the cities of her appanage that the Huguenot cause was to be supported in their cities. In Paris, Pibrac was able to win a concession for her: both the king and the queen mother agreed that when she was resident in Nérac the city should be treated as neutral—provided that her husband kept away from it.

The war made no difference at all to the gaiety of life in Nérac, unless perhaps it added a touch of glamor and excitement. Musicians and jugglers and comedians still found their way thither, assured of a warm welcome and generous fees; jewelers, costumers, goldsmiths, silversmiths plied their craft without diminution. Occasionally, there was a shortage of male company but this was of very brief duration. Despite the prohibition, the King of Navarre returned again and again to the gay little town, for Fosseuse—"my girl" as he called her —still remained with her mistress in order to satisfy the proprieties. And with Henri came his young men, all attracted to this honeypot of a pleasure dome where the most delectable and highborn girls of France were to be had for the asking. The conditions on which Nérac were to be treated as neutral were broken, and Biron, the royalist general, immediate took advantage of the fact. Tired of chasing the elusive Navarre through the wild mountain country, he waited until his quarry was dallying in Nérac and then brought up his troops. A sudden heavy rainfall incapacitated the arquebusiers who were to make the assault and, as a sudden, desperate bid to bring off a coup, he ordered up the artillery and sent seven or eight volleys into the town, one ball of which actually hit the castle in which Marguerite was staying. She was furious, despite the fact that Biron had a perfect right to take advantage of the violated conditions, despite the fact that he had always been most scrupulous in his conduct toward the king's sister during this regrettable war, even returning to her unread some of her letters that his men had captured. He now sent a trumpeter to apologize for that unlucky shot, but she sent the man back with the haughty message that Biron "might perfectly well have allowed me to enjoy the pleasure of seeing the king my husband in Nérac, that I was extremely offended at his conduct and that I should complain of it to the king." The sheer audacity of Marguerite's actions sometimes achieved the most unexpected results: she did indeed complain to the king and he did indeed—probably to his own surprise—discipline Biron for doing his duty.

But this war was merely a "fire of straw," as a royalist remarked contemptuously; almost everyone involved was seeking a way to end it without loss of prestige. In the autumn of 1580 Alençon offered his services as mediator to his brother and he arrived in Nérac bringing with him a handsome young equerry, Harlay de Chanvallon, and a seemingly limitless capacity for intrigue and mischief. Immediately on arrival he threw himself into the congenial business of pursuing Navarre's mistress, Fosseuse, and succeeded so well as to enrage his host, alarm his sister and jeopardize the peace which should have come as a mere formality. Marguerite took the young wastrel aside and pleaded with him to abandon the chase: her husband, she said, actually believed that she was jealous of his affair with Fosseuse and accused her of encouraging Alençon. Her brother agreed to look elsewhere, "caring as he did more for my happiness than his own," Marguerite tried to persuade herself. Alençon, in fact, had urgent need of troops to accompany him into Flanders, and while this pointless war raged in the south, he was being denied the glory that was his by right. He therefore abandoned Fosseuse, hurried through the treaty and, in the spring of 1581, left Nérac for the north, taking with him the beautiful Chanvallon and leaving behind a somewhat wistful, somewhat restless Marguerite.

She had been in the south for well over three years now. Nérac was beginning to lose something of its glitter, something of its attractions. The balls and banquets and more or less serious flirtations went on, but there was a certain hollowness in the gaiety. She was reluctant to admit it but the little court she had built up was essentially provincial. Her true world was the elaborate, labyrinthine world of Paris and Amboise and Chenonceaux, not this unsophisticated world of Pau and Nérac and Agen, where the men drank like Flemings and

smelled like goats, and where the older women looked askance at any
feminine activity that was not directed toward cradle or kitchen or
church. She had her own, miniature Flying Squadron, perhaps, but
she was too young to treat them with the benign tyranny that her
mother managed so successfully and too old—too mature and intelligent—to identify herself with their empty little pleasures and triumphs.

She was beginning to regret, too, the loss of a servant whom
she had treated with derision but who, she swiftly realized, had done
much to guide her through the problems that beset a landowner of
her stature. She owed much to Pibrac. Not only had he given her
excellent legal advice here in the south but had courageously champi-
oned her in Paris and even lent her money. But he had dared to
presume, playing Malvolio to her Olivia. After she had received that
preposterous letter of his, in which he had passed on his astrologer's
warning, she had replied in a towering rage. She had reason to be
annoyed; in her ambivalent position with her husband, it was hardly
tactful, to say the least, to put on paper the warning that he intended
to murder her for unfaithfulness. Pibrac wrote back pitifully, protesting that he had acted only for the best, pleading that he had done so
only because of the great love he bore her. Marguerite reacted un-
characteristically. She could be charged, with justice, with many a
social transgression—but meanness of spirit was not among them.
Now, however, she turned viciously on the man whose only real fault
was tactlessness. First she showed his pathetic lawyer's love letter to
her husband—a choice titbit which eventually found its way into the
Divorce satyrique—"she showed me her pimp Pibrac's letters and we
laughed merrily over them." Then she wrote again to Pibrac, a spite-
ful little letter, accusing him of double-dealing, expressing surprise
that a man of his years could write like a green youth. Pibrac wrote
back an immense letter, page after page of prosy argument in which
the indignant lawyer struggled with the heartbroken lover. Treating
her emotional outbursts as though they were legal documents, he
analyzed and quoted them at length, proving to any unbiased person
that he had discharged his duties honorably and competently and

with a belated pride tried to cover up his lapse. "Our fashion nowadays is full of excesses in speech. We no longer make use of the words 'to love' and 'to serve.' One adds to them 'extremely,' 'passionately,' 'madly' and similar expressions—we even invest with divinity things which are less than human."[69] But Marguerite was in no mood for a scholarly dissertation on superlatives and simply curtly ordered him to surrender his seals, thus relinquishing his office as her chancellor.

The anger and contempt with which she treated the wretched Pibrac was an index to the uncertainty of her own situation, the uneasiness with which she now regarded her own future—poor Pibrac merely received a backlash. Deep within her was the first dismaying knowledge that all was not well, and never would be well, between herself and her husband. In pursuit of her desire for independence from her family, she had identified herself wholly, courageously and at considerable cost with her husband. He had taken everything, with that disarming grin of his, but, far from giving anything in return, had gone on demanding. And at last the distasteful, ludicrous business of Fosseuse had forced her to recognize that her husband regarded his wife simply as an instrument to be used when required.

Shortly after peace had been declared Fosseuse announced a desire to take the waters at Aigues-Caudre near Pau and received permission from Marguerite to absent herself. But that was not at all what was required: apparently it was necessary that the Queen of Navarre should personally accompany her delinquent servant in order that scandal be avoided. She refused outright, for she loathed Pau. Henri lost his temper and, for the first time in their relationship, threatened her physically, swearing that he would carry her bodily to the Spa. She still refused and, reluctant to come to an open break, he accepted her conciliatory offer to send two of her other ladies-in-waiting as chaperones to Fosseuse. The offer was by no means disinterested, for one of the two girls was the discarded Mademoiselle Rebours, "a depraved and deceitful girl who was only desirous of ousting Fosseuse in order that she might supplant her in the favor of the king my husband," and who, for her own purposes, now kept Marguerite minutely informed of Fosseuse's hopeful plans.

Fosseuse's condition had now become so very obvious that Marguerite swallowed her pride and summoned the girl to her boudoir. Wisely, she did not adopt the attitude of queen to subject or even that of offended wife but simply that of a mature woman of nearly thirty to a girl half her age. She pointed out how the scandal would affect all of them and how necessary it was for Fosseuse to leave the court and keep away from the king until her child was born. In order to maintain the proprieties, she even offered to leave Nérac herself, on plea of a recent outbreak of plague, and, taking Fosseuse and a handful of servants with her, stay in a remote country house until the child was born.

Marguerite was undoubtedly acting out of self-interest, but it was an enlightened self-interest. No matter that the whole world knew that Henri de Navarre sped from bed to bed as opportunity presented itself; the fathering of a bastard among his wife's own maids of honor was so grotesque a transgression that it could bring only mockery to husband, wife and mistress alike. But Fosseuse, after listening sulkily, shouted out that she would be revenged on all who gossiped about her, that Marguerite had always hated her and she would be paid out for it. She then flounced out of the room and took her complaints to Navarre; he, at the infatuated stage of his affair, took her part and quarreled bitterly with his wife. So matters continued until the time for Fosseuse's confinement arrived.

The first Marguerite knew of the event was in the early hours of the morning when her husband urgently shook her awake. She might have reflected wryly on the times she was forced to face a traumatic situation while struggling up from sleep, for now it was to find Navarre bending over her and begging her assistance. Fosseuse's labor had started in the room which she shared with the other maids of honor, and belatedly Navarre realized just how squalid could be the scandal that resulted. Would Marguerite help? he asked, abasing himself, abjectly apologizing for his manner in the past. She reacted generously, competently, swiftly, issuing a string of orders as she hastily dressed. Navarre himself was to leave the palace immediately with all his suite and go off for a day's hunting, leaving the rest to her. She then had Fosseuse carried out of the dormitory into a separate room, summoned her own doctor and the more discreet of her servants, and personally supervised the birth. The labor was over swiftly and it was with a very real and quite undisguised sense of relief that Marguerite saw that her adolescent rival had given birth to a stillborn daughter, instead of the living son who might perhaps have opened a path for his mother to the throne of Navarre. The tiny corpse was disposed of and Fosseuse carried back to the dormitory.

Marguerite genuinely seems to have thought that it would prove entirely possible to hide the fact of the birth, wholly overlooking the excited gossip and speculation that must surely have arisen among the other maids of honor when they saw their colleague carried out and brought back a few hours later. By midafternoon the story had sped round the castle and when Navarre returned, late that night, he immediately heard its every detail. He hastened to the girl and she begged him to persuade Marguerite to visit her. This was the queen's custom whenever one of her women was sick, and if she did not do so now, Fosseuse pleaded, everyone would conclude that she had an excellent reason for not doing so. Her besotted lover agreed, and stumped off to his wife's bedroom. She was in bed. It had been a very long, very trying day and she had retired early and now was certainly in no mood to get up, dress and visit a girl who had done her nothing but harm. She said so, vigorously, pointing out that Fosseuse no longer had need of her assistance and any undue solicitude on her part would merely arouse, instead of conceal, suspicion. Navarre was furiously angry, forgetful of his abject pleas and promises of the early morning; she shouted back and the day ended in bitter mutual recriminations.

It was probably at this point that the Navarre marriage ended. It would endure, as an outward form, for another twenty years, but it was as though Navarre had hammered a wedge into a fissure that might, perhaps, have never opened wider. Massacre, religious difference, mutual infidelity, the unrelenting hostility of the king and the queen mother—none of these had done the damage achieved by Navarre's egoism, his total inability to realize that he was subjecting his wife to an intolerable degree of humiliation, his total indifference to her as a human being.

Shortly after the affair she received not only a pressing invitation from her mother and brother to visit Paris but also some fifteen thousand crowns to pay for her expenses. Reasonably, she treated the invitation with deep suspicion. It was, she believed, yet another attempt to break up her marriage, for if she and Navarre were separated, "it would prove like the breaking of the Macedonian battallion." But the invitation came when she was particularly vulnerable, smouldering over her husband's squalid ingratitude, bored with the provincial court and beginning to think wistfully of the splendors of Paris. The ready cash—that tinkling, glittering shower of fifteen thousand golden coins—was also a powerful incentive. Somehow, she was never to obtain the full revenues of her immense estates, partly through the ravages of war but mostly because she never again had such a servant as Pibrac, at once competent, honest, and devoted; already she was suffering the first of the financial crises which were to plague her for the rest of her life. The cost of her household in Nérac was borne entirely by herself; in Paris it would be heavily subsidized by the royal purse even though the price she would have to pay would be her independence. Weighing all the factors, she decided to go. And when the decision had been made, so eager was she to put Nérac behind her that she began her long journey in the depth of winter, leaving the south in January 1582.

XII

Descent into the Abyss

She traveled northward leisurely. Spring found her in Touraine among the flowers and meadows she had known as a child, and she progressed from one to the other of the great castles, each of which marked some crisis in her life—Amboise, Chenonceaux, Blois, Chaumont. It was not until late in May that she and her enormous entourage arrived at Fontainebleau, where the king and her mother were awaiting her. Their greeting could not have been more cordial; politics might have dictated the necessity of presenting a common front but infusing it, too, was that extraordinary Valois family sentiment which drew the members together even when they hated each other. In the momentary euphoria of a family meeting after nearly five years, Catherine was anxious to help her chronically penurious daughter and divested herself of the prestigious Duchy of Valois in Marguerite's favor. Supplied with new funds, Marguerite set about making a fitting background for herself. Her entourage was much too large to be lodged in the already overcrowded Louvre and, in any case, the windfall allowed her to maintain that independence she cherished. She therefore bought the imposing house recently vacated by her mother's chancellor Birague and established it as the official Navarre residence in Paris.

For it was by no means only personal vanity that urged her to such a heavy expense. During the five-month journey from Navarre she had been able to put matters in a more optimistic perspective. The relationship between herself and her husband was unchanged; they still had political need of each other, and if a girl less hostile to herself than Fosseuse could be placed in his bed, then their old mutual tolerance would be revived. To that end she had actually brought Fosseuse along with her, despite his protests, and now that she was established in Paris, she threw herself energetically into being the Queen of Navarre, dispatching a stream of informative and amusing letters to her husband. In one of her first letters she wrote to Navarre, "We shall see the king at Fontainebleau in four days' times and the day following I will send a messenger to you to tell you what happened. Five or six days later I will send another to inform you what I have been able to discover in respect of their wishes concerning us after those first greetings which are commonly marked with restraint and dissimulation."[70] She gave her husband some good advice about putting his kingdom in order: two of his subjects had been indulging in private wars and there was talk of the King of France himself traveling south to settle matters. In a later letter she returned to the problem of communication between the two courts, strongly advising him to come to Paris in person. "If you were here you would be the man on whom both sides depend. You would gain the servants you have lost, owing to the length of these troubles, and would acquire more of them in a week than you would all your life time in Gascony."[71] Mixed in with the solid political advice are nuggets of gossip, brief little vignettes of life at court: "M. de Nemours has become so very fat that he is quite deformed; M. de Guise has grown thin and seems much aged. . . . the king has been hunting for three days and afterwards we went to a concert at the Louvre which lasted all night. . . ." Each of the letters bears an imprint of sincerity, a rather desperate urge to please and to be found of use, only lightly masked by their casual tone.

Henri de Navarre rejected alike the advice and the implicit plea. He, unlike his unfortunate wife, had found his role in society and in history—and emphatically, it no longer included her. In part, his rejection of her sprang from that inner selfishness which marked his relationship with all those who had served their turn. But there was, too, some justification of his coldness toward the daughter of Catherine de Médicis and the sister of Henri III, the instigators of the Massacre of Saint Bartholomew, hostile leaders of the hostile Catholic faction. He had, altogether, good grounds to walk warily of the woman who might, after all, be simply a spy in his household, but he chose a singularly shabby way to begin his disassociation from her, again, through the shallow little Mademoiselle Fosseuse.

Marguerite had deeply shocked her mother by bringing Fosseuse to Paris with her. Catherine de Médicis could equably enough forward plans that could bring about the deaths of thousands; she was probably not above using poison as a means of disposing of individual enemies of State or family, but she believed very strongly indeed in the proprieties, particularly where the sexes were concerned. Marguerite was surprised and rather amused by her mother's vehement objections to the presence of her husband's mistress among her maids of honor, but obediently she got rid of the girl. She treated Fosseuse very generously indeed, considering all that had gone before, arranging a very advantageous match with one of the minor nobility. Henri de Navarre was beside himself with fury when he heard that his delectable Fosseuse had been removed permanently from his embraces and he promptly sent one of his staff, the Sieur de Frontenac, to reproach Marguerite and demand that she reinstate Fosseuse among her women. At this, Marguerite's long tolerance suddenly snapped, the long-disguised humiliation and bitterness welling to the surface in one of her finest letters, a generous, indignant rejection of a mean, unworthy complaint. "You say that there is nothing for me to be ashamed of in pleasing you. This should indeed be the case where it does not affect my honour—in which you too have an interest. But if you demand that I keep near my person a girl whom you have made a mother, you must surely put me to shame both because of the insult itself and the reputation I should thereby acquire. You write to me that, in order to close the mouths of the King and Queen and those who speak to me about it, I should tell them that you love her and that, for this reason, I love her too. This reason would be a good one if I were speaking of one of your servants, whether male or female. But of your mistress . . . !"[72]

Henri de Navarre was far gone in infatuation but even he might have been pulled up short by this letter. Unfortunately, however, his mother-in-law heard of his complaint and lumbered into the attack with one of her own bludgeons. In a letter so angry that in places it is almost incoherent, she treated her erring son-in-law to an historical essay on the place of mistresses at the French court. Why, her own husband had had three mistresses, and when one of them became pregnant he sent her away. And for Navarre to send his complaint "by a little gallant, presumptuous and imprudent to have accepted such a command from his master . . ." She rushed to Marguerite's defense, making it plain that though her children were now grown men and women, kings and queens in their own right, she was still their defender and arbiter of morality. "I have caused this pretty fool Fosseuse to be sent away for, so long as I live, I will not endure that those near to me, such as she [Marguerite] is shall be diminished in their affection. And I entreat you that, after this fine messenger of a Frontenac has said the worst he can to estrange you and your wife, to consider the wrong that you have done her and return to the right path."[73] Like many a man before and after him, Navarre must have reflected that, on marrying the girl, he had acquired the mother, and now congratulated himself on the four hundred miles that lay between Pau and Paris. But whether or not Catherine's letter caused the final rupture between her daughter and son-in-law, certainly the letter marked it. Marguerite's own lighthearted, sensible letters to Navarre tailed off abruptly. This was the second occasion on which her sincere attempt to behave as the Queen of Navarre and her husband's ally had been crudely rejected. There would not be a third occasion. And there was small wonder that, about now, there blossomed the last real love of her life, the affair with Harlay de Chanvallon, the handsome young equerry who had accompanied her brother Alençon into Navarre the previous autumn.

In one of her letters to Chanvallon Marguerite called him—
with a kind of irritated tenderness—Narcissus, and the name seems
curiosly apposite for one who drifted into and out of her life with the
insubstantiality of a reflection. All her previous lovers—Guise, La
Mole, Bussy, Turenne—had been very positive men of action; Harlay
de Chanvallon was far more at his ease in boudoir or ballroom than
on battlefied or in council chamberr. He was undeniably handsome
—beautiful was the word that tended to spring to people's lips; he
was elegant; he seems to have been well-meaning if rather weak. Yet
these commonplace characteristics of a not particularly well-born
young man were sufficient now to inflame a woman who had a highly
developed sense of the excellent, as well as the pick of the nobility
of France. Her glance had, in fact, passed blankly over him when they
had first met. That meeting had taken place at the council of war in
La Fère nearly four years earlier, and Marguerite certainly had seen
nothing special in her brother's equerry. But when they had come to
Nérac, at a time when her superb self-confidence was beginning to
be eroded, she had looked with greater interest on the beautiful blond
youth who made no secret of his passionate admiration. And when
they met again in Paris during that bitter period when she learned
just exactly what she was worth to her husband, it was easy enough
to fashion the sensual attraction for a handsome, not very clever
young man into an undying love affair worthy of a Greek tragedian.
Throughout her affair with Chanvallon there sounds the rather desperate note of someone trying to overcome emotional doubt with
intellectual conviction. The passionate letters she wrote to him were
wholly unlike anything else she ever penned. Even when she was
setting out to deceive, her style always remained clear, the literary
ornaments graceful and appropriate, an occasional waspish aside giving a touch of realism and humor. Her letters to Chanvallon were
wholly cerebral and in the worst possible style of Renaissance conceit, with ridiculous simile piled on ridiculous simile, the whole held
together by tortuous metaphysics that at times becomes quite incoherent and meaningless. It is difficult to imagine Chanvallon reading
them with anything but irritation and embarrassment. He seems,

indeed, to have taken fright, for not long after Marguerite's return to Paris and their supposedly ecstatic reunion, he baldly announced his engagement to the daughter of the Duke of Bouillon. Marguerite flew into a violent rage, but even now there was something contrived about her reaction, something ineradicably self-conscious and theatrical about the letter with which she dismissed her faithless lover. "Triumph, triumph over my too-ardent love! Boast of having deceived me! Laugh and mock at it with her for I shall have the consolation of knowing that her entire lack of merit will be the penalty of the wrong you have committed. When you receive this letter—the last—return it to me I beg you. I do not desire that at this fine interview to which you are going this evening it should serve as a topic of conversation to the father and the daughter."

The affair with Chanvallon might have been largely contrived, a laboriously supported intellectual fantasy, but when it had gone there was nothing to put in its place. That erosion of her self-confidence which had begun in Nérac continued, but with it now was the beginning of an erosion of her integrity. She had always been indifferent to public opinion, pursuing her way with a splendid disregard alike for moral strictures and financial solvency, but in the summer of 1582 her financial carelessness began to appear outright prodigality and waste, the people with whom she surrounded herself just a little less dependable even than those who had gone before. It was during this summer that her household fell wholly under the influence of Jean and Marguerite de Duras and their friend Madame de Béthune, a debauched trio who were to bring much trouble upon their young mistress's head. Again, she was in financial difficulties despite the fact that her mother's wealthy duchy was now added to her own. Many of her financial problems were directly of her own making, the result of a frenetically gay, almost hysterical mode of life; but many, too, were probably the result of straight theft as her officers and confidants hastened to grasp what they could before the inevitable end. Catherine de Médicis shook her ponderous head in something between anger and pity and gave instructions to her faithful servant Bellièvre to keep some watch on the princess as she danced her way to destruction. "The company we keep honours or dishonours and this holds chiefly true of Princesses who are young and think themselves beautiful. . . . Being the daughter of a king and married to a prince who calls himself a king she feels she can do what she likes—instead of rejecting every person who is not worthy to consort with a wise and good princess."

In the spring of 1583 Chanvallon returned to Paris. He had discreetly attached himself again to Alençon's staff and followed his master into Flanders, but they had a blazing row because Chanvallon had boasted in his cups of enjoying the favors of "one of the foremost ladies in the kingdom." Marguerite received back her crestfallen lover, but even this tarnished triumph was only a prelude to further humiliations; a few weeks later she discovered that she was sharing him with her established and practised rival Madame de Sauves. Irony had not yet finished with her. She fell ill and took to her bed, suffering less from a broken heart—for she knew Chanvallon's worth —than from the first visitation of that disease of dropsy which was to transform her, the golden goddess of beauty, into a figure purely grotesque. And it was her misfortune that the symptoms of that disease should closely resemble the symptoms of another condition.

It was the Tuscan ambassador who first put the suspicion into official but still secret words. "The Queen of Navarre is pregnant— or suffering from dropsy," he informed his government, and by the end of June the rumor of her pregnancy was being repeated as fact. The king her brother, who had been watching her throughout with a steady malevolence, bribed one of her women to report on her affairs. The woman provided some interesting details. Yes, M. de Chanvallon was indeed a very close friend of her mistress. Yes, he had spent many a night with her. And yes, the condition of the Queen of Navarre could indeed be attributed to the same handsome and careless young man. The rumors and accusations floated through the court and the city and came back at last to Marguerite's ears, together with the warning that her brother was planning some mischief. She reacted in her old generous and spirited manner, immediately warning Chanvallon and urging him to quit the town. Of all the letters she wrote to him, it was this last one, in which she ended the affair, that was most truly her own, a cry of pain and love unmarred by literary conceits. "Please God that on me alone this storm may expend itself. But to place you in danger—! Ah no, my life: there is no suffering so cruel to which I would not prefer to submit. How better can I show this than by depriving myself of you. Go. go."[74] And Harlay de Chanvallon went, hurrying out of Paris and of France to seek the safety of relatives in Germany, convincing himself, perhaps, that no great harm could come to a Daughter of France for a mere peccadillo. He had not played a very noble role, but he was young, frightened by the overwhelming personality of the woman who had so unexpectedly become his mistress, and even more frightened by the lethal world that was her normal milieu, a world in which a simple adulterous liaison could be construed as treason and avenged as such. Sensibly enough, he ran, and with him went the last of the reputable lovers of Marguerite of Navarre. Each of those who came after would be just a little lower in the social or moral sphere.

The storm that Marguerite feared did not immediately break. It probably would not have broken at all if her mother had been in Paris. But Catherine de Médicis had her own tragedy with which to contend. Young Alençon's Flanders expedition had ended in shame and disaster with his treacherous attempt on Antwerp and his mother had hastened to him to retrieve what could be retrieved. "Would God that you had died young," she burst out when they met. "You would not then have been the cause of the death of so many brave gentlemen." But Alençon was already a dying man, victim of that hereditary tuberculosis which had carried off his two brothers, and Catherine, who had come to chastise the rebel, stayed to comfort the invalid, knowing from most bitter experience that she would not long be troubled with this least attractive of her children.

It so happened, too, that, in that same month of August, Henri's wife Louise was also absent from Paris: at a crucial moment for Marguerite, the only two sane and constant influences upon the king were withdrawn.

Afterward, Henri defended himself by claiming that he acted

on State grounds: agents of Marguerite, he said, had attacked a royal courier and stolen a letter in which he had complained of her scandalous conduct. Certainly a royal courier was attacked on the way to Rome, but the stolen dispatches were of far greater interest to the growing Guise party than they were to the unfortunate Queen of Navarre. But whatever his pretext, his actions were informed by unadulterated sadism, a dedicated, feline cruelty carried out after meticulous planning and with the sole object at once to shatter the nerve and the public reputation of his sister. Courteously, he invited her to take the place of his absent wife at a grand ball to be held at the Louvre on the night of August 8. She accepted: in the absence of both the queen mother and the Queen of France, protocol naturally dictated that the Daughter of France should be the lady of the revels. After the banquet the king led his beautiful sister to the flower-crowed throne on its great dais, bowed respectfully and withdrew to lead off the dance. From her raised situation she would have been able to see one of the most brilliant social events in Europe, a ball at the Valois court of France, an assembly of some hundreds of men and women, dressed in somewhat garish colors, each bearing a fortune in minerals and fabrics upon his or her back, creating an intricate pattern of color and movement and sound with every outward appearance of happiness and pleasure. It was, in fact, to be the last such in which she would ever take part: when next she attended a ball in this great room, the Valois dynasty would have passed into history and she herself would be a fat and aging woman.

Sometime after the commencement of the ball, the king led a little procession toward her throne. She may, perhaps, have thought that he intended to claim her for a dance—the time had been when these two could dazzle the world with the beauty and intricacy of their movements. The procession, however, was unusual, for it was exclusively male: the king, flanked by his two favorites, the Duke d'Épernon and the Duke of Joyeuse and followed by lesser *mignons*. The presence of Épernon and Joyeuse should have warned her: both men hated her—hated her because their master and lover hated her but also because that scintillating, biting wit of hers had again and again made them a mockery in the court, sometimes to their face, sometimes by twining their names in pithy little epigrams which were delightedly repeated by those outside the royal circle of favor. And *mignons* though they might be, both were formidable men, highly intelligent and quite ruthless and determined upon her degradation. The dancing appears to have ceased when the little group arrived at the foot of the dais for the king's words were clearly audible throughout the room—so clear that the Austrian ambassador Busbecq was able to make a record of them.

Henri began by upbraiding her for her affair with Chamvallon and then went onto accuse her directly not merely of being pregnant but of actually having had a child by him. He then went back into the past and, with what seems to have been impressive accuracy, enumerated all the lovers she had had since her marriage, "naming so precisely dates and places," Busbecq remarks, "that he seemed to have been a witness of the incidents of which he spoke."[75] On and on went the hysterical tirade, while Marguerite, deserted alike by her wit and composure, sat utterly silent and motionless, her face dead white, her eyes blank with shock, until her brother screamed, as climax, that she was to quit Paris "and deliver the court from her contagious presence." She got up then and stumbled out of the silent room, and her ladies hurried her out of the palace and into her own Hôtel de Birague where she slept that night—if she slept at all. The following morning her coach and escort were waiting for her and she entered it, accompanied by Mesdames Duras and Béthune. She was in a pitiable state of indecision, likening herself to the wretched Mary Stuart, wringing her hands, praying that some kind friend would poison her. But even now her brother had not finished with her. A few miles outside Paris the coach was brought to a halt by a band of the royal archers, and Gremonville, the king's personal bodyguard, stuck his head in at the window and brusquely ordered all the ladies inside to remove their traveling masks. They refused, whereupon the man half climbed into the coach and, stretching out his hand, personally tore the mask from each of the women. Marguerite exploded. "Miserable wretch, do you dare to lift your hand against the sister of your king?" "I am acting on his orders, "Gremonville replied unarguably. What Marguerite did not know was that Chamvallon's lodgings had been raided the night before and Henri suspected that Marguerite was trying to spirit her lover away dressed as one of her ladies. Balked, Gremonville nevertheless ordered Mesdames Béthune and Duras to leave the carriage, ignoring Marguerite's protests, and proceeded to arrest eight others of her escort; only then was her coach allowed to continue on its way. About a mile farther down the road, she recognized the king's coach with her brother inside it; ostensibly, he was dining out of town; in fact, he was probably intent on insuring that his orders were carried out. As her coach clattered past his, Marguerite leaned out imploringly but he looked stonily ahead. They were never to meet again.

Henri was in a dilemma. His humiliation of Marguerite had probably been the result of the same combination of spontaneous hatred and bad advice which had led to the brief arrest of Alençon that night in the Louvre. Then, however, there had been his mother to smooth things over, to bribe and threaten and arrange, while now that archdiplomat was many miles away. It was necessary now that he should provide some justification for the public humiliation of the wife of the Huguenot leader and he went about it clumsily. He still believed—or affected to believe—that Marguerite had given birth to a child by Chanvallon, and it was to find evidence to substantiate such a charge that he had ordered the arrest of Marguerite's ladies and officers. Considerably to his embarrassment, the investigators could wring no damaging confession from either the men or the women. Torture might have produced a more satisfactory result, but by that time his mother had heard the incredible story and, though unable to return in person, had promptly dispatched the Bishop of Langres with so vehement a protest as to make Henri regret even more the situation in which he had placed himself. He took an oblique revenge on Marguerite by insisting that Mesdames Béthune and Duras be dismissed from her service because of their evil influence, but otherwise never referred again to his sister's supposed bastard. The phantom infant was to enjoy a long life in French legendry, however, furnished with identity, name and career by Protestant polemics. "He is still living," the Huguenot chronicler Dupleix recorded some years after Marguerite's death. "He is a Capuchin called Friar Ange. I was formerly acquainted with him."[76]

Meanwhile, Marguerite was in a species of limbo: her brother had ordered her to return to her husband, but her husband was debating whether to have her back. The first that Navarre had officially heard of the matter was a letter from the king explaining that he had ordered the dismissal of Marguerite's two senior ladies-in-waiting "because they were most pernicious vermin, not worthy to be endured about the person of a princess." Navarre replied with that irony of which he was a master. "The rumours of the evil and scandalous lives of Mesdames de Duras and de Béthune had indeed reached me. But I considered that, because my wife had the honour to be near your Majesties I should be wronging your natural goodness were I to be more solicitous for her good name from a distance, than your Majesties close at hand."[77] His barbed reply dispatched, Navarre sat back and awaited his brother-in-law's next move. It came immediately. The king had by now been in communication with his mother, was uneasily aware just how much of a fool he had made himself and was doing his best to get out of an unpleasant position. He begged Navarre to attach no importance to any report he might receive about his wife. It was all a mistake, a grievous calumny against a virtuous princess, a falsehood. . . .

Intrigued and scenting a political advantage in that public dishonoring of the king's sister, Navarre dispatched his counselor Duplessis-Mornay to find out more about the matter. Duplessis-Mornay was the intellectual leader of the Huguenots, a scholar and something of a puritan but also an upright and forceful man. "The Pope of the Huguenots," the Catholics called him, half in scorn but also with an unwilling touch of admiration. He was not, perhaps, the ideal person to undertake a delicate mission of this nature, being a man who ever preferred to take the war into the enemy's country, scorning hints and half-truths. But this was the very reason why Navarre—himself so devious and complex behind a simple front—chose him: this was the moment when a good, hard push could probably achieve more than a subtle approach. The fact that the Queen of Navarre might be badly injured in the process was regrettable but irrelevant.

Duplessis-Mornay pushed almost too hard. He found the king in his hesitant, unusually placatory mood and immediately went over to the attack. He ignored the incident in the ballroom, presumably because even he was reluctant to meddle in a quarrel between brother and sister, but complained justifiably of the insult which had been offered the Queen of Navarre by a common soldier who claimed to be acting expressly on the king's orders. "It is an affront which no princess of her rank has ever before received. It is impossible to conceal it. The incident took place, in the daytime, on a high road and all Europe is discussing it. The King of Navarre has reason to fear that the Queen his wife has committed some very criminal act since you yourself, Sire, have been able to treat thus your own sister. Of what is she guilty, to be so cruelly humiliated? What action ought her husband to take?"

The king tried to evade the question, muttering something about the scandalous behavior of Mesdames Béthune and Duras. Duplessis-Mornay interrupted him with remarkable boldness: "I'm not here to plead their cause. The question at issue concerns the Queen. If she has deserved the affront, my master demands justice from you against her for you are the head of the house, the father of the family. But if she is the victim of false reports, he demands that you punish openly those who have slandered her." Henri still did not take open offense, pleading first that the matter had been much exaggerated and then falling back on the feeble excuse that the matter touched the honor of his mother and brother as well as himself and he must consult them before taking any action. "That will mean a very considerable delay," said the Huguenot. "The arrow is in the wound and you make no attempt to extract it. The Queen your sister is on the way to join the King her husband. What will Christendom say if he receives her thus besmirched?" But Henri had at last had enough. "What can it say," he snarled back, "except that he is receiving the sister of your king."[78]

Marguerite was meanwhile drifting uneasily, uncertainly between Paris and Nérac. Lack of money was now added to all her other troubles. The frenetic extravagance of the past year had long since gulped down all ready cash; creditors had seized upon what negotiable income was available and now, in the sensitive manner of financiers, faithfully reflected the king's displeasure by refusing further loans. From Vendôme she wrote a truly tragic letter to her mother, swearing her innocence, offering to submit herself to a physical examination now and even a postmortem later. Catherine could do nothing but wring her hands in the face of this shame on the family, for her youngest son was now very near death and she could not abandon him even to heal the breach in the family. She did, however, send her wretched daughter sufficient money to pay off immediate debts and continue her journey south. But at Cognac, Marguerite received a curt letter from her husband, peremptorily forbidding her to cross the frontier into his realm until he had settled the matter with the king her brother.

Navarre's reluctance to receive back his wife sprang from three very different and very powerful reasons. Preeminently, he was a politician, struggling to maintain a tiny kingdom under the enormous shadow of France. Intangibles counted for much in that kind of struggle for survival, and if he took back his wife, without protest or recompense, after she had been publicly insulted by his suzeraine, he would earn the contemptuous mockery of friend and enemy alike. But shrewdly, too, he realized that that suzeraine could be forced to pay quite a substantial price for the restoration of his sister, for she was, after all, Queen of Navarre. And finally, he was again in love, this time with no pretty, empty-headed little girl but with a mature woman who combined beauty with a somewhat daunting intelligence—the twenty-six-year old Diane de Gramont, who called herself Corisande after the heroine in *Amadis de Gaul,* a piece of bluestocking affectation which, curiously, did not diminish her lover's passion. The last thing he wanted at the moment was for his wife to appear during the opening stages of the love idyll—even such a tolerant and, by now, only too submissive wife as Marguerite. She was therefore commanded to remain in exile among dreary provincial towns while her husband and brother strove to outmaneuver each other. Navarre was considerably helped by the violent extremes of Henri's nature as he adopted now the tone of offended majesty, now the tone almost of a suppliant. In the middle of October Henri dispatched Pomponne de Bellièvre to demand, outright, that Navarre receive back his wife. That had been on Catherine's insistence, but Bellièvre also carried a letter from the king which completely belied the firm words the ambassador had uttered at his audience. "Kings are often liable to be deceived by false reports," Henri wrote. "Calumny has not always respected the conduct and morals of even the most virtuous princesses—as, for example, the Queen your mother. You cannot be ignorant of all the evil that was said of her." Navarre burst out laughing after he read the letter. "His Majesty does me too much honour," he said to the embarrassed Bellièvre. "First he calls my wife a whore then he tells me that I'm the son of one."

But behind the grin, behind the lighthearted irony, the steely resolve remained unchanged: he wanted an apology from the king and, as solid damages for his wounded honor, he demanded that certain frontier towns should be stripped of their Catholic garrisons. Autumn slid into winter, winter gave place to spring and still Marguerite drifted from one provincial town to another while her husband and brother haggled over her. It was Henri III, at length, who gave way, and that for an honorable reason. It was now obviously only a question of time before his brother died and Navarre became heir presumptive, and Henri was patriot and statesman enough to put the good of the kingdom before a private vendetta. When Duplessis-Mornay arrived at his court in the early spring of 1584 on another embassy, Henri told him specifically, "I recognise your master as sole heir," and almost pleaded with him to bring about a settlement for the greater good of France. Duplessis-Mornay urged Navarre to take back his wife and then, very much aware that it was not politics alone that had led Navarre to take up such an extreme position, read him a lecture on his morals. "The eyes of all are fixed on you. The love affairs which you carry on so openly, and to which you devote so much time, are no longer seasonable. It is time, Sire, for you to make

love to all Christendom, and especially to France." Navarre ignored
the lecture but took the political advice to be reunited with his wife.
He had gained his frontier towns, gained something even better than
an apology from the king, and could also go on enjoying the pedantic
wit and beautiful body of his Corisande. There was no reason at all
why his wife should not return, and graciously he sent her permission to enter his kingdom and rejoin him.

They met again, after a separation of more than two years,
at Porte Saint-Marie on April 13, 1584. Marguerite arrived first
and took up lodgings in a house that had been set aside for her in
the little town. Two or three years earlier she would have been
exceedingly indignant at being obliged to wait until her husband
decided to join her, but she was, for the moment, quite beaten; it
was not, indeed, until she heard the cavalcade clatter into the
square outside that she was quite certain that Navarre would arrive. He entered the house and embraced her without a word,
coldly kissing the proffered cheek. Together they ascended to the
second floor where they displayed themselves formally to the
small crowd outside and, shortly after, they left for Nérac, arriving there about four in the afternoon. Later she would describe to
her mother, with a brave attempt at gaiety and confidence, the
warmth of her reception there, but there was a witness who gave
the lie to her words. He was Michel de La Huguerye, a Huguenot,
a man who had no particular liking for her either as queen or as
woman but who was so touched by her distress on that day that
he recorded it in curiously moving words. He told how the husband and wife paced back and forth, back and forth along the
great gallery of the château. No one was permitted near them so
no one knew what they were saying, though Navarre was stern
and cold and the avid watchers could see that the queen was
"bathed incessantly in tears." And later, at the banquet that night
—the banquet supposed to celebrate publicly their reunion—he
subjected her to a studied insult, for while she sat beside him,
barely able to restrain those incessant tears, "he carried on I know

not what frivolous conversation with the gentlemen about him, without either he himself or anyone else addressing the princess," La Huguerye observed, coming to the opinion that "this reconciliation would not be of long duration, and that such treatment would cause this princess to take a new part in the trouble which was about to rise."[80] He was a good prophet as well as a meticulous observer.

XIII

The Virago

In the middle of May 1584, just a month after that lukewarm reconciliation in Nérac, an unusually splendid cavalcade left Paris. It was composed of more than a hundred knights and gentlemen, to each of whom the king had given a substantial sum of money "to render him good and faithful service and make a suitable appearance," and each had equipped himself and his followers accordingly. Leading the cavalcade was the king's especial favorite, the Duke of Épernon, the man generally known as the *demi-roi* of France so sumptuous was his appearance, so arrogant his manners, so absolute his power wherever the king's writ ran. The Paris mob, free as ever with their catcalls and whistles, were nevertheless impressed and supposed that such a cavalcade, commanded by such a man, must be an embassy to some very favored, or very powerful, friend of the king's. It was not. In Épernon's personal possession were letters addressed to the King of Navarre in which the King of France "admonished, exhorted and entreated him, seeing that the life of the Duc d'Anjou his brother was despaired of, and that the news of his death was daily expected, to come to Court and go to Mass because he desired to recognise him as his true heir and successor."[81] In that month of May more than one person thought of the long-dead Nostradamus and how, against every law of probability, his prophecy regarding Navarre seemed to be working itself out. Two royal brothers had descended to the grave, the life of another was guttering to a close, there remained only the childless, debauched Henri to keep the feeble Valois grip upon the throne.

In Nérac, Navarre heard of the approaching embassy with satisfaction but no surprise. He had already made up his mind what to do about the invitation. "I cannot change my religion like a shirt," he announced proudly, being perfectly well aware that to do so would be promptly to lose all Protestant support without being in the least degree certain of gaining Catholic support. But the Épernon embassy was the first public, vital statement of the fact that he, Henri de Bourbon, was the true legal successor of the House of Valois. The odorous, shabby, garrulous little man who disliked any kind of formality therefore decreed that the king's ambassador, the Duke of Épernon, was to be received with all ceremony and honor by all his subjects—including the Queen of Navarre. Marguerite protested. She loathed Épernon and he loathed her. The last time they had met was when he had gazed up at her on her flower-crowned throne in the Louvre, exulting over the humiliation descending on her dazed head. To be asked now to receive this man of all men . . . . Navarre insisted, courteously enough but with that undertone of steel. His wife's reputation might now be nonexistent but she was a Valois of the Blood Royal, a Catholic, sister to the king, the one person who could ease the transition of the crown from Valois to Bourbon, should ever that happy event come to pass.

Some hundreds of miles to the north Catherine had foreseen her daughter's resentment and did what she could to negate it. In Épernon's embassy was that trusted counselor Pomponne de Bellièvre, who bore a letter to the smouldering young woman from her mother, together with some vehement instructions from Catherine herself. "I pray you to tell the queen my daughter not to augment further my afflictions for I know it will be much resented here if she does not receive M. d'Épernon."[82] Bellièvre added his own entreaties, arguing that she could only gain prestige by allowing someone of

Épernon's stature formally to wait upon her. "Give me orders to inform the Duc that you are prepared to give him a cordial reception." Under pressure from all sides, Marguerite gave way, although, with a flash of her old spirit, her old delight of playing with words, she remarked to those around her, "The day on which he arrives, and so long as he remains, I shall dress myself in garments which I shall never wear again—the garments of dissimulation and hypocrisy."[83] The visit, in fact, went off far better than anyone had hoped. One of Catherine's spies in her daughter's household wrote to say that the young queen and the all-powerful *mignon* had remained deep in conversation far longer than protocol demanded, as though their mutual curiosity had temporarily overcome their mutual aversion.

On June 11, 1584, François of Alençon, Duke of Anjou, Duke of Brabant, left the earth in "a bloody flux accompanied by a high fever," and the heretical Henri de Bourbon, King of Navarre, became direct heir to the Catholic crown of France. The dormant Holy League stirred and woke. Months later Pope Sixtus IV dismissed the religious protestations of its leaders as so much cant, summing up their motives with the political acumen of the Italian: "Every one of them wishes to become not a better Christian but a greater power. A hundred ambitious men, all seeking to be kings, and since they cannot all rule so mighty a state as France, trying at least to tear it apart and find a fragment on which to settle and set themselves up as mimic kings. Poor France." But though his summary was as accurate as it was pithy, it did not give due weight to the division in French society, it did not echo the despair of the Catholic majority for whom there appeared to be no choice between a homosexual king who seemed little better than an atheist and a Huguenot king who, by definition, was little better than a Satanist. The sacred law of primogeniture forced them to accept Henri de Valois: it could not force them to accept Henri de Bourbon. Throughout that summer and autumn, the groundswell built up until the Holy League was the true monarchy of France, for those who had eyes to see. The Cardinal of Bourbon was put forward as the legitimate successor to Henri, but the Red Ass had only his Bourbon blood to commend him and behind him, as behind all these deep disturbances in the State, were the Guises. Like a recurring nightmare, the names and parties and motives that men thought had been exorcised a generation before reared up again to overshadow the torn and bloody land. A three-way battle between League, king, and Huguenots—this, it seemed, was what was in store for France.

And it was at about this time that, here and there, some few moderates, some few Frenchmen appalled and disgusted by that inevitable fate, began to question aloud, if still discreetly, that Salic Law which was delivering them into chaos. Looking back some years later, Brantôme undoubtedly overemphasized the movement even while he oversimplifed and romanticized it, but he was nevertheless able to get in some telling blows at the custom which excluded a woman, no matter how able, from the throne in favor of a man, no matter how criminal or incompetent. "I would like to know if this kingdom has found itself any better for an infinitude of conceited, silly, tyrannical, foolish, do-nothing, idiotic and crazy kings, than it would have been with an infinitude of the Daughters of France—very able, very prudent, and very able to govern. I would like to know in what our last kings have surpassed our last three Daughters of France, Elizabeth, Claude, and Marguerite, and whether if the latter had come to be queens of France they would not have governed it as well as their brothers. I have heard many great personages—well-informed and far seeing—say that possibly we should not have had the evils we did have, now have and shall have. But the common and vulgar fool says, 'Must observe the Salic Law'—poor idiot that he is. Does he not know that the Germans, from whose stock we issued, were wont to call their women to affairs of State, as we learn from Tacitus?"[84] The movement, or climate of opinion, was certainly not strong enough to give Marguerite any real hope; it was quite strong enough to alarm her husband, however, and so bring her marriage to an effectual end.

The death of her brother hit her badly. Whatever the basis of their alliance, whatever her private opinions of his character and

motives, he had been her sole constant ally ever since she had stepped
onto the political battlefield. Suddenly, she was alone in an increasingly hostile world, and her reaction to Alençon's death was theatri-
cally extravagant: her court was plunged into prolonged and deep
mourning; every ornament, every piece of bright fabric was stripped
from her rooms, which were then draped in solid black. At first, after
the Épernon embassy, she had clung to a faint hope of reinstating
herself as Queen of Navarre, of taking up again her self-chosen role
of political ally to her husband. But very rapidly he disabused her of
any such idea. After Alençon's death the bewildering realignment of
forces and alliances had not merely negated her value but actually
made her seem a rival. Hindsight would show that the engrained
conservatism of France would never consent to the suspension of the
Salic Law, but at the time it seemed as though the confused situation
could produce any result, that an agonized people might grasp at any
instrument that might produce peace. And, in consequence, Navarre
would become merely consort to an heiress.

He began to freeze her out. At first she must have feared, then
later actually hoped, that his coldness was due to his passionate affair
with Corisande. It was, undoubtedly, a very strong factor. He established his mistress in Pau, which he knew Marguerite hated and
would never willingly visit, and came less and less to Nérac. For her
part, Marguerite again adopted that last remedy of the desperate wife
and began swallowing medicinal waters to encourage pregnancy.
Nothing happened—an unsurprising result, considering that Henri
slept only once with her in the whole twelve months following their
"reconciliation." By the end of the year, she had finally and permanently abandoned hope of ever being his wife in anything but name;
at the same time, there entered a sinister element into their relationship. The change was produced, on her side, by something near
hysteria, and, on his, by either a rational consideration of the situation and its logical consequences—or by a cruel and deliberate attempt to drive her away. He believed that there was a plot to murder
him and that she had a hand in it. There was, indeed, an inept attempt
made to poison him in February of 1585 and he secretly discussed

with his closest friends the possibility of bringing her to trial and executing her for it. Or so said Agrippa d'Aubigné, taking upon himself the credit for dissuading his master from the murderous intent. But though it was highly unlikely that Navarre would take matters to such an extreme, it was obvious that he and his wife had come to the end of their road. Tolerance had given place to indifference, indifference to fear and aversion, and each began to seek a way out of the impasse. At the end of March, Marguerite asked permission to spend Holy Week in her own city of Agen, a Catholic island in a Huguenot sea: willingly, Navarre gave her permission and she left Nérac with only a handful of ladies and gentlemen. Navarre fully expected her to return; it may have been that she fully intended to, but events finally parted their ways.

Agen was one of the small towns of the south which gave itself the airs of a city and so induced the visitor to accept it at its own valuation. There was a massive Romanesque cathedral with a dignified bishop's palace, a sprinkling of churches now entering their second century, and a handful of new and very handsome mansions, built by the burghers of the town before the civil war had brought the trade boom to an end. It was not a fortified town in the strictly military sense, but the citizens over the years had made the most of its excellent site, tucked in between the broad, fast-flowing Garonne on the south and a steep hill carved with ravines on the east. Twenty great towers crowned the walls, and the massive medieval ramparts and complex earthworks had been adapted by artillerymen to the new techniques of war. The royal garrison had been withdrawn as part of the bargaining for Marguerite's reinstatement, but the Agenaise had promptly formed their own civil guard. Altogether, they had good reason to believe that they could defend themselves from their Protestant neighbors during the bad times that were only too clearly coming.

They knew and liked their countess. Marguerite had found refuge here during those long months of waiting while her husband was making up his mind to take her back, and the Agenaise were keenly aware of the social and economic value of having the king's sister residing among them. It seemed to them only sensible that she, the Catholic countess of the Catholic city, should again seek refuge here from her Protestant husband. She took over one of the mansions, paying a fair rent to its widowed owner, and sent for the rest of her staff. By the beginning of April, some 325 people were on her direct payroll at Agen, and what had begun as a temporary visit began to take on a rather different aspect. But even as late as mid-April, Bellièvre, the royal agent at Nérac, believed that she was staying on at Agen only through fear—or jealousy. "I have not failed to speak of the wrong that the king of Navarre is committing in preferring the friendship of the countess [Corisande] to that of his wife," he wrote to the queen mother. "She has been constrained to return to Agen, to protect herself from the countess who is plotting against her life."[85] Catherine had more worrying matters than her daughter's unhappy marriage and was glad enough to accept her action at its face value. But by the end of the month, she had no choice but to recognize that her daughter was, in fact, leading a rebellion against the crown.

What happened in Agen between May and September 1585 is clear enough. The letters of indignant, frightened or amused observers, the town's chroniclers, the gossip of diplomats pieced together give a coherent and logical explanation. But none give a rational explanation for Marguerite's motives, she herself remained silent about them, and none of her confidantes breached her trust in them. The probability is, indeed, that she began with no clear-cut goal in mind. Those nine dreadful months during which she had wandered from one dreary town to another while her husband and brother were callously using her as a bargaining counter ended, for her, a process which had begun on that long-ago night of Saint Bartholomew when her mother had shown that she was quite prepared to sacrifice her daughter for a political gain. Loyalty had been perhaps her most obvious, most constant virtue, and she had seen that virtue repaid in the shabbiest, most brutal manner possible. When she had gained the security of Agen, she might very well have decided to remain there, in comfortable neutrality, while the forces which controlled her brother and husband fought each other to a standstill: whoever destroyed whom, she would gain. But then there had appeared a third force, the League, whose effective leader was the man she had loved and respected since she was a girl. It was obvious that, sooner or later, the Duke of Guise would be turning the power of the League not only against the husband who had rejected her, but the brother who had so often humiliated her. There was therefore every cause to be positive, to abandon those who had abandoned her and join him who had always at least tried to help her. By the end of April she had made up her mind. She summoned her secretary Choisnin and gave him a letter, together with certain secret instructions, to take to the Duke of Guise. She made an unfortunate choice of messenger: Choisnin delivered the letter but kept the instructions with the intention of using them as blackmail later.

Throughout April and the first two weeks of May there was a steady trickle of Catholic gentlemen and their retainers coming into the town. The Agenaise accepted the augmentation of their numbers —this, after all, was what was to be expected in such uncertain times. The majority of the newcomers went straight to the residence of the Queen of Navarre, swore personal allegiance to her and were enrolled in one of two brigades of men-at-arms. On May 15 the city fathers were summoned, courteously but very firmly, to a special meeting taking place in the bishop's palace. There they found their countess, enthroned with their bishop and surrounded by her court. Gracefully she recognized their salutation and then, in that rich and thrilling voice which had turned the head of many a man, she asked them to deliver over to her, personally, the keys of the citadel. It seemed that the king's marshal, Matignon, was conspiring to seize her, and even if he were not, she was in great dread of her husband, the furious Huguenot leader. The magistrates tried to defend their civic charge. Her Majesty was assured of their utmost loyalty and love, they declared, and their civil guard, together with the stout walls of Agen, would keep her enemies at bay. She heard them out, but when she spoke again, the rich and thrilling voice carried an unmistakable

threat in its tone. She was the mistress of Agen, and intended henceforth to rule it as she thought best, and if the magistrates were
disposed to argue with her, would they care to glance through the
window. They looked out and saw, drawn up in the square outside,
the two brigades of men-at-arms. An extraordinarily large number
of men seemed to have come into Agen over the past few weeks and
the strangers were more than sufficient to overwhelm the civil guard.
The magistrates gave way, sent for the key of the citadel and, before
leaving the audience chamber, in their turn swore personal allegiance
to her.

So far, Marguerite was completely in control of the situation,
her political moves sensible, her military dispositions admirable. The
two brigades were placed under the command of two men from her
own county of Auvergne, a man called Ligard and another, Jean
d'Aubiac, who was to go to his death for her. She must have heard
how Aubiac, on first seeing her, had burst out to a comrade, "What
a woman! If I could go to bed with her they could hang me an hour
afterward";[86] but while such quivering devotion would certainly not
have counted against him, it did not influence her in the appointment, and Aubiac was, in fact, an excellent soldier. Shortly after she
had taken over the citadel and replaced the civil guard with her own
brigades, her military force was strikingly augmented by the arrival
of the Bailiff of Upper Auvergne, the dour Robert de Lignerac, at the
head of a strong force of League cavalry. The main body of the
citizens were still her enthusiastic allies, enchanted alike by her manners and her liberality, for it seemed a purely technical matter that
the armed forces of Agen should be directly under her control, instead of under the control of the elected magistrates. Catherine de
Médicis did not think so. When she heard the news, her attendants
feared that she would have a stroke, so violent was her reaction.
"God has left me this creature for the punishment of my sins," she
write vehemently to Bellièvre. "Every day she afflicts me. She is my
scourge in this world."[87] But Catherine was a long way from Agen.

The next move was virtually forced upon Marguerite. Later,
her rashness was to be blamed largely upon her evil genius, Madame

de Duras, who had arrived triumphantly with her husband and promptly took charge of her old comrade's household. But though Madame de Duras and her swaggering, incompetent husband wrongly fancied themselves as political geniuses and did Marguerite very great harm, the first assaults on the neighboring Huguenot cities were an inevitable result of penning a large number of arrogant, energetic young men in the confines of a small town. At the beginning of July they marched out, attacked the Huguenot town of Tonneins, and actually placed a garrison in it. But behind the Huguenots was one of the most flexible, daring and indefatigible military minds in France—the mind of their mistress's husband, Navarre. He had watched the developments in Agen with an amused respect, but as soon as it became obvious that his wife, or the people manipulating her, would be interfering in his field, he struck back hard and remorselessly. The Catholic troops were driven out of Tonneins and the Huguenots, in their turn, went over to the offensive, driving Marguerite's troops from every one of their temporary gains, penning them again in the city of Agen.

By mid-August, the Agen adventure was turning sour. Marguerite was now in truly desperate straits for money. Always improvident and extravagant, her income now had to cover not only her usual expenses but also the pay of the hundreds of Catholic soldiers who might profess devotion to her person but whose loyalty could be very accurately measured in gold. She appealed to the Duke of Guise. He, too, was short of money and passed on her appeal to Philip of Spain, begging him to send financial assistance at once to her "in order that she whom we have established as an obstacle to her husband, may not be abandoned by her troops." Philip did nothing; he had already paid out a million crowns in subsidy to the League and was yet to be convinced that it was money well spent. In Agen the tension heightened. The citizens had totally lost their faith in their once enchanting countess. Much of her charm for them had been her liberality—that generous flow of golden coins for wine and charity and gowns and musicians which found its way into so many Agenaise pockets. At the same time they were forced to endure the presence of her soldiers, hundreds of bored, predatory, penniless young men who had no real objection to subsidizing themselves at the expense of good Catholics if wicked Huguenots were not to be found. Plague had struck the town, the weather was stiflingly hot, food supplies were becoming a worry—and it was at this stage that Marguerite decided to increase the taxes on the townspeople.

The Countess of Agen had never, throughout the whole of her rich and varied life, come into contact with ordinary people—the shopkeepers and small merchants and laborers who produced the gold she spent. Even the women and girls who performed the offices of her toilet and bedchamber were drawn for the most part from the minor gentry, people who, in their turn, lived on rents. Despite the enforced intimacy of life in the royal palaces, there was a rigid distinction between the menials who ran the great machines and the nobility who used them. A certain class of servant—such as coachmen, waiters, butlers—inevitably came into personal contact with her, but no more possessed personalities than the dogs and horses. And below these was a wholly unimaginable world; occasionally, some denizen of it, some scullion momentarily out of his milieu, might scutter across her field of vision, but it is to be doubted if she was ever actually aware of seeing such a person. He or she was simply part of the background, like the crowds in the streets through whom her litter-bearers carved a passage as though through a sea. Probably the only time she was ever aware of ordinary people was when they lined a processional route: their reaction then—hostile, indifferent or adulatory—was of personal importance to her and she might, momentarily, actually see individuals as she responded to their cheers or bridled at their silence. Otherwise her world consisted entirely of the limited but seemingly infinitely powerful members of her own class, and the parasites upon it.

In Agen, therefore, she had no real idea of what she was doing when she decreed the increase of taxes. If she thought about the matter at all, she probably assumed that the taxpayers, like herself, would merely increase their demands on another, lower class; it did not, it could not, occur to her that, at a certain level in society, an extra coin paid out in taxation meant a corresponding reduction in vital necessities, that by demanding another franc from a cobbler she was, quite literally, taking the bread from his children's mouth. A person like her husband would have been aware of such an effect and, although the awareness would not have stayed his hand for humanitarian reasons, it would have warned him to take political and military precautions. Marguerite did neither and was genuinely astonished by the storm of protest. There were more than sufficient soldiers in the town to exact the increased taxes—a task they performed with enthusiasm, for most of the gold went directly to them —but the effect was to increase the already alarming pressure of resentment.

The explosion, when it came, was entirely Marguerite's fault. The nature of her upbringing might have absolved her partially from blame over the matter of increased taxation and, in any case, the most injured and incensed of the victims were the least influential in society. But when she decided to erase fifty of the best houses in Agen in order to construct a second citadel overlooking the Garonne, she must have known that she was injuring the deepest feelings of an influential class, for she was tampering with the property of the wealthy burghers of Agen. There were vague promises of recompense, but who was to pay that recompense and when, was left in the air. In this matter she was very much a Valois, very much the princess who simply decreed and expected to be obeyed as by a natural law. Her military advisers had told her that it was necessary to demolish the houses, she assented and it was done, regardless of the fact that they were the homes of loyal citizens who had offered her shelter. Again, the overwhelming military force at her disposal enabled her decree to be executed. Her men-at-arms formed a cordon while the families were ejected from the buildings, their possessions piled carelessly, and the engineers moved in. Within a few days the fifty houses were just so much rubble, and construction began on the second citadel—now needed as much to suppress the Agenaise as to withstand the external enemy.

But she had overreached herself, forgetting that her enemies outside the city included not only Protestants but Catholics, co-religionists of the injured Agenaise. Arguably, the citizens might have loyally defended her even against these forces of the king, putting their personal loyalty and affection to her above their theoretical loyalty to a remote monarch. But her inept handling of the explosive situation lost her that vital support. The Agenaise saw ahead of them nothing but famine, ever heavier taxation, ever more arrogant tyranny and, as inevitable end, condign punishment from that distant and enraged monarch. Late on a September evening, a group of the town's leading citizens slipped out and rode the eighty-odd miles to Bordeaux, where the king's marshal, Odet de Matignon, had established his headquarters.

The deputation found the Norman in a quandary. His original instructions were clear enough: he was simply to wait, gathering together his strength until the inevitable civil war broke out, when, from that secure base in Bordeaux, he would launch his troops at Navarre, the very heart of Huguenot resistance, and—hopefully—bring the war to a sudden end. But then there had come the trouble at Agen. On the face of it, this was simply a rebellion against the king's authority and all that was required was a punitive expedition to restore the city to a proper frame of mind. But leading that rebellion was the king's sister, and Matignon remembered vividly what had happened to his predecessor Biron, who had, very properly, bombarded Nérac when that same sister was living there. He knew —all France knew—that the Queen of Navarre was in deep disgrace with her mother and brother, but one could never be certain how that volatile, erratic royal family would react in any given circumstance. The tigress in Paris, in particular, might very well turn and rend anyone foolish enough to harm her cub, no matter how furious she might be with that cub's ill behavior. The marshal had spent the last few weeks in painful indecision, wondering how he could obey the king's specific order to reduce Agen to obedience without imperiling his career, and the Agenaise deputation with its complaints and pleas for help came at an ideal moment. If the citizens themselves could be induced to revolt against their countess, then he could achieve his apparently contradictory goals. He discussed the situation with the delegates. Yes, they assured him, the Agenaise would undoubtedly revolt, provided they could be assured of military backing to counter the threat of the countess's large garrison. Matignon promised them the necessary support and the delegates departed, well satisfied. But in addition to the plans for the revolt they carried with them a document which, he earnestly hoped, was his insurance against future blame. In the name of the king he authorized the Agenaise "to capture and seize the forts, drive out and expel, by force of arms if necessary, the captains, soldiers and all men of war who were there and give him admission to the town, to hold it in obedience to his Majesty." But at the end of the proclamation, the same loyal citizens were firmly enjoined to "treat the Queen of Navarre, her ladies, and maids-of-honour with the honour, respect and very humble service which was their due."[88]

The citizens planned their coup well, coordinating movements, arranging signals, piling arms under the eyes of the garrison. Early on the morning of September 5, a group of them attacked the garrison of one of the gates, seized the gate and let in the detachment of royalist soldiers, which had come close to the town under cover of darkness. Agen was not on a war footing, and most of the men at arms were scattered around in the more comfortable private lodgings instead of the cheerless but defensible citadel. They mustered and fought well, but their opponents were no longer the amateur civil guard but the tough veteran soldiers of Matignon's command, and by midmorning the core of resistance was smashed.

Agen was a small city and Marguerite would have been able to follow, by sound alone, the course of the battle, from the first assault upon the gate to the final assault upon the citadel. But the first she seems to have known of its disastrous result was when her commander in chief, Lignerac, appeared outside her mansion with a body of cavalry and brusquely urged her to mount behind him. At the time, his action must have appeared one of selfless devotion; only later did she discover that she had placed herself in the power of a totally unscrupulous man. As Daughter of France, Countess of Agen and Queen of Navarre, her value was almost nil; but as Countess of Auvergne she had a high trading value for Auvergnat nobles, and Lignerac was the first to realize it and take prompt action. She mounted behind him; Madame de Duras mounted behind another officer and, accompanied by about a hundred gentlemen of Marguerite's household, they made their way safely out of Agen. Later, her enemies claimed that she was chased out of Agen without escort, leaving everything behind her but the clothes and jewels she was wearing. The Agenaise, in fact, treated her far more generously than she had treated them. After they had vented their rage on the garrison, they not only allowed their countess's household to leave in peace, but also allowed them to take all her possessions with them. Over the next two or three weeks a number of caravans carried her tapestries and books and wines and clothing—even the great state bed—over the hills of Auvergne to her next asylum, the forbidding castle of Carlat.

XIV

The Ark of Refuge

Some hundred miles to the north of Agen, through the wild but beautiful country of Auvergne, the great basalt rock of Carlat reared up, a black admonitory finger. The castle which dominated it was enormous, a craggy mass set on a plateau, defended by precipices. "It looked more like a robber's den than the residence of a Queen," the *Divorce satyrique* noted, one of the few accurate observations in its venom-packed length. Theoretically, it belonged to Marguerite, being part of her appanage in Auvergne; in practice it was occupied by whoever was strong enough to hold it, and a Huguenot chief had only recently been expelled from it. Marguerite—or Lignerac—could count upon the support of the local Auvergnat nobles, and it was for this reason that Carlat had been chosen as refuge if she were obliged to leave Agen.

The Countess of Auvergne entered her castle of Carlat on Monday, September 30, 1585, escorted by five hundred gentlemen who had met her on the Auvergne border. She left Carlat almost exactly a year later—on October 14, 1586—and those fifty-four weeks constitute the most mysterious period in her life. Her arrival was marked with an act of treachery, her departure with an act of murder; she appears to have become the tool, willing or unwilling, passive or protesting, of her vassals. The events in Carlat triggered off a violent reaction in Paris—so violent that her brother openly wished for her death. There is an abundance of gossip for those months, a plethora of lurid accusations and counteraccusations regarding what was supposed to have happened in that "robber's den" on its finger of black rock. But there is also a curious lack of any record of apparent motive that would articulate the several events. Out of the murky, enigmatic background the authenticated incidents stand out with melodramatic starkness, each apparently irrelevant to the other so that posterity can only speculate on the nature of the force that produced them while, inexorably, transforming the Queen of Navarre first into a tool, then into a fugitive and finally into a prisoner.

The first certain event was the treachery of her secretary Choisnin. Charpentier, her treasurer, remained on at Agen during the six weeks it took to transport all the staff and equipment from Agen to Carlat, and Choisnin took on the duties of treasurer in Carlat. When Charpentier at last arrived in Carlat and took over the post of treasurer, Choisnin presented him with the fantastic account of fifteen thousand écus—more than twice the extravagant household's normal expenditure for such a period. He demanded immediate repayment and, in addition, the sum of six thousand écus for his own temporary services. The demands were, almost certainly, plain blackmail, based on his possession of the secret instructions which Marguerite had given him to pass on to Guise. Whether or not he immediately disclosed his hand, Marguerite indignantly refused to pay his demands; he responded by addressing to his mistress a lampoon, "the most disgusting and villainous that ever was seen," and was soundly flogged for it and thrown out of the castle. Promptly he took his revenge, setting off for Paris, where he ensured that a copy of his mistress's secret instructions to Guise came into the king's hands.

Such was the curtain-raiser to Marguerite's sojourn in Carlat. And scarcely had she defied the blackmailer when she fell victim to the usurer. Desperately in need of money, as ever, she used her jewels as collateral for a loan from an Italian banker in Lyons. The man cheated her so badly that she was forced to approach Lignerac for a loan; he was prompt to oblige, grasping at the opportunity to entangle the Countess of Auvergne even further. A prolonged sickness followed, a sickness probably due more to worry and fear for the future than to any physical cause, for she had always enjoyed robust health. When she recovered, the balance of power in the castle seems to have shifted. Until then, Madame de Duras and her husband the viscount had still exercised their influence over her, but sometime in May of 1586 she had a violent quarrel with them and they left Carlat in a rage. For the first time in months she was free of their destructive influence, but she gained little; from then on the sinister figure of Robert de Lignerac loomed ever larger over the castle. A harsh, violent man, given to sudden outbursts of bestial rage, it was he who had precipitated the quarrel with the Duras in order to isolate her further for his own enigmatic purposes. The *Divorce satyrique* naturally assumed that he was Marguerite's lover; if so, he gained her bed under threat of force, for throughout, this high-spirited, intelligent and forceful woman appears to have been cowed by him. She was not as yet wholly alone in Carlat, however; as counterweight to the overbearing figure of Lignerac was Jean d'Aubiac, her young brigade commander, who had accompanied her in her flight to Carlat and now, in that gloomy castle, achieved the ambition he had announced on first setting eyes on her. The *Divorce satyrique* was predictably contemptuous of him, describing him as "red-haired, more freckled than a trout and with a red nose," but the impartial Tuscan ambassador thought him an attractive young man, good-looking and high-spirited, though inclined to be overconfident and very indiscreet. Inevitably, he and Lignerac came into conflict. Aubiac was genuinely devoted to his mistress, but that did not prevent his being aware of her political value, and Lignerac, for his part, was quick to respond to any challenge on his own ground. Throughout the summer each maneuvered for complete control of the castle and its supposed mistress, quarreling frequently but stopping just short of violence. And when violence did erupt, it was directed against a perfectly innocent third party. One morning at the end of September or beginning of

October, Lignerac burst into Marguerite's bedchamber and found
there a young man, scarcely more than a boy. His presence seems to
have been quite proper, for he was the son of her apothecary, but
Lignerac, in one of his sudden surges of rage, fell upon the boy and
slaughtered him, stabbing him so that the blood spurted out over
Marguerite's bed.

Under normal circumstances, the Queen of Navarre would
have furiously demanded vengeance upon the slayer. But over these
past few months she seems to have become not so much crushed as
bemused. Her only reaction now was terror, with a corresponding
overwhelming desire to escape from Carlat while she was still free to
do so. News came too of the advance of a royalist army, under the
command of her old enemy the *mignon* Joyeuse, penetrating deep into
the Auvergne and charged with the mission of arresting the king's
rebellious sister. Up to this point, she had been able to depend upon
Lignerac's self-interest; now, he would probably take the lead in
handing her over to her brother. On October 14, she therefore left
Carlat, accompanied by Aubiac and one of Lignerac's brothers, who
escorted her presumably in order to keep track of the golden goose
—certainly Lignerac himself made no difficulty about her departure.
Her goal was Ibois, a remote château belonging to her mother, and
it had been arranged that a certain Seigneur de Châteauneuf should
provide an escort and guide through the wild country. Yet again she
was betrayed. The escort failed to arrive, she herself was nearly
drowned crossing a river and finally, she had scarcely arrived at Ibois
when a clatter of hoofs announced the arrival of a powerful detachment dispatched by Joyeuse to arrest her on the information supplied
by Châteauneuf. Irony had not yet finished with her: the commander
of the detachment was the Marquis of Canillac, the son of her old
governess Madame de Curton.

Canillac demanded entry in the name of the king; Marguerite
parlayed, less from any hope of avoiding the inevitable than of giving
the wretched Aubiac a chance to hide. Why he was the particular
object of the royal rage no one knew outside the circle of the leading
actors in the tragedy now drawing swiftly to its close. Marguerite,

certainly, was at that time less in fear for herself than for her young lover, and while the captain of the garrison continued the delaying tactics, she hastily disguised Aubiac as best she could, causing his thick red hair to be shaved off and hiding him in a chimney. But when Canillac was at last admitted into the castle, he found and identified the young man without the slightest difficulty. He then formally arrested both Marguerite and Aubiac and sent a messenger hastening to Paris to ask for instructions in this most delicate matter.

Throughout the years of her running battle with her brother, Marguerite had relied, consciously or unconsciously, upon her mother's ultimate protection. It did not matter that Catherine de Médicis loved her son above all other humans while she reserved for her daughter something that wavered between outright dislike and an irritated affection. She was statesman enough to know that the family's good must take precedence over the individual members of it and, until now, she could always be depended on to arbitrate in the quarrel between her son and daughter. Marguerite's treachery in negotiating with the Duke of Guise had lost her, finally and completely, that formidable ally. The fact that she had been goaded into it—had, indeed, almost been forced into it to maintain her freedom—was no excuse in the eyes of Catherine de Médicis. The Duke of Guise, as head of the League, had delivered a resounding challenge to the crown—the family—and by allying herself with him Marguerite had declared herself an enemy of the family. From the moment that Catherine was convinced that the secret instructions handed over by Choisnin were genuine, she pursued her daughter with an implacable hatred that would transcend even the grave.

When, therefore, Henri learned from Auvergne that his sister was now wholly in his power, his reaction was immediate and violent, untempered by his mother's usual sensible advice. "Tell Canillac not to budge until we have made the necessary arrangements," he wrote to his agent. "Let him convey her to the Château of Usson. From this hour, let her estates and pensions be sequestrated. Let her women and male attendants be dismissed immediately and let him give her some honest waiting woman until the Queen my mother orders him to procure such women as she shall think advisable. But above all, let him take good care of her. The Queen my mother enjoins upon me to cause Aubiac to be hanged and that the execution take place in the presence of this wretched woman, in the court of the Château of Usson. Arrange for this to be properly carried out. Give orders that all her rings be sent to me, and with a full inventory, and that they be brought to me as soon as possible." But even this outburst of fury and spite did not provide a catharsis, and he continued to brood over the sorry matter, returning to it in another letter a few days later as though he could not put it out of his mind. "The more I examine the matter, the more I feel and recognise the ignominy that this wretched woman brings upon us. The best that God can do for her and us is to take her away. Regarding this Aubiac, although he merits death, it would be well for some judge to conduct his trial, in order that we may have always before us what will serve to repress her audacity, for she will always be too proud and malignant. Decide what ought to be done for death, we are all resolved, must follow."[89]

Death did follow, fulfilling Aubiac's request to the ironic gods, even down to the manner of his passing. After a brief mock trial, he was hanged. The *Divorce satyrique* had him "kissing until the last moment of his existence, a blue-cut velvet sleeve of his mistress"; the Tuscan ambassador, through his usually reliable sources, provided the macabre information that he was buried alive. A grave had been dug immediately below the gallows and he was still breathing, though unconscious, when the rope was cut and his body fell into the hole. Nobody recorded whether or not Marguerite was actually present during the execution as her brother had ordered, or what her feelings were, or why Aubiac, of all her many lovers, was the only one to suffer officially for his love. Certainly she had good grounds to fear that someone might take the king at his word that "the best God can do for her and for us is to take her away." But she still had value as a territorial bargaining piece, and the Marquis of Canillac thought it worthwhile to obey the royal instructions and took her to the château of Usson.

They arrived there on November 13, 1586, and from then until February of the following year Marguerite disappeared from sight. But she remained prominent in the plans of a large number of people from Paris to Rome via Pau and Madrid. The Duke of Guise, fighting to save her for political as well as personal reasons, was convinced that her brother and mother meditated her murder, and the Duke of Guise had access to information very close to the throne. The plot, as he heard it, was for Navarre to be married off to the queen mother's granddaughter—little Louise de Lorraine—after Marguerite's disposal had been arranged. Politically, such a move would have made good sense. Marguerite's barrenness had, throughout, been a major source of the trouble with Navarre: both the religious problem and their mutual incompatibility would have dwindled in importance if she had been able to provide that all-important heir. Where she had failed so dismally, Louise de Lorraine might well be successful. There was, too, a bonus to be gained by marrying Navarre into the Lorraines, for such a move would neatly outflank the Guises, cadets to that great house of Lorraine. Altogether, the plot bore Catherine de Médicis's Italian hallmark—the complex, interlocking details, the wide-ranging repercussions, the refusal to allow morals to affect politics. It might very well have worked had it not encountered, in the mysterious obscurity of Usson, a counterplot whose goal was much less ambitious and which succeeded precisely because a key person preferred a limited but immediate reward to large but uncertain promises. Early in February 1587, the Marquis of Canillac, Governor of the château of Usson, handed the castle over to his prisoner, the Queen of Navarre.

Friends and enemies of Marguerite were unanimous in ascribing Canillac's defection to a single cause: his seduction by his beautiful captive. "He preferred a fleeting gratification to the duty he owed his master, and suffered himself to become enslaved by her whom he had captured,"[90] the *Divorce satyrique* said caustically. Hilarion de Coste, one of Marguerite's more extravagant panegyrists, decorated the tale. "He thought to have triumphed over her, and the mere sight of her ivory arms triumphed over him, and henceforth he lived only by the favour of the victorious eyes of his beautiful captive."[91] And finally Brantôme, who really should have known better—and probably did but could not resist the picture of the captor led captive—added his hyperbole: "Poor man, what could he do? To wish to keep prisoner her who, by the power of her eyes and her beautiful face, could rivet her chains upon the rest of the world, as though they had been galley slaves."[92] The truth was considerably more prosaic, as the Duke of Guise made clear in a letter to the Spanish ambassador: "I am glad to tell you that the negotiations begun by me with the Marquis de Canillac have happily succeeded. I have persuaded him to cast in his lot with our party and, by this means, assure the person of the Queen of Navarre, who is now quite safe. And I rejoice at this as much on her account as well as the great number of places and châteaux it has brought us, rendering the Auvergne country perfectly assured to us. For it frustrates the tragic designs they are founding on her death, the details of which will cause your hair to stand on end."[93] But though it was Guise who organized the negotiations, it was Marguerite who paid the price in the ultimate coin—land.

Throughout the confused and enigmatic story of her Auvergnat adventures, from the moment that she seized Agen to the moment that she acquired Usson, there ran a single and consistent thread —the territorial ambitions of a number of Auvergnat barons, in particular Lignerac, Aubiac and Canillac. Lignerac, who actually had the prize in his hand, appears to have miscalculated and frightened her away before he could profit from his position. Aubiac was almost certainly outmaneuvered by Canillac. What means Canillac might have used to obtain his death warrant is unknown, although it is significant that the king stated it was his mother who wished Aubiac's death. Catherine had never before been particularly interested in any of her daughter's lovers, and the implication is that she was led to believe that Aubiac was involved with her daughter in that great treachery, the conspiracy with Guise, for which the only possible penalty was the death that was visited upon him. Canillac was fortunate in that he had physical possession of the prisoner at the very moment when there was a market for her person and an agent to arrange the sale. And the price he received was enormous. In return for the château of Usson—and her life—Marguerite ceded to him "all the rights that she may possess over the county of Auvergne and other estates and lordships in the said county of Auvergne . . . also the sum of 40,000 écus, payable as soon as it will be possible to discharge it and the first vacant benefices in our estates up to an annual value of 30,000 livres. . . . ."[94] At a stroke of the pen, the Marquis of Canillac became the most powerful, the wealthiest lord of Auvergne. He did not have long to enjoy the fruits of the sale: eight months after signing the document he was killed in the new war that had broken out.

Throughout her adult life, the Queen of Navarre had been haunted by the story of another, very beautiful, promiscuous and unhappy queen—her second cousin Mary Stuart, known as Queen of the Scots. Like the rest of her family she had kept herself closely informed of the dizzy, twisting patterns of Mary's life in the cold northern country, following the tragedy with a horrified fascination as, one by one, the alternative paths had closed, herding the doomed woman toward one inescapable end. For other, less involved people, Mary's career had simply been an edifying lesson in the results of hubris. For Marguerite it had a very real, very personal significance. Mary's life had frequently reflected her own, and now, six days before Guise had written that Marguerite was safe, the crunch of the descending axe in Fotheringhay Castle had spelled out the fact that no one's life was safe in these lethal times, that even a queen could shed the blood of a queen, no matter how reluctantly, for political purposes. She, Marguerite, had been granted a stay, not a cancellation of execution. Her mother, perhaps, might have second thoughts, but there were others in the land for whom her death would solve many problems. "I am waiting only to hear that someone has strangled the Queen of Navarre. This, together with the death of her mother, would make me sing the canticle of Simeon,"[95] her husband had written to his mistress. It was said lightheartedly, doubtless, with that deceptive broad grin of his, but Marguerite knew him well enough to know when he was covering a wish with a jest. By an extraordinary quirk of fate, her prison had been turned into a refuge, for Usson was not only well defended in itself but was set in the heart of League country, among people who were no less hostile to her brother than they were to her husband. Common sense dictated that she should remain in her refuge while the world outside erupted again in war. Initially, her decision was made on an ad hoc, almost day-to-day basis, but as the days merged into weeks and the weeks into months and France continued to rend itself in a paroxysm of suicidal rage, she came at last to look upon this craggy fortress as her true home and began planning not months but years ahead.

Twenty years later, when peace had at last come to the land and the castle of Usson passed into the hands of the first Bourbon king, he promptly ordered its demolition, unwilling to risk such an impregnable place falling again into rebellious hands. "The sun alone could enter by force," said Marguerite's admirer Coste, and he scarcely exaggerated. Legend had it that the castle was built on the foundations of a pagan temple, so old was it. Over the centuries it grew seemingly organically, occupying every solid footing on its steep pinnacle of rock, passing from one baron to another—but always by purchase. It came at last into the hands of Louis XI, "that good and sly fox," who turned it into a state prison, encircling it with three separate circumvallations, each garnished with massive towers. The castle shared the pinnacle with three villages, one below the other, giving the whole the appearance of a pope's triple crown, according to a topographer.

It was in this barren, rocky place, suspended between earth and sky, far removed from the luxuries that she had once accepted as necessities, that Marguerite passed eighteen years of her life, eighteen years during which she slipped painlessly—seemingly without awareness—into late middle age, while her beauty departed entirely. At first—for months—Usson remained the object of hostile attention and speculation, but as its chatelaine made no move save to root herself in ever deeper, the attention wavered and moved on, leaving the castle and its inhabitants to drift into the background, where legends in plenty were woven about them to take the place of hard fact. Marguerite was isolated, not cut off from the world. While the civil war raged around and then through Auvergne, Usson was a natural rallying point and communication center for the Leaguers, and even after the war had ebbed away, there was still a constant movement of travelers up the steep and rocky slope to visit the queen who had by then become something of a legend. And returning to the world below, they brought back impressions with which to feed the growing legends, impressions that contradicted and contrasted at almost every point, so contradictory and contrasting was the personality of their subject. Her enemies were able to make of Usson, therefore, "a Cythera for her amours," cataloging at least half a dozen young men who successively filled the place that had once been filled by such men as Guise and Bussy-d'Amboise. But these now were local lads—a strolling musician, a carpenter's son, even a shepherd— who filled her casual hours. At the other extreme, her panegyrists— and they were many—saw Usson as a species of purified Athens, an ark for virtue and nobility. "Usson, sacred and holy abode! Sweet hermitage where Majesty meditated. Thou rock, who art a witness of the voluntary seclusion of thy peerless princess Marguerite. Usson! Earthly paradise of delights, where sweet and harmonious voices combine to soothe. . . ." Thus, in an increasing tangle of metaphor and epithet, intoned the reverend Père Hilarion de Coste—ecclesiastical writers seemed to be particularly vulnerable to the princess's charm. It was to Usson that Brantôme came, bearing his own richly worked offering of praise. Marguerite read it and smiled and shook her head at its extravagances, protesting that "the charms of the picture greatly surpass the original." And as correction, she promptly wrote her own memoirs—"the work of one afternoon she claimed." That afternoon was sometime in 1595, but she took those memoirs up only to 1582, the last of the happy years, the year in which she departed Nérac for Paris, leaving it for others to trace her decline and fall as though, even now in her hard-gained tranquillity, she could not face such a task.

For dimly through the extravagances of panegyrists and detractors comes the picture of a person at last at ease with herself, a person who had recognized the limit and futility of ambitions, but did so with amusement, not despair. She probably did take lovers from cottages as from castles; she probably did make a deliberate mockery of her royal, inalienable right of "ennobling" for ignoble deeds, as when she transformed the carpenter's son Julien Date into Date de Saint-Julien. But the central core of philosophic detachment remained untouched. Years before, in her first imprisonment at her brother's hands, she had discovered that love of reading which "from this time forth provided me with this excellent remedy for the alleviation of those troubles which were in store for me. I am indebted to the sadness and solitude of my first captivity for these two blessings—the love of study and the practice of devotion, which I should never have enjoyed in the midst of the pomps and vanities of my prosperous days." So, in her high seat among the mountains of Auvergne, the months imperceptibly gave way to years unmarked by triumph or defeat, indistinguishable in their equilibrium.

But in the world outside each month marked some new atrocity, some new complication of alliance, some new betrayal. Across the Channel, Sir Francis Bacon surveyed the agonies of England's great neighbor with what, in him, passed for compassion. "The Kingdom of France that was wont to have precedence of Europe is now fallen into those calamities that, as the prophet saith 'From the crown of the head to the sole of the foot there is no whole place.' The divisions are so many and intricate—of Protestants and Catholics, Royalists and Leaguers, Bourbonists and Lorrainists, Patriots and Spanish as it seemeth God hath some great work to bring to pass upon that nation."[96] The king had been forced to side with the League to save his very head and throne but though, ostensibly, he was now its leader, the hatred he felt for Henri of Guise was by far more personal, more deadly than his enmity for their mutual enemy, Henri of Navarre, so that the popular voice was, for once, right when it nicknamed that bloody, chaotic struggle for survival the "War of the Three Henries." That phase came to an end at Blois on the bitterly cold morning before Christmas Eve in 1588, when Guise fell, like some great oak, in the king's bedchamber. It took half a dozen men to dispatch him, and when the great body at last lay quiet at the king's feet, he continued to look on it as much in wonder and fear as triumph before going off to his mother and announcing, "At last I am king of France." She was on her sickbed, an old woman of seventy-two wanting only peace, but, appalled, she struggled up: "Pray God that you do not prove to be king of nothing." She shuffled out into the cold corridors of the castle to try and avert even now the doom that hung over her son and caught a cold and died. "A few of her servants and some of her familiars wept for her and so did the king—a very little. As for Blois where she had been worshipped as the Juno of the court she had no sooner given up the ghost than she was made no more account of by any than a dead goat would have been."[97] So wrote the Frenchman L'Estoile, but her fellow country-man Cavriana, the Tuscan ambassador, pronounced at once a more Christian valediction and an accurate summary of what the king had done. "She died with great repentance for her sins against God. We all remain without light, or counsel or consolation and, to tell the truth, with her died what kept us alive. From now on we must turn our thoughts elsewhere and find some other support. The kingdom will suffer more than is believed, and the King remains without the most faithful and necessary support that he had. God help him." The prayer was not answered. Eight months afterward the avenger's dag-ger entered the king's belly, cutting short the Valois dynasty after nearly three hundred years, ushering in the Bourbon against every probability. But it could not end the war. Nothing, it seemed, would end that save total attrition. Yet slowly above the murk, above the endless, senseless slaughter, above the self-devouring frenzy of reli-gious fanaticism there began to emerge the first real king that France had seen for over a century, the stocky, scruffy, seemingly irrepressi-bly cheerful man who now called himself Henri IV of France, though most of his kingdom still mocked him as a heretic and rejected him. He fought beside the meanest of his troopers, killing and risking being killed, but behind the Gascon for whom war was a game, behind the Huguenot for whom every dead Catholic was an act of merit, was the monarch for whom every drop of French blood upon his sword was an eternal reproach. And on that day when, retreating again from the dove-gray city on the Seine, he remarked—with that trick of his of mixing truth and jest—"Paris is worth a Mass," he laid his hand on the key to the problem. He had abjured Protestantism as a boy and again as a young man to save himself; could he not now abjure it to save France? It was a calculated gamble but it worked, the deep instinctive veneration for the anointed tribal leader proving stronger than the sectarian suspicion of the apostate. On March 18, 1594, Henri IV entered Paris, the crowned King of France, to the tumultuous cheers of this bastion of Catholicism and began the work of healing the scars of thirty years of civil war.

All these events had passed Marguerite by in a kind of dream. She wrote no letters, kept no journal, so only those around her knew of her reaction to the successive reports—the murder of Guise, her first and probably only real lover; the death of her mother; the murder of her brother; the discovery that her husband was, incredibly, King of France, and she—by default at least—was queen. But though she kept herself aloof from the struggle, she also kept herself closely informed, her natural intelligence honed by the need to survive. The time for gestures, for supporting lost causes was past; as soon as she had heard that her husband had become a Catholic and received the crown, she wrote to congratulate him. And he, who recognized neither gratitude nor grudges, wrote back amiably. He had, in addition, a pressing reason to retain his estranged wife's goodwill. An heir was important to him when he had been King of Navarre; it was vital now that he was King of France. The only way he could obtain an heir was by marrying again, and the only way he could marry again was by obtaining Marguerite's active cooperation in a divorce. Rome had solemnly blessed their marriage after solemnly granting a dispensation because they were related within the forbidden degree. Rome had now to be asked to stand on its head and solemnly announce that there had never been a marriage—and that to favor an ex-heretic whose conversion to Mother Church seemed, to say the least, opportunistic.

Marguerite responded eagerly enough. At the age of forty it

was unlikely that she would bear children; she had no particular desire for the empty title of Queen of France—a title that would be borne under more or less constant threat of liquidation, judicial or otherwise. She also had enormous debts, for not only had her sources of revenue been cut off by the war but her mother, carrying that hatred to the grave, had disinherited her. Her husband agreed to pay off her debts up to the sum of a quarter of a million écus, as well as grant her a pension of fourteen thousand écus a year and, after a tussle, allowed her permanent possession of Usson, which, she told him, "she considered to be a hermitage built to serve her as an ark of safety." Henry, as king, might dislike the idea of that immensely powerful castle remaining in any hands but his, but, as ex-husband, he was glad enough to have his ex-wife safely out of the way instead of setting up her own court to rival his in Paris.

Marguerite gave her assent to the divorce proceedings in April 1593; the marriage was pronounced null and void on November 10, 1599. The six-year delay was due very largely to the king's bizarre love life. Corisande had been discarded; there had been a succession of hopeful little girls in the interim, and then came the second great love of his life, Gabrielle d'Estrées, a plump, pliable, sweet-natured girl who gave him two children and was, for all practical purposes, his wife. It was because of Gabrielle that the divorce proceedings were begun. But the Vatican disliked her because she was the friend or relative of leading Protestants; the king's advisers—particularly Rosny—disliked her because they feared the effect on the succession if her two bastard sons were legitimized and she later had more sons as queen; and Marguerite disliked her, capriciously enough, because of her immoral life. "It is repugnant to me to put in my place a woman of such low extraction and of so impure a life as the one about whom rumour speaks."[98] Poor Gabrielle resolved the deadlock by dying in childbirth, but the king, proclaiming himself eternally desolate and inconsolable, plunged headlong into the most extravagant, most bizarre episode of his extravagant, bizarre life. The girl was Henriette d'Entragues, a beautiful, cold-hearted, remorseless predator, who, backed by her father, used her elegant eighteen-year-old body to play the king, driving him into a madness of frustration which he sought to resolve in his favored manner. But Henriette and her father wanted more than passionate verbal promises: they wanted it in writing. Docilely Henri IV of France drew up a document in which he agreed to take the Demoiselle Henriette d'Entragues to wife if she became pregnant within six months from date of signing and gave birth to a son. Foolishly, he showed the document to Rosny, who promptly tore it up in front of his eyes. "Are you mad?" said the astonished king. "Would to God, Sire, I were the only madman in France."[99] But his boldness had no effect: the document was signed, handed over to the Sieur d'Entragues to become a kind of time bomb, and Henri at last bedded his new mistress.

But Marguerite had meanwhile come to the end of her empty career as Queen of Navarre. In February 1599, she signed the procuration that would commence the inexorable machinery in the Rota. Capriciously, she had wanted to declare that the marriage had never been consummated, but Henri balked at such a slight on his manhood and the request for annulment went forth on the grounds of consanguinity and constraint. In Rome, the Rota approved it and the formal inquiry was opened in the Louvre on October 15. The inquiry was undoubtedly purely a formality, for the shedding of the husk of a meaningless marriage could only be to the benefit of all parties. But, at the last, Marguerite showed, in fact, that she was killing something that was still alive. She refused to go to Paris to make her deposition before the commissioners in person because, she said, her tears might make them think she was being coerced into the divorce. It was in Usson that she made her declaration that "never did I consent willingly to this marriage. I was forced into it by King Charles IX and the Queen my mother. I besought them with copious tears but the King threatened me that, if I did not consent, I should be the most unhappy woman in the realm. Although I had never been able to entertain any affection for the King of Navarre, and said and repeated that it was my desire to wed another prince, I was compelled to obey." Then, with a single, dying flash of malice, she referred obliquely to that long-dead rivalry with Madame de Sauves: "To my profound regret, conjugal affection did not exist between us during the seven months which preceded my husband's flight in 1575. Although we occupied the same couch, we never spoke to one another." "Ah, the wretched woman," the king cried, when he read this last aside. "She knows well that I have always loved and honoured her and that she cared nothing for me and that her bad behaviour has for a long time been the cause of our separation." But it was only a momentary irritation. Grateful for her cooperation, formally he allowed her to retain the title of Queen as well as that of Duchess of Valois and all the lands that were her appanage and dowry. But still there were those rich lands which her mother had stripped from her and given to her bastard nephew, the young man known as Charles d'Angoulême, and in fighting for them she was, like one describing a great circle, to find final harbor in the city that had humiliated and expelled her twenty years before.

XV

The Return Home

Charles d'Angoulême, Count of Auvergne, was the son of Charles IX by his little Huguenot mistress, Marie Touchet. The irony that attended the last of the Valois was epitomized in the fact that the only child produced by the four Valois brothers should have been not merely illegitimate but wholly worthless. Each of the four brothers—even Alençon with his hunger for glory—had possessed at least a fleeting potential for greatness. Their nephew proved to be simply a wastrel, a man who would have been a footpad if he had been born in a lower stratum of society but who, with his high connections, was able to pass for a gentleman with unusually violent and vicious tastes. Catherine de Médicis must have hated her daughter very much to prefer to enrich this young man at her expense. An illegitimate Valois with therefore a hatred for the usurping Bourbon, permanently in need of money to pay his extravagances, he was a ripe candidate for the plot against the king which came to a head in 1602. The plot, led by Henri's old comrade Biron, was the inevitable reaction of a feudal nobility who preferred anarchy and the freedom which went with it to the firm control of a powerful lord—who, incidentally, taxed them heavily for the privilege.

From her eyrie in Auvergne, Marguerite kept a very sharp eye on her nephew as he went about his affairs, reporting the results to her ex-husband. As early as 1600, two years before the plot came to a head, she warned Henri that "this badly-counselled boy holds many places in this locality, houses which he has usurped from the late queen my mother as well as many castles, forts and defences which, for your sake, would be better demolished."[100] Henri thanked her, adding the information to the net which he was drawing around the conspirators. That particular plot came to an end with Biron's execution in July 1602, but still Charles d'Angoulême played with death. He relied—overconfidently perhaps—on the fact that he was stepbrother of the king's mistress, Henriette d'Entragues; it was certainly this relationship which led him to become involved in the next stage of the bizarre plan, that of putting Henriette's bastard son forward as heir to the throne. The plan was backed by Spanish gold and was high treason, for the king's second wife, Marie de Médicis, had already produced a legitimate heir. Henriette and her father saved their lives by surrendering that famous piece of paper which promised Henriette the throne if she conceived a son; Charles d'Angoulême went to the Bastille for eleven years and so passed out of Marguerite's life.

But he provided, unwittingly, the means for her to leave Usson. The place that had been a refuge for eighteen years had at last become a prison to her. She wanted to see the wider world in her declining years, meet again those friends who had survived two decades of war and intrigue. Above all, she wanted to return to Paris, that great city which could alone satisfy her hunger for novelty, intellectual or frivolous. Henri was still reluctant to have her too near, fearing repercussions with his new queen, fearing, too, the popular reaction to having a Valois again in Paris. He tried to distract her with the offer of various sumptuous châteaux well outside the city, but she was insistent and at last he gave way. She had given signal proof of her loyalty to him, not only by keeping him informed of the Auvergnat conspirators but even, with great generosity, offering to divest herself of her coveted title of Queen if it should embarrass him. With equal generosity he refused the offer and, in addition, granted her leave to sue the Parlement of Paris for the reversal of her mother's will in order that she could again hold those territories forfeited by her nephew.

Marguerite left Usson, her "ark of refuge" of nearly twenty years, in the first week of July 1605. Her journey to the north was a triumphant progress, nobles and commoners alike flocking out to see this legendary figure from another world. The nobles of Auvergne turned out in force to escort her to the boundaries of Auvergne. There she was met by the king's most faithful servant, Rosny, now the Duke of Sully, heavily bearded but quite bald now. She passed on to him news she had gained of yet another conspiracy against the king, that of her ex-lover Turenne, and Rosny, though openly incredulous, honorably passed the information on to his master—and found it accurate, to his surprise. At Longjumeau, Marguerite's illegitimate half-sister, Diane de France, joined the cavalcade, and in Paris itself the king's illegitimate young son and Marguerite's old lover Harlay de Chanvallon were waiting to greet her on the steps of her new home, the Château de Madrid. Their presence was, perhaps, questionable taste on the part of the king, but Maguerite greeted her ex-husband's child with perfect equanimity and her ex-lover with every appearance of unfeigned delight.

Throughout the last hour or so of her journey while she penetrated the heart of Paris, crossed the Seine from right to left bank and came at last to her new home near the Bois de Boulogne, Marguerite had professed herself astonished and delighted at the change which had come over the city. None of her three royal brothers had been particularly interested in architecture, and most of the change had taken place during the ten years that her ex-husband had been on the throne, expressing in stone the ambitions he held for all France. A few years later the Englishman Thomas Coryate admiringly described for his fellow countrymen the splendid new city that Henri IV was bringing into being. Even Henri, it seemed, could do nothing about one Parisian characteristic which impressed generations of travelers—"the evil-smelling streets, which are the dirtiest and the most stinking I ever saw in any city in my life. Lutetia! well doth it brooke being called so from the Latin word *lutum* which signifieth dirt." But everything else led him to compare the city very favorably indeed with London, whether it was the great gallows at Montfaucon on which the remains of Coligny had been gibbeted—"the fairest gallows I ever saw, which consisted of fourteen fair pillars of free-stone"—or the town's "goodly buildings, mostly of fair white stone." The number and quality of the great bridges particularly took his fancy—"the goodly bridge of white freestone nearly finished [Pont-Neuf]: a famous bridge that far exceedeth this, having one of the fairest streets in Paris called our Ladies street: the bridge of exchange where the goldsmiths live: St Michael's Bridge and the bridge of birds." Elsewhere he noted "the Via Jacobea, full of booksellers fair shoppes, most plentifully furnished with bookes and the fair build-ings, very spacious and broad, where the Judges sit in the Palais de Justice, the roofs sumptuously gilt and embossed, with an exceeding multitude of great long bosses hanging down." He admired Catherine de Médicis' Tuileries and the grand gardens of the palace, the exterior of the Louvre with its intricate festoons and, inside, he became al-most lyrical in describing the Grande Galerie, "a room which ex-celleth not only all that are now in the world but also that were ever since the creation thereof, a perfect description whereof would re-quire a large volume, with a roofe of most glittering and admirable beauty."[101] He noted other curiosities for his stay-at-home compatri-ots, in particular the Corpus Christi procession, the head of Saint Denis and the old Queen of Navarre, a tourist attraction as she swept past in her litter. For the Parisians had enthusiastically adopted in their midst the last, wayward daughter of the Valois.

The king formally called upon his ex-wife a week after she had arrived in the city. She had little difficulty in recognizing him despite the twenty years that had passed since their last meeting: the bushy beard and hair were flecked with gray, perhaps, the tanned skin was rather more leathery it seemed—that was all. What he saw was a travesty, a caricature, and it speaks much for his gallantry that he was not betrayed into some involuntary comment or gesture. Marguerite at thirty had been in the very bloom of her astonishing beauty, a stately loveliness that had combined majesty with sensuality and intelligence. Marguerite at fifty was simply a grotesque. The intelligence had survived in the still lively black eyes, together with a disconcerting spark of humor. But that was all. The peerless, glowing white skin was as raw and chafed and reddened as a washerwoman's hands, the final price paid for those deadly washes and bleaches with which she had so long treated it. The stately body had broadened and thickened intq a shapeless mass under its fussy garments. The flowing black hair that had been so perfect an instrument of coquetry, half-hiding the beautiful face, had disappeared entirely, and in its place was that extraordinary wig, made from the hair of her blond footmen, which towered up more than six inches higher than even the extravagant coiffures of the day. But undoubtedly the most disconcerting aspect of her appearance was that she seemed to be totally unaware of the change, dressing and acting as though she were still that Juno of twenty years before. During the long years of her isolation in Usson she had been the sole arbiter of fashion, renewing her garments in the style to which she was accustomed, unaware that, in the world outside, fashion was changing at an ever accelerated pace, so that when at last she emerged into it she was dressed in a style that was twenty years out of date.

After that initial shock, after the first hesitant, slightly embarrassed search for a topic of discussion, the interview proceeded with warmth and friendship. Freed at last of the necessity of pretending conjugal love, the two were able to indulge the respect, tinged with amusement, which each felt for the other. Henri stayed for over three hours, conversing animatedly about old times and old friends, but he adopted a semiserious note just as he was leaving, begging her for her health's sake to abandon her habit of turning night into day and, for his pocket's sake, to be a little less lavish in the scale of her entertainment. She laughed, replying that at her time of life it was impossible to change her habits, and he grinned ruefully and withdrew, promising to introduce her to his wife and the little dauphin in the near future. He kept his promise. A few days later Marguerite, taking the air in her litter, saw the opulent coach of Marie de Médicis approaching. Inside it, alone, was the diminutive figure of the heir to the throne. The ex-Queen of France and the future king alighted simultaneously, walked the few yards toward each other, and stood looking at each other for some moments. They took to each other immediately. "You are most welcome, *maman ma fille,*" the little boy announced gravely, using the title for this extraordinary person that he had been taught. She laughed and kissed him. "How handsome you are. You certainly have the royal air of commanding, as you will one day."[102] The following day she sent, in one of her splendidly extravagant gestures, a magnificent gift to the child—a little cupid with diamond eyes, seated on a symbolic dolphin made of emeralds, together with a little scimitar whose hilt was encrusted with gems.

Her meeting with the boy's mother was less successful. Marie de Médicis admittedly had excellent grounds to be at once wary and resentful, for she had only recently emerged triumphant but badly scarred from the running battle with her husband's mistress, Henriette d'Entragues. Almost to the end Henriette seems to have believed that he would repudiate the stupid but arrogant descendant of Lorenzo de' Medici in her favor, a belief bolstered by Henri's habit of impartially moving from Marie's to Henriette's bed, begetting children by them both. And now Marie de Médicis was called upon to welcome her predecessor into the family home, a situation that strained protocol and tolerance alike to their limits. The meeting took place on August 28 in the courtyard of the Louvre. Marguerite was standing in the center as the king and queen of France descended the great staircase. Marie stopped stubbornly at the bottom, waiting for Marguerite to advance toward her, and Henri turned to her irritably, telling her sharply that the last princess of the great dynasty of Valois was entitled to the highest honors they could accord her. Impelled by his will, Marie moved reluctantly to the center of the courtyard, and the bystanders noticed how she stood clumsy, monosyllabic, ill at ease while the Valois princess, with charming courtesy, acted as though she were a gauche visitor to be put at her ease.

Despite that unfortunate introduction, the two queens in time became excellent friends. Marguerite, perhaps, was still uncertain about her status in Paris and went out of her way, with that charm which had never deserted her, to gain the support of the royal family. And Henri, as well as his wife, accepted her overture of friendship with something like relief. The Bourbon succession to the Valois throne had been entirely legal and quite inescapable, but it was good to know that the last surviving member of the old dynasty so wholeheartedly welcomed the new. Even those conservatives of the old guard who might deplore the morals of the Queen of Navarre could not but acknowledge her high birth, and if she recognized Henri IV and his queen and children, then they, darkly influential, could not but do the same. The Parisians, who had liked her even in her unregenerate days, now delighted in her as an eccentric. Lampoons about the pretty youths in her service sped round Paris, but with them, too, were mixed stories of her astonishing generosity to the poor, of the brilliant balls she gave, of the famous dinner parties where she would propound some philosophical problem for debate and act as arbiter while the wine flowed on and on. Now and again Henri would take her to task about her mounting expenditures, waving sheafs of bills at her like some distracted bourgeois husband. The Parlement of Paris had reversed her mother's will in her favor so that she again enjoyed the revenue from the Valois estates, but even with these her income could not keep pace with the gifts poured out to the endless stream of supplicants, with the magnificent presents she made to friends, with the endowments of monasteries and with those enormous banquets and balls she gave and at which, even now, she did not disdain to lead the dance, dignified if no longer graceful. She must cut down, reduce, dismiss some of her gorgeously dressed servitors, Henri would demand, but she would only smile and refuse to promise anything and he, sometimes cursing, sometimes laughing, would order the privy purse to pay some of the more outrageous, more pressing debts.

So the closing years of her life glided by as though the dark days had never been. But there was to be one last, twisted little tragedy, a mocking echo of the cataclysmic tragedies of the past. On an April morning she was returning to her home with the young carpenter's son who had once been known as Julien Date but now swaggered around, sumptuously dressed, as the Sieur de Saint-Julien. As the coach came to a halt before the entrance to the hotel, he leaped out to help her down and at that instant another of Marguerite's young men, Vermont by name, stepped forward and shot Julien down so that he fell in his blood at the very feet of the queen. Vermont attempted to escape but was captured almost immediately. Marguerite, almost mad with rage and grief, demanded vengeance from the king, and he, genuinely shocked, promptly responded. Vermont was brought to trial that same day and hanged on the spot where Saint-Julien had died while Marguerite watched from a window. The murderer was probably obeying a family vendetta rather than suffering from sexual jealousy, but even now the aging Queen of Navarre had little difficulty in gathering young men around her whose precise relationship with her was a matter of some speculation. The very last of that line of men which began, so long ago, with the Duke of Guise was a young singer known as Villars. The charitable assumed that he was merely her protégé; the rest nicknamed the young man *"le roi Margot."*

On May 13, 1610, the coronation of Marie de Médicis took place in the royal church of Saint Denis. Henri was leaving in the near future for the Rhineland, on the opening stage of a massive attack on the House of Austria, and he had thought it advisable that his wife should enjoy, in his absence, the additional dignity and security provided by the solemn ceremony. Marguerite had given him some difficulty. She had been rather reluctant to attend the coronation which, if her path had run straight, should have been her own. Henri had been vehement in insisting upon her attendance, arguing that only thus could she publicly demonstrate her loyalty to the new regime, and she had given way. Then, to her intense irritation, she had discovered that not only would she not be allowed to wear a fleur-de-lys mantle similar to Marie's but that she was forced to yield precedence to the king's six-year-old daughter Elizabeth. Protocol, however, allowed her to wear a crown and an enormous royal mantle of violet velvet, borne by two ladies-in-waiting and, her pride assuaged, she took part in the ceremony with her usual good humor.

The following day was her birthday and she spent it outside Paris, where, according to her custom, she gave a fete. Afterward she and Scipione Dupleix, the Huguenot chronicler, were idly chatting and Dupleix casually remarked that it was curious how many great events for France had taken place on the fourteenth of the month, citing Louis XII's victory over the Venetians at Agnodel on May 14, 1509, the battle of Marignano on September 14, 1515, that of Cesirolles April 14, 1544, the raising of the siege of Metz on January 14, 1553. Dupleix had just reached the victory of Ivry, March 14, 1590, when a messenger arrived with the news that Henri IV, the survivor of more than two hundred military engagements, had been assassinated that afternoon by Ravaillac in the rue de la Ferronnerie.

Marguerite survived her husband by five years. His death made little real difference to her life except, perhaps, that Marie de Médicis turned to her more and more for advice, particularly advice in the complex social etiquette that girded life in the capital. She, the last survivor of the old regime, a legend herself and source of legends, guardian of the traditions, became the unofficial arbiter of protocol. It was she who gave the great ball when the Spaniards came to ask the hand of Elizabeth of France for the future Philip IV of Spain, presiding over it like some glittering and improbable figure from the heroic past, dressed in silver and gold and diamonds, ponderous, benign, dignified but still with an occasional witty aside which disconcerted the stiffly formal Spaniards. But thereafter the balls and banquets were less and less often, the attendance at mass ever more frequent, until at last she was hearing three a day. The end was fitting enough for one who had so improbably become the last survivor of an epoch, for she insisted on playing her ceremonial part in the opening of the States General in 1615 and caught a severe chill. And on March 27, 1615, "there died in Paris Queen Marguerite, the sole survivor of the race of Valois, a princess full of kindness and good intentions for the welfare of the State and who was her only enemy."[103]

And with her death the legends began. Some were purely fanciful, like that macabre story of the voluminous petticoat she was supposed to wear adorned with a score of pockets, each containing the mummified heart of a lover. Some were logical, as damaging as they were vicious, and these included the tale of how she had had two bastards, the one by Chanvallon, the other by the wretched Aubiac. Scipione Dupleix, the writer whom she had raised up with her own hand, granting him a sinecure at her court, repaid that generous gesture by spitting on her ghost. His *Histoire generale,* published fifteen years after her death, enshrined with the spurious verisimilitude of an historical work every vile rumor that had touched her life during twenty years of polemics. Even Dupleix felt that he might have gone too far and protested that he did so only because "she had thrown ordure on the great king [Henri IV] by her Memoirs"—a demonstrable falsehood, for self-interest alone would have assured her giving her suddenly powerful husband a favorable portrait. These legends, those pretending to be history as well as most of those obviously no more than lip-smacking gossip, held a common parentage in the mysterious *Divorce satyrique* which appeared before the death of her husband. The writer might have been Agrippa d'Aubigné, venting a last, senile venom on the woman he had always hated. Or the instigator, if not the actual writer, might have been her husband himself, seeking this hidden means of justifying his divorce from the last of the Valois. It was a despicable tactic if he did indeed employ such a means, but Henri de Bourbon, the noble savior of his country, had treated his wife throughout the greater part of their lives with something less than nobility, repaying her generosity with a squalid selfishness remarkable even in a dynastic marriage. It was the *Divorce satyrique* which provided the titbits for generations of scandalizers to pick over: the charge that she had taken her first lover at the age of eleven; the charge of incest with all four brothers; the quotable sneers—"In giving my sister to the king of Navarre I gave her to all the Huguenots of the realm," "The lads of Gascony aren't sufficient for the Queen of Navarre; she has gone to find the muleteers and the charcoal-burners of Auvergne"; the picturesque details

—the sheets of black taffeta and special flambeaux, the wooden box with which she secretly transported her lover into the Louvre—on and on for page after page the farrago runs, mixing just sufficient truth or probability to make the wilder charges palatable. There were eulogies of the Queen of Navarre in circulation, not least those of Brantôme and Coste. But they were extreme and unselective, and the public taste, in any case, ran to the spicy savors and gamey odors of the *Divorce* and of Dupleix, and these had the last word until another man, beside whom these salacious gossips were mean and shabby dwarfs, paused momentarily over her history, shook his head over this working out of fate and turned his lucid mind upon it. Cardinal Richelieu was thirty years old when she died, so that he was able to look at the active period of her life as something in the historical past and yet still connected to his present by human sympathy. "She was the greatest princess of her time, daughter, sister and wife of great kings and yet, despite this advantage, she was the toy of fortune, contemned by those who should have been her subjects and she saw another take the place that should, by right, have been hers. Her marriage, which should have been the occasion for public rejoicing, and the cause of union of the parties which were dividing the country, was the occasion of general mourning and the renewal of even more cruel warfare than before. They celebrated it on St Bartholomew's—the cries and the agonies of which resounded through all Europe. The wine of the feast was the blood of the massacred, the meats were the flesh of the innocent mixed pellmell with that of the guilty. She saw her husband in danger of his life. They deliberated as to whether they should kill him. She saved him.

"Her husband succeeded to the Crown. But just as she had no part in his affection, he gave her none in his good fortune. Reasons of state easily persuaded him to take a second wife in order to have the children she could not have. But where lesser women would have burned with envy and hatred against those who take their place, so that they cannot bear to meet them or the children with which God blessed their marriages she, on the contrary gave all her possessions to the Dauphin and made him her heir as though he was her own son.

She came to the court, lived near the Louvre and not only visited the Queen but until the end of her life paid her all the honours and dues of friendship that she might have expected from the least of princesses.

"True heiress of the House of Valois, she gave to no-one without apologising for the smallness of the gift and the present was never so large that she did not wish that it had been larger. . . . And as charity is the queen of virtues so this great queen crowned hers with giving alms so generously that there was not a religious house in Paris, not a single poor person who ever turned in vain to her."[104] So wrote Cardinal Armand Richelieu, chief minister of that King Louis XIII who should have been her son.

†

Sources
Quoted

ARTUS, THOMAS, *Description de l'isle des hermaphrodites nouvellement découverte*. Cologne, 1724.

BACON, FRANCIS, *"Certain Observations upon a libel"* in *The Letters and Life of Francis Bacon;* edited by Spedding and others. Vol 1. London, 1857.

BASSOMPIERRE, F.DE, *Mémoires*. Cologne, 1665.

BERGER DE XIVERY (ed.), *Recueil des Lettres Missives de Henri IV*. Paris 1843–76.

BRANTOME, PIERRE BOURDEILLE DE, *The Book of the Ladies (Illustrious Dames)* with Eleucidations by C.-A. Sainte-Beuve, trans. by Katharine Wormeley. Boston, 1899.

————, *Les Vies des Hommes Illustres & Grands Capitaines François de son temps*. Amsterdam, 1666.

BURGHLEY, LORD, *A collection of state papers, from Letters and Memorials left by William Cecil, Lord Burghley* edited by S. Haynes and W. Murdin. London, 1740–59.

BUTLER, A.J., *The Wars of Religion in France* (The Cambridge Modern History, Vol. III). Cambridge, 1902.

CATHERINE DE' MEDICI, *Lettres*. T.1–10. Paris, 1880–1909.

CORYATE, T., *Coryat's Crudities: Hastily Gobbled up in Five Moneths Travells*. London, 1611.

D'AUBIGNE, THEODORE-AGRIPPA, *L'Histoire Universelle*, Maillé, 1616–20.

"DISCOURS DU ROI" in *Mémoires d'Etat de Villeroi,* edited by Michaud, q.v.

"DIVORICE SATYRIQUE." See *Recueil . . .*

DUPLEIX, S., *Histoire de Henry le Grand IV du nom, Roy de France et de Navarre.* Paris, 1635.

DUPLESSIS-MORNAY, PHILIPPE DE. *Mémoires.* T. I–XI. Paris, 1824–5.

ERLANGER, P., *Henri IIII.* Paris, 1935.

L'ESTOILE, PIERRE DE, *Journal,* edited by L.R. Lefvre. Paris 1948–60.

————, *Mémoires pour servir à l'histoire de France.* (Trans. by N.L. Roelker under the title of *The Paris of Henry of Navarre.* Cambridge [US] 1958.)

FAVYN, A., *Histoire de Navarre.* Paris, 1612.

GUESSARD, M.F. (ed.), *Mémoires et lettres de Marguerite de Valois.* Paris, 1842. (See also Marguerite de Valois, *Memoirs.)*

HEROARD, *Journal,* Vol. I, in Michaud, q.v.

HUGUERYE, M.DE LA, *Mémoires inedits de Michel de la Huguerye.* Paris, 1877.

MARGUERITE DE VALOIS, *Memoirs: Written by Her Own Hand.* Trans. by Violet Fane. London, n.d. (See also Guessard.)

Memoires de l'Academie de Clermont-Ferrand.

MERGEY, JEAN DE, *Mémoires* in Ser.I, t.9 of Michaud, q.v.

MERKI, CHARLES, *La Reine Margot et la fin des Valois.* Paris, 1905.

MICHAUD, JOSEPH FRANCOIS, *Nouvelle collection des memoires pour servir a l'histoire de France depuis le 13e jusqua la fin du 18e.* Paris, 1850.

MOTLEY, J. L., *The Rise of the Dutch Republic.* London, 1873.

NOUE, D. DE LA, *Mémoires* in Series I, t.34 of Michaud, q.v.

PEARSON, HESKETH, *Henry of Navarre.* London, 1963.

PEREFIXE, H. DE BEAUMONT DE, *History of Henry IV,* trans. by J. Daunce. London, 1663.

PONTRARCHAIN, *Memoires,* in Michaud, q.v.

Recueil de diverses pieces servans à l'histoire de Henri III. Cologne, 1663. (The "Divorce Satyrique" appears on pp. 193–221.)

RICHELIEU, CARDINAL DE, *Mémoires sur la regne de Louis XIII* in Series I, t.7–9 of Michaud, q.v.

ROEDER, RALPH, *Catherine de' Medici and the Lost Revolution.* London, 1937.

SEWARD, DESMOND, *The First Bourbon: Henri IV, King of France and Navarre.* London, 1971.

†

Notes

1   *Lettres de Catherine de Medicis.*

2   Marguerite, *Memoires,* p. 66.

3   Brantôme: *The Book of the Ladies,* p. 154.

4   *Ibid.,* p. 159.

5   Ibid., p. 166.

6   For this conversation and what follows: Marguerite, *Memoires,* pp. 74–86.

7   The whole despatch in Williams, p. 48.

8   Marguerite, *Memoires,* p. 83.

9   Nicot to the queen mother: in Williams, p. 46 n.

10   Quoted in Favyn: *Histoire de Navarre.*

11   Jeanne d'Albret to her son: letters in Williams, pp. 62–63.

12   Sully, p. 77.

13   Letters quoted in Williams, p. 62.

14   Brantôme: *The Book of the Ladies,* p. 162.

15   The whole report in Williams, pp. 67–69.

16   Marguerite, *Memoires,* p. 87.

17   Brantôme: *Les Vies des Hommes.*

18   Quoted in Roeder.

19   D'Aubigné, *Histoire Universelle* III, p. 303.

20   "Discours du roi."

21   Ibid.

22   Ibid.

23   Marguerite, *Memoires,* p. 94.

24   Ibid., p. 95.

25   Mergey, *Memoires,* p. 202.

26   "Discours du roi."

27   Marguerite, *Memoires,* p. 96.

28   Ibid., p. 98.

29   Sully, Vol. I, p. 91.

30   Marguerite, *Memoires,* p. 100.

31   *Lettres de Catherine de Medicis:* Documents inedits, Book IV.

32   Péréfixe p. 37.

33   Estoile, *Journal,* I, p. 244.

34   Artus, p. 38.

35   *Lettres de Catherine de Medicis,* Book VIII.

36   Marguerite, *Memoires,* p. 106.

37   Estoile, II, p. 39.

38   Ibid., p. 42.

39   Ibid., p. 44.

40   The whole story in Marguerite, *Memoires,* 109 seq.

41   Ibid., p. 120.

42   Berger, pp. 81–82.

43   Estoile, *Journal,* II, p. 75.

44   Marguerite, *Memoires,* p. 137.

45   Ibid., p. 147.

46   D'Aubigné, *Histoire Universelle* II, p. 187.

47   Estoile, *Journal,* I, p. 63.

48   Ibid.

49   Marguerite, *Memoires,* p. 151.

50   Ibid., p. 167.

51   Ibid., p. 201.

52   Estoile, Journal, II, p. 110.

53   Motley, p. 755.

54   Sully, p. 127.

55   The whole entry in Strickland, p. 204.

56   Marguerite, *Memoires,* p. 207.

57   Ibid., p. 209.

58   Ibid., p. 226.

59   *Lettres de Catherine de Medicis,* Book VIII.

60   Ibid.

61   Brantôme: *The Book of the Ladies,* p. 175.

62   Estoile, *Journal,* III, p. 29.

63   D'Aubigné, *Histoire Universelle,* Book V, p. 381.

64   *Recueil,* p. 201.

65   Ibid., p. 202.

66   Quoted in Merki, p. 247 n (2).

67   Guessard, p. 202.

68   Ibid., p. 239.

69   Ibid.

70   Ibid., p. 281.

71   Ibid., p. 285.

72   Ibid., p. 289.

73   *Lettres de Catherine de Medicis,* Book VIII.

74   Guessard, p. 474.

75   Quoted by Merki, p. 283 n1.

76   Dupleix, p. 595.

77   Quoted by Merki, p. 288.

78   The whole in Duplessis-Mornay, p. 290.

79   Estoile, Journal, I, p. 164.

80   Huguerye, II, p. 315.

81   Estoile, *Journal,* I, p. 171.

82   *Lettres de Catherine de Médicis.*

83   Cited by Merki, p. 307.

84   Brantôme, *The Book of the Ladies,* p. 173.

85   *Lettres de Catherine de Medicis:* Book VII. Appendix.

86   *Recueil,* p. 210.

87   *Lettres de Catherine de Medicis,* Book VIII.

88   Quoted in Merki, p. 334.

89   Both letters in Merki, p. 350.

90   *Recueil,* p. 209.

91   In Williams, p. 333.

92   Brantôme, *The Book of the Ladies,* p. 183.

93   Merki, p. 356.

94   Cited in *Memoires de l'Academie de Clermont-Ferrand,* Book VIII.

95   In Merki, p. 354n.

96   Bacon, *Certain observations.*

97   Estoile, III, p. 231.

Notes

†

98	In Merki, p. 395.
99	Sully. I, p. 291.
100	Guessard, p. 347.
101	Coryate, p. 36
102	Heroard: *Journal* I. p. 144.
103	Pontrarchain. ed. Michaud II, p. 51
104	Richelieu. *Memoire* . . ., ed. Michaud, I, p. 92.

Index